THE FAUVES

JEAN-PAUL CRESPELLE

THE FAUVES

NEW YORK GRAPHIC SOCIETY, GREENWICH, CONNECTICUT

Translated by ANITA BROOKNER

Jacket illustrations:
VAN DONGEN. Portrait de Fernande.
MANGUIN. Quatorze juillet à Saint-Tropez.

61,828

Contents

List of Illustrations

18 Les Régates à Bougival. 1905.
23 $^7/_8$×28 $^7/_8$ ins.
New York, Mr. and Mrs. Werner E. Josten.

19 La Danseuse du " Rat Mort." 1906.
28 $^3/_4$×21 $^1/_4$ ins.
Paris, M. et Mme André Fried.

20 Paysage aux arbres rouges. 1905.
25 $^5/_8$×31 $^7/_8$ ins.
Paris, Musée National d'Art Moderne.

21 Voilier sur la Seine. 1906.
21 $^1/_2$×28 $^7/_8$ ins.
New York, Mr. Robert Lehman.

22 Vase de fleurs. Before 1910.
28 $^3/_4$×23 $^7/_8$ ins.
Washington, National Gallery of Art.
Chester Dale Collection.

23 Le Jardinier. 1905.
27 $^1/_8$×37 $^3/_4$ ins.
Paris, private collection.

24 The Seine at Carrières-sur-Seine. 1906.
21 $^1/_4$×25 $^5/_8$ ins.
Paris, M. Guy Roncey.

ANDRÉ DERAIN (1880-1954).

25 Portrait of Vlaminck. 1905.
16 $^1/_8$×13 ins.
Rueil-la-Gadelière, Mme Berthe Vlaminck.

26 Les Péniches. 1904.
31 $^1/_8$×38 $^1/_4$ ins.
Paris, M. B. J. Fize.

27 Chatou. 1905.
31 $^7/_8$×51 $^1/_4$ ins.
New York, Mr. and Mrs. William S. Paley.

28 Portrait of Matisse. 1905.
18 $^1/_8$×13 $^3/_4$ ins.
London, Tate Gallery.

29 Big Ben. 1906.
31 $^1/_8$×38 $^5/_8$ ins.
Troyes, M. Pierre Lévy.

30 Coucher de soleil. 1905-1906.
31 $^7/_8$×39 $^3/_8$ ins.
Saint-Tropez, Musée de l'Annonciade.

31 La Femme au châle. 1908.
31 $^1/_8$×24 $^3/_4$ ins.
Paris, M. B. J. Fize.

32 The Houses of Parliament. 1906.
31 $^1/_8$×39 ins.
New York, Mr. Robert Lehman.

33 Charing Cross Bridge. 1905-1906.
32 $^1/_8$×39 $^3/_8$ ins.
New York, private collection.

34 Sur la Tamise. 1906.
25 $^5/_8$×39 $^3/_8$ ins.
Paris, private collection.

End of Chapter V, pages 171-218

RAOUL DUFY (1877-1953).

35 Le Yacht pavoisé au Havre. 1904.
27 $^1/_8$×31 $^1/_2$ ins.
Nice, Mme Raoul Dufy.

36 Vue de l'église Saint-Gervais. Before 1905.
19 $^1/_8$×13 ins.
Avignon, Musée Calvet.

37 Les Ombrelles. 1905.
23 $^5/_8$×28 $^3/_4$ ins.
Paris, Dr Roudinesco.

38 Le Bal Champêtre. 1906.
18 $^1/_8$×21 $^5/_8$ ins.
Paris, private collection.

39 Le Bassin à Honfleur. 1905.
23 $^5/_8$×28 $^3/_4$ ins.
Paris, Dr Roudinesco.

40 La Plage de Sainte-Adresse. 1906.
21 $^1/_4$×25 $^5/_8$ ins.
New York, Mr. and Mrs. John Hay Whitney.

41 Le Bateau Pavoisé. After 1900.
21 $^1/_4$×22 ins.
Lyon, Musée des Beaux-Arts.

42 Voiliers au Havre. 1905.
21 $^1/_2$×25 $^5/_8$ ins.
New York, Mr. and Mrs. John Hay Whitney.

43 Les Affiches à Trouville. 1906.
25 $^5/_8$×31 $^7/_8$ ins.
Paris, Musée National d'Art Moderne.

44 Les Bains du casino Marie-Christine à Sainte-Adresse. 1904.
25 $^5/_8$×31 $^7/_8$ ins.
Paris, Musée National d'Art Moderne.

OTHON FRIESZ (1879-1949).

45 Portrait of Fernand Fleuret. 1907.
29 $^7/_8$×23 $^5/_8$ ins.
Paris, Musée National d'Art Moderne.

46 Le Bec-de-l'Aigle. 1906.
25 ³/₄×32 ¹/₈ ins.
New York, Mr. and Mrs. Werner E. Josten.

47 L'Estaque. 1905.
13×18 ¹/₈ ins.
Paris, Musée National d'Art Moderne.

48 Paysage à La Ciotat. 1905.
13×16 ¹/₈ ins.
Paris, Musée National d'Art Moderne.

49 Oliviers en Provence. 1909.
25 ⁵/₈×31 ⁷/₄ ins.
Paris, private collection.

GEORGES BRAQUE (born 1882).

50 L'Estaque. 1906.
19 ⁵/₈×24 ins.
Paris, Georges Braque.

51 Seated nude. 1907.
21 ⁵/₈×18 ¹/₈ ins.
Paris, private collection.

52 Le Port de L'Estaque. 1906.
23 ⁵/₈×28 ³/₄ ins.
Paris, private collection.

53 Maison derrière les arbres. 1906.
14 ³/₄×18 ¹/₈ ins.
New York, Mr. Robert Lehman.

54 La Ciotat. 1906.
15×18 ¹/₈ ins.
Paris, private collection.

55 Paysage à La Ciotat. 1907.
15×18 ¹/₈ ins.
Paris, Georges Braque.

56 Le Port de La Ciotat. May 1907.
25 ⁵/₈×31 ⁷/₈ ins.
New York, Mr. and Mrs. John Hay Whitney.

57 La Calanque. 1907.
16 ⁷/₈×21 ⁵/₈ ins.
Paris, private collection.

58 Paysage à La Ciotat. 1907.
23×28 ins.
Chicago, Mr. and Mrs. Leigh B. Block.

End of Chapter VI, pages 235-296

GEORGES ROUAULT (1871-1958).

59 Self-portrait. 1921
18 ⁷/₈×12 ¹/₄ ins.
Paris, private collection.

60 Nude c. 1906.
12 ¹/₄×10 ins.
Paris, Musée National d'Art Moderne.
Girardin collection.

61 " Les Poulots." 1905.
27 ¹/₂×20 ¹/₂ ins.
Hem (France), M. Philippe Leclerq.

62 La Noce à Nini Patte-en-l'Air. 1905.
20 ⁵/₈×26 ¹/₈ ins.
Paris, private collection.

63 La Parade. 1907.
25 ⁵/₈×38 ins.
Montreux, M. Max Bangerter.

64 Nu au miroir. 1906.
27 ¹/₂×20 ⁷/₈ ins.
Paris, Musée National d'Art Moderne.

KEES VAN DONGEN (born 1877).

65 Self-portrait. 1905.
Monaco, M. et Mᵐᵉ Kees Van Dongen.

66 Anita. 1905.
31 ⁷/₈×51 ¹/₄ ins.
Monaco, M. et Mᵐᵉ Kees Van Dongen.

67 Le Promenoir des Folies-Bergère. 1907.
Monaco, M. et Mᵐᵉ Kess Van Dongen.

68 Fernande. 1905.
39 ³/₈×31 ⁷/₈ ins.
Paris, private collection.

69 Le Clown. 1905.
29 ¹/₈×23 ⁵/₈ ins.
Paris, Mᵐᵉ Lucile Manguin.

70 La Ballerine Borgne. 1905-1906.
31 ⁷/₈×21 ¹/₄ ins.
Paris, private collection.

71 La Femme au Chapeau. 1908.
39 ³/₈×31 ⁷/₈ ins.
Paris, private collection.

LOUIS VALTAT (1869-1952).

72 La " Fiesta." 1896.
7 ¹/₂×9 ¹/₂ ins.
Paris, Dr. Jean Valtat.

73 La Jetée. 1905-1906.
14 ³/₄×21 ⁵/₈ ins.
New York, Mr. and Mrs. Henry Ittleson.

74 Voilier dans la baie d'Agay. 1905.
7 ¹/₂×9 ¹/₂ ins.
Paris, Dr. Jean Valtat.

75 Femme sur un banc. 1896.
18 $^7/_8$×24 $^3/_8$ ins.
Paris, Dr. Jean Valtat.

76 Les Rochers rouges d'Anthéor. 1908.
31 $^7/_8$×39 $^3/_8$ ins.
Paris, Dr. Jean Valtat.

CHARLES CAMOIN (born 1879).

77 La rue Bouterie. Before 1914.
30 $^3/_4$×24 $^3/_8$ ins.
Paris, Mme Ginette Signac.

78 Le Moulin Rouge. 1904.
22 $^7/_8$×29 $^7/_8$ ins.
Menton, Musée.

79 Le Port de Marseille. 1904.
25 $^5/_8$×31 $^7/_8$ ins.
Le Havre, Nouveau Musée.

80 Portrait of Marquet. 1904.
36 $^1/_4$×28 $^3/_4$ ins.
Paris, Musée National d'Art Moderne.

HENRI MANGUIN (1874-1949).

81 Quatorze juillet à Saint-Tropez. 1905.
24×19 $^5/_8$ ins.
Paris, Mme Lucile Manguin.

82 Landscape with figures. Cavalaire. 1905.
28 $^3/_4$×23 $^5/_8$ ins.
Paris, M. Francis Junker.
(formerly collection of Mme Lucile Manguin).

83. Nude. 1905.
13×16 $^1/_8$ ins.
Paris, Mme Lucile Manguin.

84 Portrait of Mme Henri Manguin. 1900.
25 $^5/_8$×21 $^1/_4$ ins.
Paris, Mme Lucile Manguin.

85 Femme à l'ombrelle. 1905.
24×19 $^5/_8$ ins.
Paris, Mme Lucile Manguin.

JEAN PUY (1876-1960).

86 Nude. 1902.
41 $^1/_2$×29 $^1/_8$ ins.
Paris, private collection.

87 La Femme au fauteuil. *c.* 1924.
31 $^7/_8$×25 $^5/_8$ ins.
Saint-Jeoire (France), Dr. Paul Gay.

88 Femme lisant. 1902.
18 $^1/_8$×15 ins.
Paris, private collection.

89 Reclining nude. 1906.
12×18 $^1/_2$ ins.
Geneva, M. Oscar Ghez.

End of Chapter VII, pages 311-332

VASSILY KANDINSKY (1866-1944).

90 Landscape with a factory chimney. 1910.
26 $^1/_8$×32 $^1/_8$ ins.
New York, Solomon R. Guggenheim Museum.

91 Murnau. 1909.
13 $^1/_4$×17 $^1/_2$ ins.
Munich, Dr. Kurt Martin.

ALEXEI VON JAWLENSKY (1864-1941).

92 The red shawl. 1909.
21 $^1/_4$×19 $^1/_4$ ins.
Munich, private collection.

93 Nikita. 1910.
33 $^7/_8$×29 $^1/_8$ ins.
Wiesbaden, Städtisches Museum.

KARL SCHMIDT-ROTTLUFF (born 1884).

94 In the studio. 1910.
29 $^7/_8$×33 $^1/_8$ ins.
Hamburg, Kunsthalle.

95 Summer. 1913.
34 $^1/_2$×40 ins.
Hannover, Städtische Galerie im Landesmuseum.

ERNST-LUDWIG KIRCHNER (1880-1938).

96 Girl in front of a mirror. 1912.
39 $^3/_4$×29 $^1/_2$ ins.
Düsseldorf, private collection.

97 The artist and his model. 1907.
59×39 $^3/_8$ ins.
Hamburg, Kunsthalle.

CASIMIR MALEVITCH (1878-1935).

98 Les Dévots. Before 1912.
29 $^1/_2$×38 $^3/_8$ ins.
Amsterdam, Stedelijk Museum.

AUGUST MACKE (1887-1914).

99 By the Blue Lake. 1913.
23 $^5/_8$×19 $^1/_8$ ins.
Karlsruhe, Staatliche Kunsthalle.

FRANZ MARC (1880-1916).

100 Red horses. 1911.
41 $^1/_2$×73 ins.
Rome, M. et Mme Paul E. Geier.

I   1905: Scandal at the Salon d'Automne

In 1905 Paris was still a predominantly nineteenth century city. Life was regulated by the pace of the horse-drawn cab, although the Metro and the first motorcars were already in existence. Street cries had not yet become obsolete.

Vlaminck, the most famous of the Fauves, has left a happy description of the Paris of his youth in his Memoirs: " 1900—the noodle period, as it has been described by Paul Morand—was a time of great tranquility, of settled ideas, employment and money. Half of Paris seemed to be perpetually strolling round with a little cash in its pockets. Life was considered more engrossing than one's career or one's prospects. People lived on very little, made do with what they had. In the restaurants you could eat as much bread as you could manage, although conditions were rough enough at home—oil lamps, water from a pump in the courtyard. A bathroom was a fantastic luxury.

"Paris had a kind of happy provincial routine. The streets were roughly paved and smelt of horse dung. Small shops had not yet been crowded out by big stores; craftsmen and artisans were independent. People knew how to take their leisure. Each district of Paris had its own distinctive character, and the first Metro stations were in the Art Nouveau style; Russian loans were considered gilt-edged, and the five-franc piece was really worth five francs. The cost of living was steady, unemployment rare. The middle-classes, comfortably ensconced in their Louis-Philippe armchairs, hummed the *Valse Bleue* or *Les Cloches de Corneville* and admired the pictures—varnish and all—of Bonnat, Bouguereau and Henner. In 1900 Monet, Sisley, Renoir and Cézanne were still regarded as revolutionary painters."

We can add a few details to this picture. Women wore corsets, bustles and buttoned boots; men, frock-coats, top hats, hard collars and pale lemon gloves. Moustaches were compulsory, except for waiters, who were forbidden the privilege until they went on strike in 1907. Beneath the trees of the

Cours-la-Reine, with its coconut sellers, Punch-and-Judy shows, and wooden horses, little girls in flounced dresses ran after their hoops, and soldiers in red trousers made up to beribboned nannies and incidentally provided genre painters with an extremely popular subject.

At Maxim's the last of the professional cocottes, wearing full complement of jewels, flounces, frills and plumes, pursued their task of getting rich foreigners and provincials to part with their money. That well-known pasha Edward VII could take his pleasures tranquilly in the houses of the rue des Moulins, knowing that such interludes were marked " Visit to the President of the Senate " in his official diary. The middle-classes and the workers shared the less arduous recreations of dancing at the Moulin Rouge or at Bullier's, or boating at Chatou. Society was vulnerable and almost childlike in its trusting satisfaction, but such stability was to be short-lived, and the first rumbles could be heard by anyone who gave a mind to such matters.

One of the first warning signs of impending change appeared at the Grand Palais, temple of official art, which a mistaken leniency had caused to be thrown open to the revolutionary painters of the Salon d'Automne. The curtain rises on the Fauve drama. There are many versions of the exact context in which the critic Louis Vauxcelles is reported to have uttered his famous phrase about the wild beasts (fauves). Penetrating with Matisse into the room in which the highly explosive pictures of Vlaminck, Derain, Marquet, Puy, Rouault and Matisse himself were hung, he caught sight of a neo-Florentine sculpture of a child's head by the sculptor Marque and indicated it slyly as " Donatello among the wild beasts! " Another version has it that the remark was inspired by Matisse's heavy hairy overcoat, which made him look like a bear. Whatever the truth of the matter, the phrase was coined and quickly became known. Vauxcelles himself repeated it the following day in his review of the exhibition in the newspaper *Gil Blas*. The Fauves, thus brought into being, accepted the label with a certain fierce satisfaction.

The critics reacted in their usual way to the colour of these brilliant canvases, which, in Vlaminck's own words, looked as if it had been squirted straight from the tube. Camille Mauclair, the most conservative of them all, wrote in *Le Matin*, " They have thrown a pot of paint in the public's face! "—hardly an original phrase since it had been first used by Ruskin of Whistler in 1877. But it was a good description all the same. Criticism had not been so violent since the days of the Impressionists: the discreetly bourgeois Nabis had attracted little attention outside their own small circle.

What precisely made the event so combustible? From a list drawn up by Vauxcelles and a double page spread in *L'Illustration* for November 4, 1905, we can establish what was hanging in the famous room.

Matisse showed: *La Robe japonaise*, *La Fenêtre ouverte*, *La Femme au Chapeau* (a portrait of his wife), *La Promenade*.

Manguin showed: *La Sieste, Sur le balcon, Sous les arbres, Les Chênes-lièges, Le Pré*.
Derain: a *Self-portrait, Le Séchage des voiles*, and three landscapes of Collioure.
Vlaminck: *La Vallée de la Seine à Marly, La Maison de mon père, Crépuscule* and *L'Etang de Saint-Cucufa*.
Marquet: *Anthéor, Menton, Agay, Les Roches rouges du Trayas*.
Valtat: *Paysage d'Anthéor*, two seascapes, *Portrait de femme, Intérieur*.
Puy: *Matinée nonchalante, Flânerie sous les pins, Le Chemin modeste, Souvenirs de Concarneau*.

In the same Salon, but in other rooms, Rouault was showing several works from his series *Pitres et Cabotins*. Cézanne had sent his *Baigneuses*, Vuillard *La Musique*, and the Douanier Rousseau his *Lion dévorant une antilope*. The Russian colourists from Munich, Jawlensky and Kandinsky, were also represented, and it was at this exhibition that they met Matisse and the other Fauves, who were to exercise such an important influence on their own development.

The purpose of *L'Illustration*, which reproduced some of these pictures in a double page spread, was certainly not to encourage modern painting. The editor, whose own tastes were confined to the works of his brother Marcel Baschet, the peasant anecdotes of Dagnan-Bouveret, the cloudy pastels of Guinerand de Scevola and the yachting scenes of du Gardier, simply wanted to amuse his conservative readers at the expense of both the Fauves and the few critics who had been brave enough to offer a serious description of what they had done. The supporting text had a veneer of impartiality but left little doubt as to what the editor of the great bourgeois weekly really felt. "Why, we are asked, does *L'Illustration* affect to ignore the existence of the Salon d'Automne when it devotes a whole number to the traditional Spring shows? Foreign and provincial readers who are unable to reach the Grand Palais would be pleased to have some idea at least of the works of these little-known masters who have been so warmly praised by serious newspapers like *Le Temps*. We have therefore set aside two whole pages and reproduced as best we can a dozen or so of the most striking canvases in the Salon d'Automne. Unfortunately, we cannot give you the colours, but at least you will be able to judge the design and composition. Should any of our readers feel surprise at our choice, would they be good enough to read the lines printed underneath each picture: these are the opinions of the most distinguished art critics in Paris and we shelter behind their authority. We should simply like to point out that though critics once kept their incense for the established masters and their sarcasm for the beginners, things are very different today." Under the illustrations were printed a series of captions taken from articles by Gustave Geffroy *(Le Journal)*, Louis Vauxcelles *(Gil Blas)*, and Thiébault-Sisson *(Le Temps)*.

Other critics left subtle irony to *L'Illustration* and went straight for the heavier weapons of scorn and abuse. Generally speaking, the painters who had exhibited in the Fauve room were described as decadent and incoherent, and were recommended to take a course at the Ecole des Beaux-Arts. J.-B. Hall wrote that the room was the headquarters of " pictorial aberrations, chromatic madness, and the fantasies of men who, if they were not so obviously practical jokers, would deserve the Spartan regime of the Ecole des Beaux-Arts." " Recriminations are useless," he went on, " either these young people are right or the Salon d'Automne is enjoying their joke. Why put all these maniacs together and show their work to the public if it has no aesthetic value ? What is the meaning of this new farce ? Who is protecting them ? Does someone in a high position imagine that their efforts signify the birth of a new style ? The effect is deplorable ... and a serious loss of prestige for the Salon d'Automne. It has landed us with parasites who will be difficult to get rid of, for how can their presence be explained to a selection committee that has honoured Carrière and Courbet ? What have the daubs of Messrs. Matisse, Vlaminck and Derain got to do with art ?"

Marcel Nicolle found the means of improving on a previous performance in an article published in *Le Journal de Rouen* on November 20. " Now the most astonishing room in this astonishing Salon. All attempts at description, judgement or criticism are defeated. What we see—apart from the materials used—has nothing to do with painting. Formless streaks of blue, red, yellow and green, all mixed up, splashes of raw colour juxtaposed without rhyme or reason, the naif and brutal efforts of a child playing with its paint-box. We can do little more than record the names of these phenomena, whose art, by our standards, at least, is either raving madness or a bad joke. MM. Camoin, Derain, A. Marquet, P. Girieud, Manguin, Henri Matisse—one of whose works in the same style was bought by the State last spring—Jean Puy, Maurice de Vlaminck, P. Laprade, and Mlle Jelka-Rosen."

After such outbursts the favourable opinions seemed very feeble indeed. Nevertheless, the Fauves had attracted the attention of serious critics like Vauxcelles and Gustave Geffroy who were to become champions of the new style. Another critic, a newcomer called André Gide, also gave them an article. " I spent a long time in this room and listened to what people were saying. When I heard someone exclaim in front of a Matisse, ' But it's sheer madness!' I was tempted to reply, ' On the contrary, this is the result of a theory. Everything can be explained or deduced and intuition plays no part in it. I have no doubt that when M. Matisse paints that woman's forehead apple-green and that tree-trunk bright red, he is able to give his reasons for doing so. This painting is entirely reasonable. It is even pedantic.' "

But such intelligent and sensitive remarks (how many people read Gide in those days ?) had little effect on the crowds whose curiosity had been stimulated by the newspapers. The press was completely indifferent to the experiments of the young painters and had no thought beyond flattering the muggily conventional artistic tastes of the public. (It is worth recording that conservatism in these matters is by no means the exclusive province of the middle class. In 1904 D. H. Kahnweiler saw two cab drivers convulsed with fury at the sight of some pictures of London by Monet in Durand-Ruel's window. They were enraged by what they could not understand.)

The critics therefore had a field day with their witticisms and their condemnations. A few years later, young Roland Dorgelès, a leading Montmartre practical joker, brought a psychiatrist to the Salon d'Automne and took down his "diagnosis" of several Fauve and Cubist paintings. The main target was the reserved and circumspect Matisse, who thus found himself promoted to leadership of the movement much as Manet, forty years earlier, had reluctantly become the leader of the Impressionists. Matisse did not dare go back to the Salon. He sent his wife. Loitering by her husband's pictures, she recorded the remarks and jeers of the public, who came mainly for a good laugh. Six months earlier, at the Salon des Indépendants, both Vlaminck and Derain had sold a painting. The secretary of the Salon told them that a prospective buyer was offering 100 francs apiece for their landscapes. They were overjoyed. Recognition at last! But it turned out that the buyer, a rich man from Le Havre, had chosen their work because he could find nothing more hideous in the whole Salon to give to his son-in-law, who collected modern paintings. This son-in-law was André Siegfried, the future Academician.

The Fauve scandal was unpremeditated and unexpected, a matter of pure chance due mainly to the organizer, Desvallières, who wanted to have all the most highly coloured pictures hanging together to form a consistent group. Without Desvallières's decision, they might never have come together at all, and their paintings left scattered amongst those of the other exhibitors.

It is not difficult to explain the outbursts of violence, the bad temper verging on hatred, sparked off by this incident. The Fauves were seen as dangerous revolutionaries, threatening the rigidly compartmented class system of the bourgeoisie. They were attacking some of the most respected institutions of that society: the Institut, the Ecole des Beaux-Arts, the Salon, the whole artistic establishment.

In 1905 the bourgeoisie was on the defensive. The Dreyfus affair had recently weakened the prestige of the army, and Combes's anti-clerical campaigns had aroused antagonism in powerful ecclesiastical circles. In the same year, the break between Church and State became final, and a new revolt of the Catholic peasants of the Vendée was feared. Anarchists had almost succeeded in killing Alfonso XIII of Spain as he drove through Paris, and a disquieting series of strikes in the city centre seemed likely to turn into an insurrection. Abroad, the clouds that were to release the storm of 1914 were already gathering. The bourgeoisie sensed that its supremacy, its ideals, its way of life, and, most frightening of all, its security, were coming to an end. The glitter of

Parisian life was getting a bit tarnished. The ruling class, alerted by its instinct for self-preservation, registered the shock of these events and decided to defend more vigorously the institutions it had created.

In the sphere of art, official resistance was no less strong than it was in social and religious affairs. All the great aesthetic revolutions of the nineteenth century were greeted either with indifference or savage opposition. Under pressure from the Institut, the director of the Ecole des Beaux-Arts, Roujon, who hoped to become a member of the Académie, managed to get part of the Caillebotte bequest refused in 1894. (Only forty of the sixty-seven pictures were accepted.) When Vollard, who was anxious to keep the paintings in France, asked Bénédite, the curator of the Luxembourg Museum, to shelter the rejected works in his store-rooms, he received the indignant reply, " A public officer enjoying the confidence of the State cannot become a receiver of canvases that the commission has rejected!" The paintings went to America and Germany, like the two hundred watercolours bequeathed by Jongkind, which were also refused by the Museums Committee.

When Vollard offered a Gauguin to a client, he was told, " I will never buy the work of a man who abandoned his wife and children!" When President Loubet visited the Exposition Universelle of 1900, Gérome stopped him at the door of the Impressionist gallery and said, " Don't go in, Sir. It's a national disgrace."

In 1905 resistance was as strong as ever, and the Impressionists were only barely tolerated. It was not until 1907 that Clemenceau, urged by his friend Monet, lost patience, opened up the store-rooms where Manet's *Olympia* had languished for seventeen years, and had it hung in the Louvre. Van Gogh was still considered a madman and Cézanne a failure (among others, by Emile Zola, an otherwise unlikely champion of academic painting). The most important event of the artistic and social season was still varnishing day of the Salon des Artistes Français, held every may at the Grand Palais. Preparations were made weeks in advance and women ordered special outfits for the occasion. You were " out of it " if you were not seen lunching at Ledoyen's (salmon with *sauce verte, jambon aux épinards*) with the most fashionable painters, presided over by the amiable Harpignies, just before the opening.

Miguel Zamacoïs has left a lively description of the event in his book of memoirs entitled *Pinceaux et Stylos*. " Varnishing day meant a general mobilisation of painters, sculptors and engravers, who wandered through the rooms forming groups in front of works which had attracted attention through their merit, their subject matter or their size. There were lively and sometimes excited discussions, but passions belonging more properly to the spheres of politics or metaphysics had not quite ousted aesthetic preoccupations. Teachers took a paternal interest in their pupils' contributions, pupils made uninhibited comments on their masters' contributions, and there was a great

Matisse, self-portrait

murmuring of prognostications about future rewards 'medals, mentions, the *Prix du Salon* and so on. Botticelli had just been rediscovered, and artists' wives, mistresses and models made strenuous but not necessarily expensive efforts to present themselves in outfits garnished with shawls, crowns of flowers, iron headbands and earphones of hair, Art Nouveau jewellery in previously neglected materials such as horn, cornelian, agate, coral, inferior pearls and base metals, inspired, after the Japanese example, by various botanical shapes. The almost theatrical aspect of the women was echoed by shades of the *Vie de Bohème*, men with broad-brimmed hats wearing voluminous cravats over high buttoned velvet waistcoats, baggy trousers tapering at the ankle, and occasionally capes like those worn by the cavaliers of Velazquez."

The great event of varnishing day was of course the visit of the President of the Republic. He arrived in an open carriage drawn by four white horses. President Loubet would trot diligently round the galleries, in which the painters could be seen standing to attention beside their works. President Fallières would greet the organizers with the kind of remark equally suitable to a commercial or industrial fair: " I have confidence in you. I look to you to point out the way." The contents were more or less standard from year to year : uniformed and moustached generals, nymphs rising from pools, statesmen in frock coats, Sarah Bernhardt (who exhibited her own sculptures) in a Venetian robe, musketeers standing stiffly to attention, jovial pastrycooks, Reichshoffen cuirassiers, Moorish sirens, Iceland fishermen, Italian and Breton landscapes. The President rewarded the prize-winners with a vague and cordial remark and sent them off happy for another year. In its review, *L'Illustration* set exactly the right tone when it stated, " The two Salons (i. e. the Artistes Français and the Nationale) have opened their doors. But these are more than Salons; these are palaces brought to life by art." Typical works included Charles Lenoir's *Vision antique*, Charles Walhain's *Petite escapade*, Lapara's *Les étapes de Jacques Bonhomme*, Brispot's *Billet de logement*, Cayron's *Doux repos*, A. Guillou's *Pour l'absent*, Louis Baader's *Le quart d'heure de Rabelais*, Detaille's *La Chevauchée de la gloire*, and, the only canvas to have survived this field-day for sociologists, Willette's *Parce Domine*.

These titles prove conclusively that what the public wanted was anecdote. All classes wanted to be moved, uplifted, charmed, melted, instructed or amused by a picture that told a story. Painters in the service of a self-congratulatory society had not only to produce a flattering image of it, but to demonstrate the great events of its history and religion, and stimulate patriotism, martial valour and filial devotion. The picturesque triumphed. Even certain nudes—opulently modelled, splendidly hairless—were allowed as forming a recognizable part of hallowed Gallic tradition.

The artist was a kind of official whose role was not without importance in society. The first rungs of the ladder were climbed at the Ecole des Beaux-

Arts. Once he had been received in a studio, the young painter, provided he were talented and of a pliant disposition, could pass without hindrance through the various stages that led to fame and fortune : Prix Chenavard, Prix de Rome, Salon des Artistes Français, State commissions for public buildings, a professorship, the Institut de France, the Villa Medici, perhaps even the Académie Française. The successful artist was an important element in the life of the Third Republic. He received invitations to the Elysée on evenings when white ties and decorations were worn.

A whole series of rites were designed to prepare the pupil for his career as a privileged artist. The practical jokes were always grotesque and sometimes as cruel as initiation ceremonies. Professors looked on with a tolerant eye and occasionally laid aside their dignity to grace the famous *bal des quatz'arts*. The Salon artists felt they had a mission and they were not mistaken, for their art perfectly reflected the taste of the time. For the sake of convenience, the territory was divided up as follows : Detaille : battles; Cormon : ancient history; J.-P. Laurens : History with a capital H; Brispot : history of a less imposing variety; Dagnan-Bouveret : peasant scenes; Bouguereau (who died in 1905) : the approved type of nude; Carolus-Duran : woman of fashion; and Bonnat : Presidents of the Republic.

But not all these conformists were simply mediocre executants exploiting and reproducing innocuous themes, and it would be a mistake to dismiss them as categorically as the critics of the time dismissed the innovators. Some of them had considerable talent but they went to great lengths to hide it. It is only today that the studies and sketches of men such as Cals, Ziem, Carolus-Duran, Meissonier, Théodule Ribot, Harpignies and Albert Besnard are being seen in a newer and truer light. Rouart, Berthe Morisot's son-in-law, had a study by Bouguereau among his collection of Impressionist masterpieces. Robert Rey tells us that strolling one day through the Luxembourg, of which he was Director, with Vuillard, he made a joking remark about Friant's ponderous *Toussaint*. " Certainly," replied Vuillard. " But look at that still life of chrysanthemums carried by the woman in black. I wish I had painted that."

When they forgot their public and painted for their own pleasure, these respected academic artists were sometimes capable of great things. But in their official commissions, they allowed all considerations of form to be obliterated by the importance of the subject matter. The autonomy of their means of expression escaped them; André Chamson rightly remarks that their great weakness was the poverty of their inner lives. Technical skill usurped the place of talent, and recognized patterns that of creative imagination. Hence those innumerable and boring rigmaroles which clutter up the storerooms of many a provincial museum. Very few painters were as conscientious as Gérome, who made long journeys to the Crimea and Egypt in search of local colour. Even Gérome's interest was documentary rather than plastic : like

Masters of Academic Painting

DETAILLE (1842-1912). His picture, *Le Rêve*, had made him the official painter of French military glory and a famous man. A pupil of Meissonier, he never wandered far from his master's orbit, and even took a house next door in order to see him more often. Like Meissonier, he had a passion for historical reconstruction and was an authority on military costume. Paul Poiret once asked his advice about dressing the corps de ballet at the Opera in Napoleonic costume. "I found him," he writes, " in his court-yard, painting a cannon surrounded by policemen disguised as Napoleon's infantry. I told him the purpose of my visit. Effortlessly, almost without turning his head, he recited the colours worn by every Hussar regiment in 1815." A tireless worker, Detaille executed a number of large public commissions in the sentimental military vein of the time: *Les Vainqueurs, Salut aux blessés, Victimes du Devoir*, etc.

BONNAT (1834-1923). To a certain extent Bonnat played the part in his own time that Lebrun, David, and Ingres had played in theirs: he was a dictator of the arts and his influence was deplorable. It was on the recommendation of Bonnat that the State refused Toulouse-Lautrec's bequest; the artist's mother then presented it to the Museum at Albi. Bonnat's dark and heavy style, which he believed to be in the great seventeenth century Spanish tradition, was ridiculed by students in his own lifetime. He was nevertheless a celebrated painter of official portraits, especially of Presidents of the Republic, and he charged enormous prices: e.g. *Fallières*, 50,000 gold francs. A man of strange contrasts, Bonnat had no illusions about himself. He appreciated the Impressionists, and once, when showing Degas his admirable private collection, which he bequeathed to his home town of Bayonne, he assured him that none of his own work would be included. A member of the Institut, professor at the Ecole des Beaux-Arts, Grand Cross of the Legion of Honour, he was a well-known sight at official receptions. But he was not

Detaille, Meissonier, and Roybet, he was a slave to historical reconstruction. The *chers maîtres*, who were professors at the Ecole des Beaux-Arts and recipients of Salon medals, were members of a privileged class. They were rich : a Bouguereau could sell for 730,000 NF, a Bonnat was worth 350,000 NF, and Meissonier's *1814* fetched 920,000 NF at the Porto-Riche sale. They were decorated : Meissonier was awarded the Grand Cross of the Legion of Honour and was a member of the Conseil de l'Ordre. When he died in 1891, Emperor Wilhelm II felt moved to send a telegram of condolence to President Sadi Carnot. They lived wealthy and elegant lives in their Renaissance or neo-Gothic mansions around the Parc Monceau. It is interesting to note that all the official art of the Third Republic came from the fashionable seventeenth arrondissement. Cormon lived in the rue de Rome; Roybet, who supplied France with several regiments of musketeers, in the rue de Prony; and Detaille and Meissonier occupied neighbouring houses in the Boulevard Malesherbes. Roll, Lhermite, Gervex and Paul Chabas lived nearby. Only Bouguereau showed some independence and lived on the Left Bank, in a vast studio in the rue Notre-Dame-des-Champs. Ironically enough, it was taken over after his death by a Fauve, Othon Friesz.

The studios of these painters were as full of bric-à-brac as a junk yard: moth-eaten uniforms of Napoleon's Guard, bishops' chasubles, lacquered Japanese armour, divans covered with Turkish carpets and Spanish shawls, cabinets encrusted with ivory and mother-of-pearl. Green plants in Chinese pots were more or less obligatory. Gérome, the most original of them all, and a considerable traveller, worked at his canvases seated on a Malayan hen-coop.

Miguel Zamacoïs has left an excellent description of the atmosphere in which such painters worked. "Edouard Detaille's studio, which I visited occasionally, was an exact reflection of the famous military painter's appearance and way of life. Everything was clean, tidy, polished, ready for parade. The artist, fully-dressed, clean-shaven, not a hair out of place, would paint standing before an easel or perched on a step-ladder. Occasionally he might relax to the extent of wearing an informal jacket made by a good tailor. In front of him would be a uniformed model, seated astride a fully harnessed, life-size horse of papier mâché. His palette (immaculate) would be in his hand, and he would greet me—I was a young boy at the time—with great kindness, asking questions about my small world, especially my studies … Then he would invite me to take a walk around. This was fascinating because his studio was like a military museum (he did in fact leave his collection to the Invalides). Rows of cardboard heads, which Detaille himself had painted, bearing wigs, carabineers' helmets, shakoes, hats decorated with silk cords or feathers, of all kinds and of all countries, were ranged on shelves against one wall. Around and about were panoplies of sabres, swords, bayonets, lances and armour from all over Europe."

completely spoiled by his own success, and often helped students in need of money. His aversion for Toulouse-Lautrec seemed to spring not so much from dislike of his art as from disapproval of his way of life. Lautrec, however, remained loyal to him. "What are they all laughing for?" he once asked loudly in the middle of a Salon. "That man knows how to work!"

Mme Steinheil, in whose arms Félix Faure died, had just left a sitting with Bonnat early to go to meet her lover. Bonnat dined out with great success on his connection with the case, and would produce a letter from Mme Steinheil excusing herself for leaving early, because, she said, she had to meet some ladies at the Elysée.

BOUGUEREAU (1825-1905). Bouguereau began life as a business man and retained his original hardworking habits throughout his career as a painter. Every year he painted twenty huge pictures crowded with nude nymphs (a good selling line). For a change, he painted portraits and still lifes. Art students found him and his work a rich subject for irony. The greatest irony, however, was the fact that whereas his nudes sold for enormous sums and were hung in all the best drawing-rooms, similar subjects treated by Toulouse-Lautrec were considered obscene. Vollard once recommended Bouguereau to a certain Russian count who had come to Paris to commission forty pornographic paintings.

CAROLUS-DURAN (1838-1917). A native of Lille, he made his name both literally and figuratively by changing his original "Charles" to "Carolus", adding a hyphen, and suppressing the final "d" of Durand. His *Femme au Gant*, a portrait of his wife, who was said to be a natural daughter of the Czar, had an enormous success, and he became the most popular portraitist of the Second Empire. A flashy personality, dressed like a comic opera idea of a bohemian artist, Duran was three years older than Monet, five years younger than Manet, and a friend of both. Unlike many academic artists he was not hostile to Impressionism and

These painters defended morals, broadcast the glories of history, and interpreted messages from the Almighty, and were therefore well looked after by the Government, the civil service, the conservative press and established critics. They were praised in the most extravagant terms. When Albert Besnard, a shameless pasticheur of the Impressionists (Degas said of him: "He is using our wings to fly"), had an exhibition at the Galerie Georges Petit, the critic of *L'Illustration* spoke of "brush-strokes that have not been seen since Rubens, Goya and Delacroix."

Unenlightened collectors paid out huge sums for these indifferent works. The most resounding was an extraordinary character called Chauchard, a multi-millionaire and owner of the Grand Magasin du Louvre, who was known as the "Linen King". At the beginning of the century this man exercised a real dictatorship over the arts. A slave to Meissonier's cavaliers and Bouguereau's nymphs, he was vain, gross and dull, and dreamed of having his coffin followed by a cortège of friends carrying the paintings he had decided to bequeath to the Louvre (he did in fact leave to the Louvre Millet's *Angelus*, forty Corots, as many Meissonier's—including *L'Homme à l'épée*, *Le Lansquenet et son lévrier*, *Gentilhomme frisant sa moustache*, *Grenadier en faction*—pictures by Théodore Rousseau, Diaz etc.). He had a naive pride in his Grand Cross of the Legion of Honour, and this earned him a vengeful quip from the journalist Jean de Mitty, who had just been made a Knight of the Order. Meeting the "Linen King" at the Café Napolitain, Mitty was condescendingly greeted with the words, "Well, young man, I congratulate you. I started in the same way. First I was a Knight, then an Officer, then ..."

"Then you bought the whole bolt!" said Mitty.

By virtue of his fortune, Chauchard was the official protector of *l'art pompier*. Léo Larguier recalls the vernissage of the Salon of 1903: "People practically stood in line as he passed by. Even a straggler up from the provinces would have known who he was. Surrounded by his general staff, he could be recognized a mile off. Like Napoleon, he wore a redingote and a white waistcoat. Quickly he clasped a few hands, nodded a greeting, turned a compliment: This year's Salon was of exceptional quality ... but one would need weeks to see everything ... Too much talent, much too much ... and taking a semi-professional stand in front of some predictable nude or dreary landscape, he would sketch an ineffably artistic gesture with his gloved hand.

"He was escorted by the Chancellor of the University. Artists presented to him would mumble, ' *Monsieur le Ministre* '—but with their eyes on Chauchard. Sovereigns do not prolong their visits, and his stay was always short. The Minister of Education would accompany him to his carriage, and he would return to his sumptuous mansion in the Avenue Velazquez which he had filled with pictures chosen for him by dealers."

even learned something from it, but his fundamental lack of interest in plastic problems made his work lifeless and superficial and, in Thadée Natanson's words, " his impressive name, his way of life, and the scale of his success remain a classic warning to painters who get excited by their own fame, and who paint for reasons other than the joy and torment of their art."

BESNARD (1849-1934). Another fashionable painter. He ended up as Director of the French Academy in Rome. He too learned from the Impressionists, applied their *peinture claire* to the sort of genre scenes popular with collectors, and had a great success. Certain of his portraits, however, are not without merit, and this is particularly true of sketches for larger, more elaborate works.

CORMON (1845-1924). This singular artist had the distinction of teaching both Van Gogh and Toulouse-Lautrec, but not for a moment did he ever suspect their genius. When they were recognized and famous he ignored them. At the end of his life he was outraged to learn that another of his pupils, Francis Picabia, had aquired a notoriety which owed nothing to Cormon's teaching. At the same time, he confused him with Picasso, whom he also condemned. His real name was Piestre but he adopted the pseudonym of his father who was connected with the stage. During the Second Empire he gained a reputation for exotic compositions with titles such as *La Mort de Mahomet, La Mort de Radva, roi des Louka.* He then switched to ancient history. A tiny little man, he turned out vast pictures of cave-dwellers, which were highly favoured in anti-clerical circles, where more conventional scenes, representing our ancestors as Adam and Eve, were not well received. His atelier was one of the most important at the Ecole des Beaux-Arts; he trained hundreds of pupils who in return had a high regard for him.

The upper reaches of official art conformed to a strict hierarchy. After the death of Meissonier and Gérome, Detaille was held in highest regard, closely followed by Bonnat, Bouguereau, Carolus-Duran, Albert Besnard and Cormon. These in turn were surrounded by lesser men like Lévy-Dhurmer, who painted bloodless pastels, Jules Lefèbvre, specialist in nymphs for American millionaires, Didier Pouget, who turned out acres of mauve heather, Chocarne-Moreau, the jovial pastrycook man, and Brispot, whose production consisted entirely of musketeers. Their works, which today litter the Flea Market, could command twenty or thirty thousand gold francs. This would seem to explain why such painters were so anxious to protect their public from the impact of new ideas. One of them, according to Miguel Zamacoïs, even hatched a fantastic plan to create an Order of Painters. " This painters' corporation," he proposed, " would only admit those who had proved their ability in a technical examination. Such men alone would then have the right to put letters after their names, which would assure the public of their professional standing in exhibitions ... Naturally, the examination and the degree would not deprive them of the right to explore the most daring new directions, as far removed as possible from classicism and academic routine, but the letters after their names would reassure the public that they were following such a course deliberately and not through ignorance ..." This grotesque proposal sheds an interesting light on the mentality of academic painters before the first World War.

Nevertheless, it should not be assumed that this was the only attitude adopted when innovations threatened to destroy the old equilibrium. Life in the *Belle époque* had its darker side, and even the comfortable bourgeoisie was aware of it : it was reminded of the fact every time an anarchist's bomb exploded. Pacifism was rife in working-class and intellectual circles; clerics and anti-clerics were in constant and vociferous argument. Important men, society itself, were mercilessly taken to task by certain satirical journals—*Gil Blas, L'Assiette au Beurre, Le Rire*—while more enlightened members of the middle-classes thronged to the *Chat Noir* to hear Jehan Rictus recite his savage verses. Many artists had anarchist leanings and associations. Maximilien Luce, who upheld the policy of *Le Libertaire*, had serious reasons for fearing the arrival of the police. The art critic Félix Fénéon, who was a strong supporter of the new style, was imprisoned for having boasted of his friendship with the anarchist Emile Henry, who was later guillotined.

Several of the Fauves, notably Vlaminck, Van Dongen and Dufy, had anarchist contacts. Vlaminck, whose association with *Le Libertaire* began in about 1900, contributed the proceeds from the sale of a painting every year until 1939. Unknown to the working-classes and denounced by the bourgeoisie, who dismissed them as Marxists, the Fauves were not entirely unrecognized. Certain collectors took a passionate interest in their work, notably the

Avant-garde Salons

The Salon des Indépendants

This Salon was founded in 1884 by Odilon Redon, Seurat and Signac, and had neither selection committee nor prizes. It was held every May in the former municipal conservatories in the Cours-la-Reine, principally so that artists could exhibit work done during the winter. It was presided over by Signac, aided by Maximilien Luce. Signac named Matisse as president of the hanging committee in 1905 and thus brought about the first group exhibition of the Fauves, for Matisse invited Vlaminck and Derain to hang pictures together with his own and Marquet's. Notoriety, however, did not come until the Salon d'Automne of the same year. At first, Vlaminck and Derain resented Signac's air of superiority and his manner, which was that of a sergeant major addressing new recruits to the camp. Signac was, in fact, a fairly overwhelming personality. In 1905 he was a successful man with the best part of his career behind him. His important book, *De Delacroix aux Néo-Impressionnistes*, had appeared ten years earlier. He was extremely bourgeois and given to loud and categorical pronouncements. A cultivated and passionate man, he was devoted to Stendhal, on whom he wrote a book which still commands respect. But he was by no means an intellectual; he was very fond of sailing—at one stage he owned more than thirty boats—and spent half his life sailing round France. With his friend Person, he even got as far as Constantinople. It was Signac who discovered Saint-Tropez and Collioure. The Fauves were disconcerted by his authoritative and incisive manner, but this hid a heart of gold which

deputies Marcel Sembat and Denys-Cochin, Auguste Pellerin, the manufacturer of " Tip " margarine, who sold his valuable collection of pictures by Manet (including *Le Bar des Folies-Bergère*) in order to buy works by Cézanne (he eventually owned 180), and the Russian merchant-prince Shchukin, who was the patron of Matisse and Picasso. Younger men, with more limited resources, bought paintings by Vuillard, Bonnard and Matisse, Vlaminck and Derain, which could be had for little more than a hundred francs. Some of them formed an association called *La Peau de l'Ours* which played a leading part in the development of modern art and the decline of academic painting. They pooled their resources—each contributed 250 francs—and every year put aside a sum for the purchase of new pictures. These circulated among the shareholders according to a fixed rule.

When *La Peau de l'Ours* was founded in 1904, it was decided that the entire collection should be sold ten years later in order to prove that modern painting was a " good risk." On March 2, 1914, the sale took place at the Hôtel Drouot, before an audience of important dealers, painters and critics, notably Apollinaire and Max Jacob, who wore a magnificent cloak with a crimson lining for the occasion. According to André Salmon, who was also present, the event was as important for modern painting as the battle of Hernani had been for the Romantic theatre. The result was an unexpected triumph, which demonstrated without a doubt that the new style could command high prices. It launched the vogue for modern art considered as a form of speculation. Here are some of the prices :

Bonnard's *L'Aquarium* : 720 francs.

Derain's *La Chambre* : 210 francs.

Dunoyer de Segonzac's *La Mare* : 800 francs.

Gauguin's *Le Violoncelliste* : 4000 francs.

Matisse's *Feuillages au bord de la Marne* : 2000 francs, and his *Compotier de pommes et oranges* : 5000 francs.

There was applause when Picasso's rose period *Famille de saltimbanques* reached 11,500 francs. The picture went to the United States. The shareholders of *La Peau de l'Ours*, who had come to the sale expecting to be able to buy back their favourite pictures, were both overjoyed and dismayed : they could only retain a quarter of the paintings for themselves. But academic art had received a mortal blow, and the new style had successfully imposed itself on the art market. That same year in New York, a Bouguereau nymph could still command 100,000 francs, but ten years later his pictures were selling in the junk shops at 1000 devalued francs apiece.

Critics in favour of the new style were nevertheless isolated and had some difficulty in making themselves heard. Vauxcelles, Thiébault-Sisson and Geffroy were exceptional cases. It was writers, and most of all poets, whose enthusiasm contributed so greatly to the success of the Fauves and later of the

Marquet, self-portrait

he allowed free rein when he was sure of a man's worth. He hated pretence, falseness, pastiche and the wrong sort of ambition. The first meetings between Signac and the Fauves were stormy, but peace was soon made, and they remained faithful to the Salon des Indépendants until 1910.

The Salon d'Automne

The Salon d'Automne was founded in 1903 to offset the confusion and proliferation of styles that flourished at the Salon des Indépendants. The founders were Renoir, Marquet, Vuillard, Rouault, Desvallières and Maurice Denis, and they chose as their president the architect Frantz Jourdain who was known for his sympathy towards modern painting. The choice was unfortunate for Jourdain soon revealed an implacable hostility to the more daring trends. Though he supported the Fauves, he hated the Cubists, and Vollard relates that when war broke out in 1914, Jourdain exclaimed, " Good! This will finish Cubism!" His treatment of the Douanier Rousseau, whose pictures he hung in dark corners, earned him the disapproval of Picasso and his friends, and of Apollinaire who celebrated the event with a satirical poem. The evening opening of the first Salon d'Automne, on October 31, 1903, was a memorable occasion in the annals of Parisian life. The organizers had succeeded, after some difficulty, in obtaining the basement of the Petit-Palais for the event, and among the fashionable personalities attending were the comtesse de Noailles, Robert de Montesquiou, Marcel Proust and Léon Blum.

Unfortunately this success had no sequel. Public response to the first Salon was cool, and the curator of the Petit-Palais, who was hostile to modern art, used this as a pretext to refuse to let the premises another year. In this he thought he was striking a blow for the Establishment; in fact, he brought about its first defeat. Henry Marcel, who had replaced Roujon as the Director of the Ecole des Beaux-Arts, decided to take a different line from his predecessor, and allowed Jourdain to take over the Grand-Palais,

Cubists. Max Jacob discovered Picasso at the very beginning of his career as an art critic. He was so wild with enthusiasm that he put himself completely at Picasso's disposition, and defying his natural indolence, went to work in a big store in order to support him and enable him to paint. Apollinaire, impressed by the pictures of Vlaminck and Derain, defended all newcomers to the Salon des Indépendants and the Salon d'Automne with a fervour that arose more from his native generosity than from his knowledge of art. On re-reading his articles, one is not entirely surprised to learn that he praised Benjamin Rabier and Picasso in almost the same terms. His taste was volatile, but one thing is certain : though he may have over-estimated certain mediocre painters, he never missed an artist of real talent.

A few dealers gave the new painters their support, notably Durand-Ruel, who almost ruined himself for the Impressionists; the Bernheim family, who were devoted to the Nabis; Vollard, to whom Cézanne owed the fact that he was recognized before his death; Clovis Sagot, Braque's first dealer; Soulié, a former clown; and Berthe Weil, the first to buy Picasso's work. Most of these had galleries in the rue Laffitte, which became a well-known pilgrimage route for young Fauves who had broken with the Academy or the Ecole des Beaux-Arts.

As we shall see, the Ecole des Beaux-Arts played a very important part in the formation of the Fauves. Some of them were permanently marked by the influence of their extraordinary master, Gustave Moreau. Others attended the Academies Julian and Carrière. The Académie Julian, which had been the cradle of the Nabis, counted Matisse, Derain, Marquet, Jean Puy and Valtat among its pupils. It had been founded after the war of 1870 by a young painter, Rodolphe Julian, for a rather unusual reason. He had a favourite model, a magnificent Auvergnat with the muscles of an athlete, but not enough commissions to keep the man fully employed. Rather than let him pose for rivals, Julian decided to open his own academy in his studio at 37, rue Fontaine, and by this means kept his model employed all day. He also allowed women to work alongside his male students : Louise Breslau and Marie Bashkirtseff were his pupils. At the time when the Fauves attended its life class, the Academy was situated in the rue du Faubourg Saint-Denis.

The Académie Carrière was founded by the well-known painter of foggy pictures of mother love, who was popular with everyone, Impressionists and *pompiers* alike. Derain, Matisse, Puy, Laprade and Chabaud often worked there.

Very young painters had no chance of exhibiting at the Salon des Artistes Français if they did not follow one or other of the accepted masters. They consoled themselves by showing their paintings in the two Salons open to experiments : the Salon des Indépendants and the more serious Salon d'Automne, for which the pictures were selected by a committee. Established

which was normally reserved for the very conventional Salon des Artistes Français. Thus the Salon d'Automne was launched on its famous career. Matisse, Van Dongen, Derain, Vlaminck, Manguin, Friesz, Jean Puy and Valtat joined the original exhibitors, and until 1914 the Salon was the stamping ground for all the important movements in modern art: Fauvism, Cubism, Futurism and Orphism.

artists and famous masters like Rodin exhibited there alongside complete beginners.

These two Salons played a vital part in discovering and promoting the artists who were to revolutionize painting at the beginning of the century. The importance of the Salon d'Automne was augmented by the retrospective exhibitions that brought the complete works of Gauguin (1904-1906), Manet (1905) and Cézanne (1907) to the public eye. These exhibitions, especially the first and last, had an enormous effect on the direction of the Fauve movement. This, then, was the social and artistic scene in the automn of 1905. The Fauve bonfire was to burn fiercely for a few years, then, just as abruptly, to be extinguished. But its sparks lit other fires which illuminated all the painting of the first half of the twentieth century, fires which, in the form of Abstract Expressionism, are still alive at the present day.

The sources of Fauvism

When Rouault as a young man showed Degas his paintings and apologized for the influences only too obviously reflected in them, Degas replied: "Everyone must have a mother and father." Without going back to the Middle Ages, it is possible to see inklings of Fauvism in certain aspects of the work of Delacroix, in Daumier's generous use of paint, and in the later landscapes of Courbet, in which the lyrical feeling imposes an increasingly vigorous colour and handling. But the two main sources of Fauvism are Gauguin and Van Gogh.

It should be made clear that Fauvism is merely a term of convenience. It was never an organic movement like Impressionism, Cubism or Surrealism. The Fauves were a mixed group with no recognized leader, no exponent of theory, and their ideas were often at variance. Matisse and Vlaminck, for example, differed on practically everything. The few principles that were evolved came later. Fauvism was essentially the untrammelled expression of the artist's personality.

It is easier to describe the Fauves in terms of what they disliked rather than what they liked. The dozen or so young painters grouped under the Fauve banner were reacting against the atmospheric naturalism of the Impressionists, the slightly decadent charm of the Nabis, and of course against any form of academic art. Their paintings were the reflection of their artistic personalities and consequently in no way bound to any form of objective representation.

"Nature is only a hypothesis," as Dufy remarked to a collector, puzzled by one of his landscapes. Maurice Denis, one of the first Nabis to take an interest in the Fauves, defined Fauvism in these terms: " It is painting divorced from contingencies, painting for its own sake, the pure act of painting. All qualities of description or personal reflection have been excluded from the work of art. These painters are searching for the absolute."

Long after the Fauve bombshell had burst, Othon Friesz explained what his friends were trying to achieve: " To render the sunlight effect through a technique of colour orchestrations and transpositions of their own to which their emotion toward nature inspired them and which intense and enthusiastic research proved to be correct." Matisse, speaking to the publisher Tériade in 1929, added a few details: "These were the ideas we had then: construction by means of coloured surfaces. A desire for a greater intensity of colour, the actual quality of the paint being of minor interest. Reaction against the representation of light by a diffusion of local colours. Light was not suppressed, rather it was expressed by a conjunction of intensely coloured surfaces. In my picture *La Musique*, I chose the bluest of blues for the sky. The surface was coloured to saturation point, that is, to the point at which it communicated the idea of absolute blue. It was the same for the green of the trees and the vibrant vermilion of the human bodies. With these three colours I established a harmony of light as well as purity of tone. One more point: colour was proportioned to form. Form was modified by the interplay of neighbouring coloured areas. The impact comes from the coloured surface, which the spectator grasps in its entirety."

The Fauves wanted to convey emotional shocks with the aid of forms reduced to their essentials and with pure colour. But colour was the first item on their programme of reform. Disregarding realism, they used colour simply with an eye to the picture surface, with only the effect in mind. The stronger the colour, the greater its effect, which led them logically to the ultimate step of using colour straight from the tube. Some sought to increase the vibration of their colours by adopting the divisionist technique of the Neo-Impressionists, but this rudimentary pointillism did not imply acceptance of Neo-Impressionist theories of atmospheric realism. As Matisse and Derain learned more about Gauguin, this trend was abandoned.

The need to express themselves in colour led the Fauves to reject most of the principles of traditional painting to which both Impressionists and Neo-Impressionists had adhered: linear and atmospheric perspective, chiaroscuro, modelling, and attention to detail. Economy of means was stressed in order to increase the expressive force of the painting. Hard-hitting was the order of the day.

Despite their lack of cohesion, the Fauves shared certain characteristics. The most violent and resolute members of the group (and the ones who gave it its character and sense of purpose) were from the north, which might explain their love of red and other bright colours. Matisse came from Cateau-Cambrésis and Vlaminck, although born in Paris, was of Flemish origin. The southerners were all minor figures. Most of them were sturdy and well-built, with fair complexions, red beards and blue eyes. They had little interest in poetry, the theatre or literature, and had few contacts in intellectual circles. Their emotive temperaments were better attuned to music. Braque played both the accordeon and the guitar. Vlaminck earned his living as a music teacher until he was thirty, and both Matisse and Dufy played the violin. Derain played the organ and the harpsichord.

Several of the Fauves, as we have seen, were either anarchists or anarchist sympathisers. With the exception of Matisse, they tended to adopt eccentric form of dress as a means of stressing their opposition to bourgeois standards. Vlaminck sported a painted wooden tie and a red scarf to go with his bowler hat. Van Dongen and Braque wore blue overalls, and Manguin baggy Zouave trousers. They were more often to be seen in the bistros of the Halles or Montmartre than in the literary cafés of Saint-Germain. It is doubtful whether they ever met, as did the Nabis, around a tea-table.

Despite their differences, they all passed through similar or parallel stages of evolution : discovery of Impressionism, understanding of its weaknesses, and finally admiration for Gauguin and Van Gogh. Their reaction, however authentic, was not the first of its kind. Gauguin had led the revolt against the Impressionists, although he owed his formation as an artist to them. He was one of the first to perceive the inadequacy of their art. " They study what the eye sees," he said, " but they do not penetrate to the mysterious centre of thought itself." Here he states the question of the spiritual importance of a work of art. Gauguin considered that painting should be symbolic, poetical and plastic, and his mature works were diametrically opposed to those of the Impressionists. He restored the autonomy of the picture, or, as Jean Cassou says, " He led painting back to its primitive and essential function, which is to draw plastic signs on a two-dimensional surface." This idea was of enormous consequence in the development of modern art in general and of Fauvism in particular.

To satisfy his mysticism and his sense of poetry, Gauguin turned to primitive art, not so much from deliberate choice as from an instinctive, almost unconscious, desire to return to the origins of his personality. His early childhood in his great-uncle's mansion in Peru, his journeys as a navigator and then an ordinary seaman in the navy, had given him a Baudelairean vision of a world composed of strange forms and colours. To the end of his life and throughout his various peregrinations, he clung to certain pre-Columbian vases collected by his mother; they figure in many of his paintings. " Primitivism is a source of strength for me," he said—a statement which conditioned Nabis, Fauves and Cubists to an interest in exotic and primitive art. He went to Brittany not solely in order to live cheaply, but to find a more primitive existence. Gauguin, whose technique had been formed through contacts with Monet and Pissarro between 1883 and 1887, began to define his ideas and to communicate (i. e. impose) them on the younger painters in his entourage during his second stay at the Pension Gloanec in Pont-Aven in the summer of 1888. Although many years of adventure were already behind him, he had still to find his own artistic personality, paint his most significant works, and live out the painful conclusion of his extraordinary destiny. He had just returned from Martinique, matured by the failure of the expedition, and was beginning to see how he could give concrete shape to his ideas. The canvases he had brought back showed that he had already abandoned the bright dabs of the Impressionists in favour of rather timid flat coloured areas. He was groping for a simpler, more summary form of art, and his conception suddenly crystallized when he met Emile Bernard, who was also staying at the Pension Gloanec. Gauguin was then forty years old and Bernard just twenty, an ethereal youth with a tendency to mysticism, a vivid imagination and a remarkable gift for exposition. The two had met before, in 1886, in the dining-room of the Pension, but Gauguin had taken little notice of the young art student, a fugitive from the Atelier Cormon.

In his memoirs, Emile Bernard tells of this first, disappointing, meeting. " I had a room in the town where I slept, read and worked, and I went to the Pension only at mealtimes. Gauguin sat opposite me, with a painter friend, Charles Laval, beside him. One day he took me to his studio and showed me canvases that reminded me very strongly of Pissarro and Puvis de Chavannes. I was not very enthusiastic, and he consequently lost interest in me."

Two years later everything was different. Bernard had already painted several pictures in a new technique on which he had been meditating for some time. Simplified shapes were outlined in black, and these outlines defined the coloured areas which were broadly and flatly painted. Some of these works had been hung in the dining-room of the Pension and Gauguin was immediately impressed. Here was something that connected with his own experiments. He therefore greeted Bernard with more warmth and went to his room to see the pictures he had brought back from Saint-Briac. " He thought they had great character," writes Bernard, " and he liked the bright colours and the simplicity of technique. Then he took me to his studio in Mme Gloanec's attic. I found that his style had become more personal and distinct. He still divided his tones, and this destroyed the general colour effect and gave the pictures a slightly muddy appearance. I told him this, as politely as I could, but also assured him of my regard for his talent. Some time later there was a saint's day in Pont-Aven and ... I painted some Breton women in black dresses seated in a meadow which I deliberately made a greenish yellow. Gauguin was very impressed by this picture which demonstrated my ideas on colour and summed up the results of my experiments with colour effects. ' The more you divide the tone, the more you weaken it,' I told him, ' and that makes it look grey and dull.' He wanted to work this out for himself, so he borrowed some of the colours I had used, such as Prussian blue, which the Impressionists

"It therefore became necessary ... to envisage a complete liberation, to break all the windows, even at the risk of cutting one's fingers ... to produce a brilliant solution to the problem. I don't say a *final* solution, because we are dealing precisely with a relative art, rich in every kind of technique, capable of reflecting all the emotions of man and nature, adapting itself to all individuals at all times, in joy and suffering. It became necessary to fight body and soul, to fight all schools—all, without exception—to challenge not only official painting but the Impressionists, the Neo-Impressionists, the old and the new public. To renounce the wife and children who disowned you. Neither insults nor poverty matter. All this, as part of one's activity as a man. As part of one's work. A method of contradiction if you like. To tackle the strongest abstractions. To do everything that was forbidden and to reconstruct more or less successfully, without fear of exaggeration, or even with exaggeration. To learn again, and once one has understood, to learn yet again: to overcome all the timidities, however ridiculous the process. Before his easel, the painter is a slave neither to the past nor to the future, neither to nature nor his neighbour. He is himself, always himself."

Written in Atuana in September, 1902.

Racontars de Rapin (Falaize).

"Where does the execution of a picture begin and where does it end ? When deep feelings are at work, when they burst forth and thought shoots up like lava from a volcano, isn't that a moment of creation ? Brutal, if you like, but great, almost superhuman ? The cold processes of reason have had nothing to do with this outburst, but who knows at what moment in the soul's history it began ? Its origins are unconscious, perhaps. Have you noticed how, when you recopy a sketch with which you are pleased, which was done in a moment of inspiration, you

had banished from their palettes and which he did not have with him. He then painted *The Vision after the Sermon*, which earned him the title of ' the creator of symbolism.' "

Despite its grudging tone, this account is of great importance. Bernard spent the rest of his life trying to prove that he was the real inventor of Synthetism, but his efforts were in vain. Gauguin found in the method a means of giving total expression to his genius for rare decorative richness, while poor Bernard, whose temperament was arid and intellectual, never emerged from a particular form of sham mediaevalism. From the beginning there was a striking contrast between the cold and limited theoretical character of his work and the amplitude, boldness and vigour, almost truculence, of Gauguin's pictures. Synthetism was born from this encounter, and Synthetism meant that the picture was composed in terms of the subject, that lines were reduced to the essential, perspective was abandoned (figures were placed one above the other), chiaroscuro was redundant, as was relief, and flat areas of colour were encompassed by a black line like the panes in a stained glass window. Gauguin even distorted his figures in order to add to the expressive force of his composition.

His meeting with Bernard had freed him from the last traces of Impressionist influence and enabled him to give full expression to his powers in pictures such as *La Belle Angèle, Bonjour M. Gauguin, Le Christ Jaune, L'Eveil du Printemps,* and *Nirvana,* all of which were to have an enormous influence on subsequent painting.

In order to avoid tourists, Gauguin took refuge in an inn belonging to the Gloanec family near Le Pouldu, and there conscripted a number of young painters who became his disciples. These included Meyer de Haan, the strange Dutch gnome with disturbingly phosphorescent eyes, whom he portrayed in *Nirvana,* Charles Laval, his companion on the journey to Martinique, Armand Seguin, and Charles Filiger. For several years—interrupted by his journey to Arles and a few trips to Paris—Gauguin comported himself as the leader of the movement. Through the pipe smoke at the main table he made pronouncements in a voice rendered all the more authoritative by the fact that he knew what he was talking about. The conversation, however, was not always so serious. Gauguin was a first class practical joker : he conducted the mock trial of a woman staying in the house who was suspected of trying to seduce one of the other lodgers, he painted the farm pigs red, and fed the geese on cherries soaked in brandy. Finally, the inhabitants of Pont-Aven became heartily sick of him : the parish priest of Nizon refused Gauguin's offer of *La Vision après le Sermon,* and Angèle Satre, the model for *La Belle Angèle,* was horrified by the painting. This did not stop Gauguin from writing to his wife, "I am working very successfully here. I am recognized as the leading painter in Pont-Aven, although I'm not a penny the richer for it. People fight for my

somehow diminish it, particularly if you correct the proportions or the faults that reason condemns. I sometimes hear remarks like, " the arm is too long ", etc. Yes and no. No, if by making it too long you are attaining some kind of poetic truth (of course, the whole picture must be consistent). Yes, if you happen to be Bouguereau, whose whole artistry lies in the kind of witless precision that clamps you to the chain of material truth."

Letter to Daniel de Monfreid.

L'Art de la Peinture (Seghers).

advice and I am foolish enough to give it—and in the end they make use of it without due acknowledgement."

The character of his advice can be judged from his letters. In the autumn of 1888, still excited by his experiences at Pont-Aven, he wrote to Emile Bernard from Arles, where he was visiting Van Gogh : " I am quite out of my element in Arles; I find the countryside and the landscape trivial and uninteresting. Vincent and I agree on very little, especially in painting. He admires Daumier, Daubigny, Ziem and the great Rousseau, all of whom I detest. On the other hand, he can't bear Ingres, Raphael and Degas, all of whom I admire. I always say, ' You're right, Brigadier,' for a bit of peace. He likes my paintings very much, but when I am at work on them he always finds something wrong. As for colour, he treats paint like Monticelli and I hate the business of working the surface ..."

He goes further in another letter to Bernard : " You discuss shadows with Laval and ask me if I care ... As an explanation of light, yes! Look at those admirable draughtsmen, the Japanese; they show life in the open air and in the sun without shadows, using colour as a combination of tones only ... giving the impression of heat, etc. Moreover, I think that Impressionism is an entirely new departure in art, completely distinct from a mechanical process like photography, etc. ... Going on from there, I want to get as far away as possible from anything that creates the illusion of a thing, and since a shadow is a perspective effect of the sun, I am inclined to do away with it.

" But if a shadow is a necessary element in your composition, that is quite another matter. If you leave out a figure but put in the shadow, that is an original idea and you will have planned the strangeness of the effect, like putting a crow on the head of Pallas rather than a parrot. So, my dear Bernard, put in shadows if you judge them useful; leave them out if you don't. You are the master, not the other way round."

The tone of the letter gives a clear indication of the relation of teacher and pupil that existed between Gauguin and Emile Bernard.

On his return to Paris after the dramatic Christmas night in Arles when Van Gogh's reason gave way, Gauguin was welcomed and fêted by a large group of young painters which included Sérusier, Laval, Moret, Anquetin, Maurice Denis, Ibels, Ranson and Bonnard. He was regarded as the head of a new school of painting. He never sought the title; on the other hand, he did nothing to disclaim it. He lived at the Cité Boulard with his former colleague Schuffenecker (who had also given up stockbroking to become a painter), and received his young admirers in Schuffenecker's studio or at the Café Volpini. They introduced him to the circle of Symbolist writers and poets, and welcomed him as one of themselves. " Good for Symbolism!" he is said to have exclaimed, happy to have found a receptive audience.

Vlaminck, self-portrait

The Nabis

There were two batches of Nabis: 1) the pupils of the Académie Julian —Sérusier, Maurice Denis, Ranson, Bonnard, Ibels, Vuillard, K.-X. Roussel —who were directly influenced by *The Talisman* brought back from Pont-Aven by Sérusier, and 2) those who joined the movement later, Lacombe, Rippel Ronai, Vallotton, Verkade, Ballin. The movement was fairly short-lived. As a group, the Nabis cannot be said to exist after 1900. Each member answered the demands of his own temperament, of his tastes and aspirations, and followed a personal line of development which sometimes had very little in common with the theories which originally united them. But the principal Nabis, Sérusier, Ranson, Maurice Denis, Bonnard and Vuillard, remained on close and friendly terms with each other.

SÉRUSIER (1863-1927). Called "the Nabi with the flowing beard," Sérusier was the enthusiastic, possibly over-enthusiastic, apostle of Gauguin's theories. He even posed for Maurice Denis in order to send Gauguin the money. He was enormous, emotional and talkative, always gesticulating, always ready for an argument. He had a fine tenor voice and at one point thought of making singing his career. He was twenty-five when he met Gauguin, and his dynamic personality had already given him a certain ascendancy over the other young painters at the Académie Julian. He remained faithful to Gauguin to the very end, although a certain coolness made itself felt during the latter's last visit to Paris, inspired no doubt by Gauguin's attitude towards the Nabi rituals, for which Sérusier was responsible. Sérusier was one of the first (and one of the few) Nabis to become interested in the Fauves. In a letter to Dom Verkade, dated May 31, 1906, he wrote, "A new group of painters, all aged between thirty-five and forty, and all trained at

Gauguin's influence spread, largely through the efforts of an enthusiastic young painter called Sérusier, the treasurer of the Académie Julian. He figures in one of the most celebrated anecdotes of modern art. Sérusier was at Bois-d'Amour, near Pont-Aven, and under Gauguin's direction was painting a landscape on the lid of a cigar box.

" How do you see the colour of that tree ? " asked Gauguin.

" Yellow."

" Well, use your very best yellow."

" How do you see the colour of the earth ? "

" Red."

" Then use your very best red."

Overcome, Sérusier returned from Pont-Aven and converted the future Fauve painters at the Académie Julian, who baptised his little panel *The Talisman*. " I met a kind of genius there called Gauguin," he told them, showing them his little study, the paint not yet dry. " He showed me what real painting is : ' If you want to do an apple, draw something round ... ' "

Maurice Denis has left an account of the effect of *The Talisman* on himself and on his friends : " For the first time, in a paradoxical and unforgettable form, we were presented with the revolutionary idea of ' a flat surface covered with colours assembled in a certain order.' In this way we learnt that every work of art is a transposition or a caricature, the passionate equivalent of an original sensation. This was the beginning of a development to which H. G. Ibels, Pierre Bonnard, Ranson and Maurice Denis all contributed. We began to visit places quite unknown to Jules Lefèbvre, the head of our school : the mezzanine of the Goupil Gallery in the Boulevard Montmartre, where Van Gogh's brother showed us pictures painted by Gauguin in Martinique, works by Van Gogh, by Monet and Degas, and Tanguy's shop in the rue Clauzel, where we discovered—with what emotion, you can imagine—paintings by Cézanne ..."

Elsewhere Maurice Denis tells us what Gauguin meant to the young painters who were to form the Nabi group. " He freed us from all the restraints that the idea of copying imposed on our painters' instincts. The theory of equivalents gave us the means to do this. We derived it from his expressive imagery: it gave us a right to be lyrical, and we learnt from his example that if it were permissible to paint a tree vermilion because it appeared very red to us at a particular moment, then we might also interpret our impressions by means of certain formal exaggerations, stress the colour of a shoulder, push the pearly white of a carnation to extremes, distort the symmetry of a branch... Gauguin had the privilege of illuminating these young minds with the dazzling revelation that art is above all a means of expression. He taught them, perhaps unintentionally, that a work of art must be decorative. Finally, he proved in

the Ecole des Beaux-Arts by Gustave Moreau, has just come into being. They claim to paint their *sensations*. This is even worse than wanting to paint nature. The results are poor but their ideas are intelligent and could even be fruitful. In the main, they are the same as the ideas we had fifteen years ago at Huelgoat. But we had something else, which they lack: a feeling for harmony in the construction and colour of a picture."

Like all the Nabis, Sérusier was a cultivated man with a taste for mysticism. He remained a fervent Theosophist until his death. Unfortunately, his painting, despite an occasional strength of colour, does not reflect the generosity of his temperament. His pictures give off an aura of pedantry, calculation, and sheer tedium. He spent his last years in Brittany in search of a primitive atmosphere and also of the peace and quiet which his vivid personality needed.

Maurice DENIS (1870-1943). According to Sérusier, this " Nabi of the beautiful icons " was the power behind the group. An extremely devout Christian, he had decided as a child to be a religious painter, and with Desvallières did a great deal to revive religious art which had fallen into the worst kind of mediocrity. His subtle and lucid mind fitted him for the position of theorist of the group. He was only twenty when, in 1890, he published in *Art et Critique* the famous definition that was to become the golden rule of modern painting: " A picture, before it is a war-horse, a nude woman, or any kind of anecdote, is above all a flat surface covered with colours assembled in a certain order." His own religious compositions, in which pictorial interest was completely sacrificed to the demands of the subject, were a contradiction of his own dictum. Despite the economy of his drawing, which is reminiscent of that of Puvis de Chavannes, his large frescoes, painted in unrelieved " pastel " shades, are chilling in the extreme. Yet he enjoyed the brilliant colours used by the Fauves, and supported them in his articles and reviews immediately after the Salon d'Automne of 1905.

his own work that grandeur is nothing without simplicity, clarity and consistency of pigment ...

" There was something quintessential and profoundly true in his savage art, his sturdy common sense, his vigorous naiveté. The paradoxes that he uttered in conversation—no doubt in order to appear just as pretentious as his companions—contained basic doctrines, essential truths that no art of any period can afford to deny. He gave painting a new lease of life. He was a kind of Poussin without the classical culture, a Poussin for our times. Like Poussin, he taught us to will freely and frankly, and to him synthesis and style meant much the same thing."

To these young people, Gauguin was the most important man of the century, greater than Courbet, Manet or Renoir. He had, moreover, the advantage of a colourful past—he was descended from the Incas of Peru, he had given up an important position on the Stock Exchange in order to devote himself to painting. Very few painters knew Cézanne, who was so remote from Parisian artistic circles that he was practically a myth, and it was impossible to see how much Gauguin owed to him. It was not until the Cubists that Cézanne's teachings bore fruit.

The veneration with which the members of the Académie Julian approached Gauguin did not conceal the enormous difference between him, the rather corpulent buccaneer, and the cultivated and sensitive young bourgeois with their rather timid appetites. Even his physical appearance—his mountebank's outfits : emblazoned waistcoats, royal blue cape, astrakhan hat—contrasted strangely with their sober middle-class dress. There was also a marked discrepancy between his sensual tastes (" I like my women fat and depraved," he used to say), and their thirst for purity. The impression that his uninhibited bragging must have produced on Mallarmé's Tuesday gatherings in the rue de Rome, attended by Verlaine, Maeterlinck, Pierre Louys, and Paul Valéry, or Paul Ranson's Saturday teas, can be imagined. Toulouse-Lautrec loathed him, and, to his fury, nicknamed him " The Professor."

Though their admiration for him persisted, relations between Gauguin and the Nabis eventually cooled, and he soon grew tired of his rôle as head of a school. What he wanted from these young painters was first and foremost recognition of his genius, and eventually some form of material support. It was the Nabis who, at his request, mobilised their friends and brought them to a sale of his pictures which was meant to finance his first trip to Tahiti. They also organized a memorable banquet for him and Verlaine. A few days later, on April 4, 1891, Sérusier, Verkade and Ballin accompanied Gauguin to the Gare de Lyon.

The seed sown by Gauguin was to germinate and bear fruit. But as he became increasingly engrossed in his painting and his own personal drama, he hardly

He died on a note of anti-climax. Having travelled the world in search of poetic themes, he was run over by a lorry in the Avenue de l'Observatoire. At his own request he was buried wearing the habit of a Franciscan tertiary.

RANSON (1864-1909). Of all the Nabis, Ranson had the strongest feeling for stylized forms, arabesques, and the kind of naturalism that distinguishes the English Pre-Raphaelites. His art is clearly connected with the Art Nouveau style that flourished around 1900. He would be completely forgotten had he not contributed, with Maillol, to the revival of the art of tapestry.

Ranson was the son of a deputy and Mayor of Limoges. His parents died when he was young and he was brought up by his grandmother. Wealthy, irritable and unstable, he was given to long periods of depression. His studio at 26, Boulevard du Montparnasse, which the Nabis had promoted to the rank of "Temple," was the scene of their weekly meetings, in which charades and games were interspersed with esoteric discussions on aesthetic and metaphysical problems. Although himself a bourgeois, a Protestant, and a Socialist, Ranson was full of contempt for the bourgeoisie. For him, there were only two categories: artists and bourgeois. Artists wore broad-brimmed hats, velvet trousers, and had high ideals. Bourgeois were ugly, stupid, and craven. Each had their own music, their own plays, their own literature.

Despite the slight stupidity of this conception, Ranson was popular, and his premature death was a great shock to his fellows Nabis. His widow, France, whom he had married when she was seventeen, decided to continue to direct the Academy which he had started in the rue Victor-Massé. The Academy, which was later moved to the rue Joseph-Bara, counted Vuillard, Sérusier, and Maurice Denis among its teachers and was one of the most important centres of artistic activity in the great days of Montparnasse.

gave this a thought. Finally, Symbolists and Nabis got on his nerves and he made fun of their vocabulary, rhyming " *cyntaise* " with *foutaise*.

The Nabi movement, brought to birth by *The Talisman*, reached rapid maturity; then its members went their separate ways, and Gauguin's theories were forgotten. Their works apart, the Nabis were characterized by a certain schoolboy pretentiousness which came out in a liking for ritual meetings, nicknames, and a secret language. Vuillard was known as " the Zouave," Bonnard as " the Japanese Nabi," Maurice Denis as " the Nabi of the beautiful icons," Sérusier as " the Nabi with the flowing beard," the tall thin Verkade as " the obeliscal Nabi," Vallotton as " the strange Nabi," Lacombe as " the sculptor Nabi," and Meyer de Haan as " the Dutch Nabi." All this was very close in spirit to afternoon recreation at the Lycée Condorcet, where in fact most of the leading Nabis had first met. The name Nabi (which means " prophet " in Hebrew) was bestowed on them by one of their colleagues, the poet Cazalis (known as Ben Calyre), who was taking a course in Hebrew civilization under Professor Ledrain. A complete vocabulary was evolved : the studio became the " ergastulon," pictures were " icons," and the long-suffering bourgeoisie were " pelitchim "—Hebrew for philistine.

The Nabis' letters are excellent examples of this taste for childish yet high-handed mystification. In 1889, Sérusier wrote from Le Pouldu to Maurice Denis : " Alas! alas! Armorica (Brittany), beautiful Armorica, the land of pious men, calls me; he who is about to depart will not see thy well-loved face this year before the red leaves fall."

Another example (quoted by Agnès Humbert in her book on the Nabis) is a letter in which Sérusier, writing to Ranson, announces the arrival of Meyer de Haan at Le Pouldu.

" Venus Day, one hour before the going-down of Helios, and finished on the Lord's day at the same hour.

" In thy hand my words and my thoughts!

" A pilgrim with his loins bound up in the land of Armorica, steward of (here a sketch of Helios, the sun), I live in harmony. By my side is de Haan, the Dutch Nabi, who knows the Hebrew Bible and even chants the words of the Nabis in the primitive rhythms; he also lives in harmony though troubled in his spirit. For the matters I have been turning over in my mind during the time of the winter mists now preoccupy him." The greetings at the end were carefully worded : " To the sublime incarnation of the eternal feminine, who with thee combines in perfect harmony, offer the homage of the pilgrim Nabi, and take my words and my thoughts in thy hand." His signature follows in French and Arabic.

As important as the secret language were the secret meetings. Every month, the Nabis ate a ritual meal in a bistro in the Passage Brady; the member chosen to give the address held a sculptured staff like a bishop's crozier. According

BONNARD (1867-1947). Bonnard, who was to become the most famous of all the Nabis and to rank with Picasso and Matisse as one of the greatest of all modern artists, was an inconspicuous young man who surveyed the world with a clear eye behind his pince-nez. Paradoxically, this tremendous colourist originally painted in extremely subdued greys and browns. The sight of *The Talisman* changed all this, and in about 1898 his palette became enriched by coppery tones similar to those of the Fauves. When he left the Académie Julian, he turned his attention to the decorative arts and covered screens and fans with witty and nervous compositions whose effortless drawing reflects his passion for Japanese prints.

Shy and solitary by inclination, Bonnard had few friends but kept them all his life. He was indifferent to fame, indifferent to comfort. His colour took on an increasing richness, which caused him to be compared with the Impressionists, but Bonnard's style, with its controlling sense of synthesis, has a strength and a significance which many Impressionist pictures lack.

His death touched off a series of lawsuits. With an innocence incredible in a former law student, he made a false will on his wife's death, assuming all her property in order to avoid death duties. The discovery of this will after his own death resulted in one of the most extraordinary legal tangles of the century.

VUILLARD (1868-1940). Vuillard's development is practically the opposite of that of Bonnard. He started painting in a series of brilliant, almost Fauve colours inspired by *The Talisman*, and evolved towards a style of half-tones and nuances manipulated with prodigious sensitivity. Of all the Nabis, Vuillard was the most interested in the surface of a picture, and used gouache and gum in order to obtain the large matt colour areas which give his work its particular freshness and calm.

He was a bachelor and his life was dominated by his love for his mother. She was his favourite subject, and he painted many pictures of her in her hideous little home which he transformed

to Vollard, these dinners came to be known as " the marrowbone dinners " because of a marrowbone which hung from the key of the lavatory, greatly in demand. Women were not allowed to attend these functions but the enchanting France Ranson was admitted to meetings held in Ranson's studio every week. As it was not possible to turn her out of her own house, she was designated a " luminary of the Temple " and commanded to pour out the tea. New Nabis such as Lacombe and Rippel Ronai, the Hungarian, were received at the Temple, which was also the scene of a ridiculous but touching " wedding " between Maurice Denis and Marthe Meunier. Although a devout Catholic, Denis went through the whole charade : he and his bride sat on a decorated platform, bound together by lengths of white tulle, and were then censed by the other Nabis. Denis was very much affected and wept freely. One can imagine Gauguin's comments.

These apparently childish activities can be justified to a certain extent. The Nabis were predominantly intellectual and mystical in outlook; they felt as great a need to escape their bourgeois origins (except for Vuillard and Denis, all came from very respectable families) as to avoid the formulae of Impressionist and academic painting. Hence the creation of a world of their own. Some, like Sérusier, were theosophists, read Maurice Schuré, and maintained contacts with the Rosicrucians. Maurice Denis was a practising Christian; Verkade was converted and entered the monastery of Beuron, Mögens Ballin, a Danish Jew, was also converted and led such an exemplary life that his canonization has since been proposed and adopted. All their lives, the Nabis scorned or ignored material circumstances—another contrast with Gauguin. They were in the main well-off, and their demands were modest.

The influence of the Nabis was felt mainly in the sphere of the applied arts : printing, posters, book-illustration, tapestry, pottery, stained glass. They had a knack of breathing new life into dying crafts. They also had considerable influence on other artistic and cultural activities. The musicians Duparc, Chausson, Debussy and Vincent d'Indy were their friends and shared their ideals. In the theatre they maintained close contact with Lugné-Poë, another former pupil of the Lycée Condorcet, Firmin Gémier and André Antoine. They were fervent supporters of Alfred Jarry, and supplied both extras and *claque* for the first performance of *Ubu Roi* at the Théâtre de l'Oeuvre on December 10, 1896. They accepted Gauguin and his theories because he seemed to be leading the revolt against Impressionism. They considered researches on light and the breaking-up of form of little importance, nor did they care for the real appearance of things : realism meant decadence and sterility, and naturalism had produced nothing worth-while. In Gauguin's paintings, objects were given a density and a personality of their own, quite remote from atmospheric preoccupations. Like Gauguin, the Nabis wanted to give the picture back its autonomy, to make it meaningful. To this end,

Derain, by Vlaminck

into a jewel of pattern and colour. A scholarship boy at the Lycée Condorcet, he was about to go to Saint-Cyr and train to be an army officer like his father when he met Ker-Xavier Roussel and decided to be a painter. His mother, who adored him, set up a workroom as a corset-maker in order to increase their income. She enjoyed the company of the students he brought home, and the " Temple " meetings usually ended up in Mᵐᵉ Vuillard's workroom.

The Nabis considered Vuillard to be the most intellectual of their members, but unlike his friends he had no metaphysical preoccupations. He was not even very interested in Symbolism, but was passionately fond of poetry and literature; his friends included Mallarmé, Paul Valéry, Lugné-Poë and the staff of the *Revue Blanche*, which was edited by Thadée Natanson, a former pupil at the Lycée Condorcet. Once famous, he was elected the favourite portraitist of the bourgeoisie, although his portraits are not always the most attractive examples of his work. His greatness lies in his ability to convey the poetry of ordinary life. He is the most outstanding of the intimist painters.

they adopted Synthetism and abandoned the gradated tones and broken touch of the Impressionists. They gave up primary colours and concentrated on blacks, bistres and earths which they applied in broad unmodulated areas. Like Gauguin, they were interested in primitive cultures, Japanese prints and popular imagery, and they helped to launch the vogue for the arts of remote civilizations. Looking back on these years, Maurice Denis says, " The schema of the Japanese painters did not satisfy our need for simplification. We combined elements from primitive and Far Eastern idols, Breton calvaries, figures from tapestries and stained glass windows, with echoes of Daumier, Cézanne's gauche version of Poussin in pictures like *Les Baigneuses*, and Pissarro's heavy peasant style."

But their collective temperament—intellectual, prone to doubt and compromise—made them stop half way. Brilliant colours disconcerted them; lacking the dynamism to persevere, they settled for a more delicate style, relying on muted colour harmonies and lilting arabesque. This, however, was not uniform. Sérusier continued to use bold colours, while Bonnard became one of the greatest colourists of the century. Although they missed the point of Gauguin's message, they were careful to stress the poetical meaning of a picture, and often added numerous symbols.

Their weakness lay in the fact that they tended to indulge their fondness for arabesque and occasionally descended to a style of decoration not too far removed from the Art Nouveau they professed to despise. Their real distinction lay not in their crusading activities (they were reformers rather than revolutionaries), but in their taste, the refinement of their means of expression, their touching ability to convey intimacy. No style has caught the tranquility of the home, the sweetness of family life and affection, the inherent poetry of daily tasks, the charm of parks and public places so well as that of the Nabis. The Fauves, who made their appearance shortly after the Nabis had broken up as a group, thought little of them; they lumped them with the Impressionists. Only Marquet, who attended the Académie Ranson, when Maurice Denis and Vuillard were teaching there, maintained any kind of contact. The Nabis, for their part, had attained a level of cultural and personal development which made them disinclined to pay much attention to a group of young firebrands. Only Sérusier and Maurice Denis took an interest in their work, and through the lesson of the Fauves' violence rediscovered some of their own youthful ardour.

Moreover, the Fauves discovered Gauguin independently of the Nabis, learned for themselves his lesson of strong colours worked in flat unmodulated areas, and understood his message that a picture is an end in itself. Like the Nabis, they discovered primitive art through his example, but unlike Gauguin, they perceived its plastic possibilities rather than its symbolism, a lesson which they passed on to the Cubists. Not all the Fauves, however, were influenced

Van Gogh: "Colour alone can express certain things"

" You understand that this combination of yellow and red, of green dulled down with grey, and the black lines that emphasise the contours, produces a feeling of oppression ... Moreover, the subject of the great tree struck by lightning, the sickly greenish pink smirk of the last autumn flower, confirm this feeling. Another canvas shows the sun rising on a field of young corn: lines converging toward the horizon, furrows mounting high in the picture space towards a wall and a range of mauve hills. The field is violet and yellow-green: the white sun is surrounded by a great halo of yellow. In this picture, as a contrast to the first, I have tried to express a feeling of calm and of great peace ... I mention these two pictures, particularly the first, to remind you that to give a feeling of anguish, there is no need to paint the Garden of Gethsemane, and that one can paint gentleness without depicting the protagonists of the Sermon on the Mount."

Letter to Emile Bernard.

" A technical problem: tell me what you think of it in your next letter. I'm going to put black and white on my palette and use them just as they are when I get them from the colour merchant. When—and remember that I'm speaking of a simplified scheme of colour such as the Japanese use—when I see in a green field, with a pink path, a gentleman dressed in black ... reading *L'Intransigeant*, and above him a simple cobalt sky, why shouldn't I paint him in unmixed black and the newspaper in unmixed white ?

For the Japanese painter makes an abstraction of the reflection and paints flat colours one beside another, with characteristic lines indicating the movements and the forms. In another connection, when one paints a combination of colours expressing, for example, a yellow evening sky, the harsh flat white of a wall seen against the sky must be done by mixing the crude white with a neutral colour because the sky would give it a slightly lilac overtone. Again, in this simple landscape,

by Gauguin. Matisse, who discovered Gauguin's last works in the course of a visit to Daniel de Monfreid at Collioure in the summer of 1905, saw in their simplified colour areas a means of personal escape from Neo-Impressionist pointillism (*Le Bonheur de Vivre*, painted shortly after this visit, accurately reflects this discovery). But Vlaminck denied that he owed anything to Gauguin. " Paul Gauguin's painting always seemed to me cruel, metallic, and lacking in natural emotion," he wrote. " Interposed between Gauguin and his pictures, I sense a fanatical desire for novelty, a desire to create an original effect at all costs ... Gauguin is always absent from his own work. Everything is there, except the painter himself. There is no feeling, and perhaps it has never affected me simply because it lacks the unity it would have possessed if his heart had played a greater part in it." Speaking of Van Gogh, the major influence on his early years, Vlaminck added, " Van Gogh's art is human, sensitive, alive; Gauguin's is cerebral, intellectual, stylized."

This judgement establishes once and for all the two main currents of Fauvism. Matisse, Marquet, Friesz, Dufy and Braque were all influenced by Gauguin; Vlaminck, Derain and Van Dongen were influenced by Van Gogh. Yet this division was not hard and fast. During his stay at Collioure with Matisse in 1905, Derain adopted Gauguin's decorative style and his use of broad flat colour areas, while Matisse experimented with Van Gogh's typical dabbing brush-stroke.

The Fauves were attracted by Van Gogh's dynamism, his ability to translate his sensations into colour, and a certain baroque feeling for movement, qualities easier to assimilate than the allusive and intellectual style of Gauguin. Van Gogh's emotional intensity suited their temperaments and strengthened their own preconceptions. His contempt for an exact reproduction of nature, the direct and sometimes brutal tone of his paintings, underlined by deliberate distortion and brilliant colour, spoke directly to their understanding. Also —and this is important—they preferred Van Gogh as a man. Like many of their own group, he was self-taught; painfully, he had found his own way, far from academies and schools. Vlaminck, in his Memoirs, conveys something of the shock caused by the Van Gogh exhibition at Bernheim's in 1900. " At that time Bernheim was in the rue Laffitte, between Durand-Ruel's and the Boulevard des Italiens. The gallery consisted of two rooms : the first, which you entered directly from the street, and a smaller one behind it. The lighting was poor. A spiral staircase led to the first floor where the director had his office.

" Van Gogh was known to only a few artists and a small number of collectors. Tanguy, half dealer, half colour-merchant, and Le Barc de Boutteville, at the bottom of the rue Le Pelletier, sold or tried to sell a few of his canvases. They asked modest prices—fifty or a hundred francs—and it was eleven years before fifty or so of his pictures were brought together at Bernheim's. There were

44

Manguin, self-portrait

which is meant to represent a white-washed hut on orange earth (orange because the southern sun and the brilliant blue of the Mediterranean bring out an orange which corresponds in intensity to the colour scale of the blues), the black notes of the door, the windows and the little cross on the roof ensure that the contrast of black and white is as agreeable to the eye as the combination of blue and orange."
Letter to Emile Bernard.

" Colour alone expresses something; one can't do without it, one must profit from it; what is really beautiful is also true."

" Whether it is of a figure or a landscape, painters have always tried to convince people that their picture is something other than the representation of nature as one might see it in a mirror, something other than an imitation—a sort of re-creation."

" The painter of the future is a colourist such as has never been seen before."

" To express the love of two lovers by a marriage of two complementary colours, their identity, their oppositions, the mysterious vibrations of the area in which they mingle. To express the thought in a head by the flash of a light colour on a dark ground. To express hope by a star. The ardour of a human being by a ray of setting sun. This is certainly not realism, but is it not something which truly exists ? "

Letters to Théo.
L'Art de la Peinture (Seghers).

seascapes, harvest scenes, Provençal landscapes, *L'Arlésienne*, a self-portrait, cypresses, sunflowers, the *Chambre à Coucher* and *La Nuit Etoilée*.

" Until then I had known nothing of Van Gogh. His discoveries seemed to me decisive, but precisely because I felt unlimited admiration for the man and his work, he seemed to rise up in front of me like an adversary. I rejoiced in his lesson, but it gave me a severe jolt! " Both Derain and Matisse, who went to the exhibition with him, were equally overcome. Later Vlaminck said, " At that moment, I loved Van Gogh more than my own father."

These were not idle words; in spite of his poverty and the need to support his wife and children, Vlaminck made heroic efforts to buy one of Van Gogh's pictures. But he failed to raise the necessary four hundred francs.

Van Gogh, who had first come to Paris in 1886, painting landscapes in sombre colours relieved with highlights, discovered the idea of pure colour only when he went to Arles. In Paris, under the influence of Pissarro and Signac, he had given up using blacks and bistres, and had painted a few Montmartre landscapes in an overtly Impressionist style. Once in contact with the light of the South, his palette changed completely and he was able to communicate his deepest feelings through the medium of colour. It is interesting to note that the Fauves, Vlaminck in particular, naively believed that Van Gogh was a purely instinctive artist. In this they were greatly mistaken, for his obsession with colour depended on precise theories on which he had meditated for some time and which are abundantly expounded in his letters to his brother Théo and Emile Bernard. His ideas may be summed up as follows :—

Only the artist's reaction to his subject matters.

Colours are symbols. Red and green, for example, symbolize the terrible passions of men. Colours do not have to correspond to reality.

Colour can replace tonal values, perspective, chiaroscuro, even, to a large extent, relief.

He laid particular emphasis on the suggestive powers of colour. In a letter to Théo, he explained, " In my picture, *The Café at Night*, I wanted to express the idea that a café is a place where one can ruin oneself, go mad, commit a crime. By contrasting light pink, blood red, burgundy, Louis XV and Veronese greens with yellow-green and a hard blue-green in an atmosphere of subterranean sulphur yellow, I tried to express the subversive attraction of a drinking den."

Thus, while Gauguin taught the Fauves that a picture is an end in itself, that it is a decorative whole achieved by allusion and economy of means, Van Gogh incited them to use pure colour as a form of lyrical expression. He strengthened them in their belief that the artist's reactions to his subject matter are of primary importance and encouraged them to paint pictures in which temperament and emotion are more important than reason and analysis. In a prophetic letter written to Théo from Arles in 1888, he stated, " Contemporary

47

painting promises to become more subtle, more musical and less like sculpture; in short, it promises colour! "

The three Fauve groups (from the studio of Moreau, from Chatou, and from Le Havre) had only to follow the lines laid down by Gauguin and Van Gogh. Gauguin, at Bois d'Amour, had advised Sérusier to paint his tree yellow. The Fauves, in a kind of sun-struck delirium inherited from Van Gogh, decided on red.

III The studio of Gustave Moreau

Paradoxically, many of the Fauves, and Matisse in particular, received their training in the studios of the Ecole des Beaux-Arts. The most important of these studios was that of Gustave Moreau.

Moreau was a sophisticated artist who specialized in rather thin-blooded " visions," and he shared with David the distinction of having trained more painters than any other teacher of the nineteenth century. He must have been a man of exceptional qualities, for his many pupils were unanimous in their admiration for him. Rouault, his favourite disciple and spiritual heir, who also became the curator of the museum which he left to the State, almost worshipped him. Louis Vauxcelles wrote of him that " he brought minds to birth," and for this reason he was venerated by his pupils, who included Matisse, Desvallières, Marquet, Manguin, Camoin, Evenepoël, Ary Renan, Piot, Flandrin, Milcendeau, Lehmann and Bonhomme. The Belgian painter Evenepoël, who died of typhoid at the outset of a brilliant career, wrote to his father, " We came away from his house with greater enthusiasm in our hearts, and with our ideas and feelings about art enormously uplifted."

Moreau was a strange creature, physically small, and crippled by an inferiority complex. After a timid onslaught on the world of fashion—he had a charming tenor voice and could be persuaded to sing—he retired from society and lived with his aged mother in a little mock Renaissance house in the rue de La Rochefoucauld. Since his mother was deaf, he could only communicate with her by writing. After her death, he became a complete recluse, seeing few people apart from his favourite pupils. This seclusion did not impress Degas, who disliked him and described him as " a hermit who knew the railway timetable." Degas also criticized his painting, remarking that " Moreau thinks that the gods of Olympus wear watch chains." These taunts soon dissuaded Moreau from exhibiting his works. He had been strongly influenced by Chassériau, whom he had greatly admired in his youth, and from whom he inherited a taste for Orientalism, overloaded architecture, jewels and rich materials. He had an advanced taste for religious mythology which formed the subject of all his pictures. Moreau, who as a child had received no religious instruction and was not even baptized, subsequently suffered from a form of religious frustration which turned him into a passionate student of every cult. Finally he became a theosophist. At the end of his life he was living in a world of debased Christian fantasy, in which Leda and the Swan served as symbols of the Incarnation.

He died the death of a sage. Cancer caused him atrocious suffering, but he refused sedatives. " I want to keep my brain intact to the very end," he said; " it is my most precious possession."

Progressive and reactionary painters alike made fun of his pictures, which are weighed down with allusions and symbols. But the Symbolists, naturally enough, admired him. Huysmans and Jean Lorrain proclaimed him the most representative artist of the movement. " Gustave Moreau is a wizard," wrote Jean Lorrain. " He can boast of having forced open the doors of mystery, of having disturbed a generation. To a whole group of artists, now avid for the mystical and the supernatural, he has bequeathed a subversive taste for voluptuous and legendary deaths. Oh! the dangerous attraction of the accoutrements and perversities of ancient cults! Curiosity about the ritual fornications of ancient religions has become an exquisite obsession for *fin de siècle* aesthetes." After the Symbolists, the Surrealists claimed Moreau as one of their forerunners.

Contemporary opinion has reduced Moreau to a kind of Odilon Redon minus the talent, a master of the sham and the fake. His gods and goddesses, sphinxes and heroes, loaded with ornaments and draperies, strike languid and declamatory attitudes and disport themselves in scenery worthy of a Hollywood technicolour epic. This only throws into sharp relief his curious role in the evolution of modern painting. This cold and laborious artist (according to Renoir, he could not even draw a foot properly) left his mark on an entire generation. The fact of the matter is that Moreau was enlightened and perceptive when dealing with the work of others. Unlike the other professors at the Ecole des Beaux-Arts, he did not demand that his pupils should slavishly imitate his own style; he only asked that they should be completely themselves, and it can truthfully be said that the ones he loved the best were the ones who were least like himself. " He trusted their gifts," wrote Thadée Natanson, " often more than they did themselves, and almost always before they did." For those who only wanted to learn the business of picture making, he acted as an effective guide, pointing out the way to an academic career, awards, and one of the Academies. Not all his pupils were geniuses : far from it. They included Maxence, Bussy, Sabatté, Piot and a certain Marcel Beronneau who simply copied his master.

Other teachers at the Ecole des Beaux-Arts regarded him as a heretic, and recriminations were frequent and prolonged. He was once seen emerging from a selection committee meeting shouting, " The swine! the swine! " His teaching, based on museums rather than an academic system, appeared completely revolutionary. He would take his pupils to the Louvre and lecture passionately on its masterpieces. " I owe my knowledge of the Louvre to Gustave Moreau," said Matisse. " We had stopped going there. Moreau took us and taught us how to look at the masters. He had strange and diverse enthusiasms. One day, he could look at nothing but Raphael; the next, Veronese. One morning he arrived proclaiming that Chardin was the greatest master of them all. He could understand and explain all the great painters to us, while Bouguereau only asked us to admire Giulio Romano. One Saturday Moreau exclaimed, ' I've just seen an acrobat by Lautrec in the window of a newspaper kiosk. It's awfully clever.' " Certain of his remarks to Matisse and Marquet throw light on the Fauves' most extreme positions : " What does nature matter ? It is only a pretext for the artist to express himself. Art is an endless pursuit of the right form to express our inner feelings." " I don't believe in what I see or what I touch. I only believe in what I can't see, what I can only feel. My intellect and reason seem ephemeral, of doubtful reality; only my innermost feelings seem eternal and unquestionably real." " The most durable artists are those who interpret nature, who put into their works the chromatic imagination needed to become a colourist."

Applying principles like these, he obliged his pupils to paint creatively, not to imitate. In his view, the artist's main task was to make beautiful things which were of value in themselves. To this end, all technical means—form, colour, pigment—were valid.

Moreau was perfectly aware of his profound originality. " I am the bridge over which you will pass," he would say to his pupils, and then add, " Perhaps I annoy you sometimes. All the same, I wish I had someone who knew his business as my master."

When he died, his studio was taken over by Cormon who set his course for a return to academism. Most of Moreau's favourite pupils left. Matisse, with some reservations, recognized his debt to Moreau and was fond of repeating one of his precepts : " In art, the more rudimentary the means, the greater the intensity of feeling." He would have had some difficulty in denying Moreau's influence on his own work, and Vlaminck makes no bones about it when he says, " Gustave Moreau's art was little more than a collection of accessories and attributes, which obliterated the model under a weight of trinkets, pearls, crosses, diadems and swathes of material. Though Matisse thought he had got right away from this, he was in reality steeped in it; it became part of him, and ornamentation and accessories are of major importance in his own canvases. He does not deck his model with jewels, but he does compose his picture with the blue designs of a tablecloth, the stripes of the curtains, the yellow pattern on the wallpaper and the markings of the odalisque's trousers. His sinuous outline gives the picture the appearance of a coloured drawing which lacks both modelling and depth. The general effect is attractive and reflects a decorative and skilfully composed palette; but his colour, which tends to become refined and delicate, lacks density, has no weight or substance. It is more like a water colour or a lithograph ..." This is especially true of his post-Fauve period, the period of the windows at Nice and the odalisques.

One fact is incontrovertible : it was through Moreau's tender care that Matisse was able to reach his full stature as a painter. Moreau, who called him his " intimate enemy," told him, " You are going to simplify painting." He exacted from Matisse's father an assurance that he would be allowed to continue his studies; " I have no fears for him," he told the cautious grain merchant, " he is one of my best pupils." His support was decisive for Matisse, who would otherwise have gone straight back to the dusty lawyer's office from which he had escaped only with the greatest difficulty. His career was slow to develop and had been considerably hampered. He was born at Cateau-Cambrésis in 1869 and brought up at nearby Bohain en Vermandois where his father was a grain chandler. As a child he gave no signs of any particular talent and had even been considered hopeless in the drawing classes at his school in Saint-Quentin. He was therefore quite ready to go into law and was articled in Saint-Quentin to a solicitor appropriately named Bonconseil.

It was here that he showed his first signs of independence. He was by no means a model clerk; sometimes he incorporated fables by La Fontaine into lengthy legal documents. No-one ever found out.

He began to paint shortly after he had his appendix removed. While convalescing he was interested to see his neighbour in the next bed painting a picture and decided to have a shot himself. His mother was delighted to find a simple means of distracting him; she herself was fond of decorating porcelain plates. She brought him a little box of oil paints, and his first canvas, signed Essitam (his own name spelt backwards), was a copy of the lithograph inside the lid, showing the banks of a river with a mill. This, as he said, was a glimpse of paradise for him. He copied many lithographs and read Goupil's manual " containing everything a painter should know." When he left hospital he registered at the Ecole Quentin de La Tour and went there every morning to copy plaster casts before going on to the lawyer's office.

For a long time this was a secret between his mother and himself, since his father was a man of fixed principles with a luke-warm attitude to the arts. He thought that all artists starved. " You'll get over it," was all he said when Matisse finally confessed that he wanted to be a painter. He then pretended to give in, thinking his son would return to the fold when he had had his head. He was nearly right. Matisse's first days at the Académie Julian, which he entered in October, 1891, were disappointing. Led by Sérusier, the Nabis had just left, and the atmosphere had once more become markedly academic. Bouguereau, who taught there with Gabriel Férier, rebuked Matisse on his first day. " You are rubbing out your charcoal with your fingers. That's dirty. Get a rag and some chalk. And draw that plaster cast on the wall ... You must learn perspective. But first you've got to learn how to hold a pencil."

Disgusted, he joined the evening classes at the Ecole des Arts Décoratifs, where he met Marquet, who had been there a year, and with whom he felt himself to be in immediate sympathy. For some reason Matisse refused to obey the studio usher's order that pupils should remove their hats when the professor entered the room. " I'm afraid of draughts," he is supposed to have said. This pig-headed attitude appealed to Marquet who was from Bordeaux and six years younger, and the outcome was a fortnight's rustication and a friendship that lasted half a century.

Matisse's disappointments continued, however, for he failed the entrance examination to the Ecole des Beaux-Arts. Discussing this difficult period with Robert de Saint-Jean in 1948 he remarked, " I didn't understand a word of those drawing lessons at the Cours Yvon where my early works were corrected by teachers who were categorical but far from clear. Should I have understood if they had been men of ability ? I doubt it. Once I was lucky enough to hear Rodin's comments on my drawings. They were completely irrelevant ... But this is no reflection on Rodin because an artist rarely understands, and is therefore incapable of communicating, his own particular gift. A teacher doesn't always know what he is teaching; most studios remind me of Brueghel's *The Blind leading the Blind* ..."

Better times came when Gustave Moreau noticed some of his drawings in the casts room at the Ecole des Beaux-Arts where students were allowed to work and in 1893 admitted him to his studio without an examination. Rouault and Manguin had already been there a year, together with Desvallières, Piot and Evenepoël, for whom he had a particular regard. Marquet joined them in 1898 with Linaret and Camoin. These last were not greatly influenced by Moreau's teaching, for he died a few months later.

Taken by his master to the Louvre, and helped by that master's enthusiasm, Matisse began to discover himself. To train his eye and his hand he made numerous copies, particularly of Philippe de Champaigne's *Dead Christ*, Poussin's *Echo and Narcissus*, Raphael's portrait of Castiglione, Giorgione's *Tempesta*, Chardin's *La Raie*, and Delacroix's *Enlèvement de Rebecca* (this last in black and white). One of these copies, of a *Hunt* by Annibale Carracci, was bought by the State and today hangs in the Hôtel de Ville at Grenoble. Others, including two splendid copies of Chardin's *La Raie* and Philippe de Champaigne's *Dead Christ*, signed H. M., were discovered in 1922 in the attics of the Louvre by

Robert Rey, then Director of the Beaux-Arts. Matisse was told of them and took them back.

This copying gave Matisse a technique and a taste for silver greys and thin paint. Still following Moreau's advice he visited the dealers of the rue Laffitte in search of works by the Impressionists, Gauguin and Van Gogh. But it appears that he was not yet sufficiently mature to derive any benefit from this early contact with the painters of light and colour. " I was more or less inclined to agree with Rodin, who dismissed Gauguin as just another oddity," he remarked. His relations with Pissarro were more fruitful. This guardian angel of the Impressionists was always interested in young painters and had even been influenced by Seurat; he gave Matisse the benefit of his opinions and his experience.

In 1896 Matisse was all set for an honourable career as an academic painter. He was a protégé of Puvis de Chavannes, and was admitted to the Salon de la Nationale despite the opposition of Béraud. He exhibited two *Dessertes*, an *Intérieur d'Atelier* and a *Liseuse*, which Félix Faure, the President of the Republic, bought for his daughter's room at Rambouillet. The following year he was appointed an associate of the Salon and was thinking seriously of becoming a teacher of drawing. A trip to Brittany with the painter Wéry in the summer of 1896 led him to abandon the idea of a traditional career in the arts and to join forces with the innovators of the day. In the course of this trip he discovered Impressionism, simplified his drawing, and lightened his palette. At Belle-Ile he met an Australian painter, John Russell, who talked about Van Gogh and his work and gave Matisse one of Van Gogh's drawings. The effects of this journey became visible immediately after his return to Paris. During the winter of 1896-1897, he painted a *Desserte* (now in the Niarchos collection) in a distinctly Impressionist manner. Pissarro, who had been following and encouraging his development, advised him to go over his picture and eliminate the white spaces in the centre of the canvas. This he did. All traces of grey disappeared from his palette, and with the exception of a brief interlude in 1902, he remained faithful to the claims of colour.

1898, the year of Moreau's death, was nevertheless a happy one for Matisse, marked by two important events : his marriage and his first contact with the warmth and light of the Mediterranean. His wife, Amélie-Noëlle-Alexandrine Paraye, was from the Roussillon, and they were married on January 8, 1898, at the Church of Saint-Honoré d'Eylau. A memorable cook, she was to be a courageous and indispensable companion during the difficult days ahead. Moreover, she accepted Matisse's natural daughter Marguerite and brought her up with a care that was increased by her own fear that her husband did not love her enough.

Amélie accompanied him on a brief trip to London, where he discovered Turner, and she was also with him when he discovered the Mediterranean.

At last he had discovered his true element: the sun, which, as Picasso said, " he had in his blood." He spent almost a year in Ajaccio, then moved to the outskirts of Toulouse, where his wife's parents lived, to paint in a state of continued delight. The canvases he took back to Paris after his long absence were boldly coloured, with thick paint applied in slashing strokes. They bore no relation to his previous works. Chrome yellow, cobalt blue and emerald green exploded in a pre-Fauve symphony.

As soon as he returned he left the Beaux-Arts, where Cormon had just succeeded Moreau. The history painter received him coldly.

" How old is Matisse ?" he asked the studio usher at the first lesson.

" Thirty-seven."

" Does he know what he's doing ?"

" Yes, sir."

" Then he'll have to go."

Matisse, unrepentant, decided to go his way alone. He returned to the Louvre and made more copies of Chardin, then, with Marquet, went sketching in places like Arcueil and the Luxembourg gardens. The two artists were impressed by the art of Toulouse-Lautrec and drew at the Moulin de la Galette and in the cafés of Montmartre. At the Petit-Casino, Matisse noticed Mistinguett, then at the outset of her career. Marquet developed an unrivalled virtuosity in this genre and his sketches of this period reveal him as one of the most gifted draughtsmen of his time.

In order to draw from the nude, the two friends enrolled at the Atelier Biette in the rue de Rennes, where Carrière was an instructor. Carrière was famous for his vapourish pictures of motherhood (" the model moved!" Degas once said of one of them). He was a mild and self-effacing man, and he and Matisse never exchanged a single word. Yet the young Fauve could have learned a great deal from Carrière, who was an artist of complete independence. Frantz Jourdain describes him in his Memoirs as " a kind of psychological freak, an exceptional character who disturbed his more rational colleagues and apparently took pleasure in ignoring the normal code of living. He had nothing in common with the greater number of his contemporaries, did not share their tastes, needs, appetites, passions or principles, yet he made no conscious attempt to be singular or to think of himself as exceptional." Of Alsatian origin, Carrière had had a difficult and unhappy life. He married very young and had six children, one of whom died in hospital because he couldn't afford to look after him at home. Poverty, which he accepted with a kind of fierce dignity, dogged him throughout his life. His fame coincided with the development of the cancer which was to cause him great and prolonged pain before it finally killed him. He was a man of complete integrity and once refused to sign a contract for 100,000 francs a year (which would have given him security) because he knew he could not honour it. A non-conformist and a supporter of Dreyfus, Carrière knew that he was boycotted by the other Salon painters and for their benefit exaggerated his inelegant manners. When visitors came in the evening, he would take an already opened bottle of rough red wine from a cupboard and slop it into thick glasses standing on a bare table. " Those who attended Carrière's classes realized that he was an exceptional teacher," adds Jourdain. " Certainly he rarely bothered to correct the drawing of a nose, a knee, or a muscle, but he did inspire his audience with a passion for art. He found the right words to explain how nature should be interpreted, pointing out the harmonious links connecting humanity with the world, the country-side, the sky and the trees; he communicated the deep and powerful mystery of things, showed the nobility of the humblest forms of nature's creations, showed also how the spirit shines through matter. He was orator, poet, philosopher and moralist, and he had the gift of awakening in young people a feeling of reverence for life."

It is a pity that Matisse did not catch the attention of such a man, although it is probable that Carrière's artistic ideals were too remote from the ones which Matisse, Marquet, Puy, Laprade and Derain were then following. These men formed the first Fauve group; Vlaminck came in later through his friendship with Derain.

At this period Matisse was painting mainly nudes, in a harsh and rather brutal manner. His palette was explosive: violet madder, emerald green, vermilion, cadmium yellow. Jean Puy, writing of this period, states, " He did not hesitate to introduce extreme and completely arbitrary methods. For example, the lateral planes and the shadows under the eyebrows were painted in almost pure vermilion, and this intensified the general colour of the head and the prominence of the nose and forehead. Sometimes the nudes would seem to be enclosed in an envelope of orange."

On his return from the south Matisse installed himself at 19, Quai Saint-Michel, where, a few years later, he was joined by Marquet. It was a curious household, a kind of second Bateau-Lavoir: the central staircase led off in all directions and in addition to Matisse and Marquet the building also housed a number of other artists, notably Flandrin and his mistress, Marval, a former model who had taken up painting to prove to her lover that anyone could do it. Well-built and statuesque, she was famous for her eccentric dress and the cascades of brightly coloured flowers of which her pictures were composed. This period was a time of creative fertility, personal happiness, and material difficulties for Matisse. The critics and collectors whose attention he had attracted with his early *Liseuse* were discouraged by his new manner and gave him up. His father, who had answered numerous demands for financial assistance, put his foot down. On more than one occasion he was forced to go home to his parents at Bohain, leaving his wife to run a hat shop in the rue de Châteaudun and to support their two little boys, Jean and Pierre, on the proceeds. (Hats always inspired Matisse. His mother had also been a milliner and many of his models wear some very impressive creations.) In 1900 he reached the depths of poverty and discomfort when he was forced to take a job as assistant to the painter Jambon who had been commissioned to decorate the Grand Palais for the Exposition Universelle. With Marquet he painted chains of laurel leaves on travelling bands. It was laborious and uninteresting work and it had to be done in a crouching position. He recalled this miserable period in a conversation with Francis Carco in 1941. "What a job! I have never known such complete degradation. The clever ones got themselves dismissed after a fortnight and collected an indemnity. There were waiters, grooms, a whole pack of scoundrels on whom Jambon had to keep a sharp eye. Unfortunately he didn't like the look of me. One day as I was whistling he said, 'Well, Doctor, you're having a good time, aren't you?' I was so fed up that I answered, 'Some hopes here!' That did it. I got my money and the sack. I had to try and get a job somewhere else." Obeying one of those mad impulses to which people with no money are particularly prone, he tried to get himself taken on as an attendant at the Opera, without success.

In the studios people were beginning to call him " M. le Docteur," or " Herr Professor," because of his gold-rimmed spectacles, well-shaped beard, and slightly pedantic manner. Even when drawing from the nude at the Académie Carrière, he gave the impression of writing out a prescription. " I remember," writes Thadée Natanson, " an extremely well-groomed man wearing spectacles whose gold rims were outshone by his reddish hair and beard. He spoke with assurance, without affectation, and it was only afterwards that one became conscious of his extreme prudence. His spectacles—especially before he changed to horn-rims—emphasized the academic quality of his pronouncements." " I never saw him laugh," says André Salmon. He must have been unlucky with his timing, for Matisse, despite his schoolmaster's appearance was, as numerous witnesses have attested, a high-spirited companion with a taste for practical jokes. All his life he spiked his conversations with slang and studio jokes. He was seen, with Marquet, at many fancy-dress parties. In 1913 he turned up at Van Dongen's in a long clerical robe; this came off to reveal an undershirt inscribed with the names of unmentionable diseases. The same year he sat on a panel to elect the first queen of the Quartier Latin. Later, he was given to attending dances at festival time in Nice wearing a mask. Nevertheless, he never went beyond a certain point. The sculptor Pierre de Léonardi remembers an evening at the Rotonde when Modigliani set fire to a Russian newspaper that Lenin was reading; Matisse angrily snatched the crackling sheet from the future dictator's hands.

1901 was a wretched year. His first Fauve period was over and his material difficulties caused him to retreat in some measure from the isolated position he had adopted. He may even have thought that his experiments in colour were leading him in the wrong direction. His painting became more temperate, with a greater attention to realism and a clear concern for design and composition. For a better understanding of volume he turned to sculpture, and at the Ville de Paris school, rue Etienne Marcel, executed a *Jaguar devouring a Hare* after Barye.

One side of his character is clearly revealed by the fact that at the time of his greatest poverty, when he had no coal for a fire and was forced to paint wearing gloves and a heavy overcoat, he still managed to buy a Cézanne study of *Baigneuses* from Vollard, a Gauguin *Head of a Boy*, and a plaster model by Rodin. The following year he acquired two Redon pastels, although his family was living on nothing but dried vegetables sent by his mother. When he bequeathed his Cézanne to the Petit Palais in 1936, he wrote to the curator, Raymond Escholier, " I have had this canvas for thirty-seven years and I know it pretty well, though not completely, I hope. I drew strength from it at critical moments in my life as an artist, as well as faith and perseverance. For this reason I am asking you to give it the position it needs in order to be seen at its best. It should have light and should be viewed from a distance. Its colour and design are rich, and distance reveals the vigour and tension of its structure and its exceptional sobriety of tone." He must have had unusual strength of will not to sell this work when Cézanne's prices were beginning to rise. One very black day he almost succumbed, but the potential buyer failed to keep the appointment. Not all his colleagues experienced the same difficulties. Manguin, Puy, and Camoin, for example, learned how to compromise with their love of pure colour and sold their paintings for good prices. But the time when Matisse would overrule the protests of the public and win over both critics and collectors was not far distant.

Another trip to the south in 1904, this time to Collioure (which he was to revisit frequently), confirmed him in his earlier ideas on colour. Vollard, who saw the pictures painted at this time when he visited the Quai Saint-Michel, decided to give Matisse his first one-man show. Roger-Marx wrote a short preface for the catalogue, but the results were disappointing : only one canvas was sold, to Olivier Saincère, a future secretary-general at the Elysée. But from this moment progress was rapid. With this money and his wife's savings Matisse managed to take his family to Saint-Tropez to spend the summer with Signac. This was the second turning-point in his career. In the euphoria of the Mediterranean sunshine he adopted the Neo-Impressionist technique of pointillism to give greater intensity to his coloured surface. Making no attempt to convey the atmospheric qualities of the landscape, he used the divisionist technique to give his tones the greatest possible vibration, isolating his colours by areas of white canvas.

Signac, who had been living at Saint-Tropez since 1892, had rapidly inveigled all his old Neo-Impressionist friends—H. E. Cross, Maximilien Luce,

Van Rysselberghe, and Lucie Cousturier—down to seen him. His villa, "*La Hune*," overlooked the *Crique des Graniers*. Eventually he invited the younger artists whom he had met at the Salon des Indépendants, Manguin, Camoin, Matisse and Marquet. The remote little harbour was the ideal place for artists in search of the simple, free and inexpensive life. It was almost impossible to get there except by sea, which pleased Signac and his friend Person who were fond of sailing, or, if one were particularly adventurous, by the local train and a narrow twisting track on which derailments had ceased to excite any comment. An asthmatic cargo-boat brought meat, vegetables and fruit once a week from Marseilles. Barrels of raw *vin rosé* were piled on the quayside waiting for the luggers which would take them on to Nice. This idyllic situation lasted until about 1930. At the outbreak of the second World War the Saint-Tropez of the vineyards and the fishing smacks had become the "Saint-Trop" of vacation fantasy, and the painters had disappeared with the rest. During his stay with Signac Matisse made studies which he worked up in Paris into *Luxe, Calme et Volupté,* his first undoubted masterpiece and the first picture to excite the abuse of the visitors to the Salon des Indépendants. It was bought by Signac. Dufy, on seeing this picture, was converted to Fauvism. " When I saw it," he said, " I understood all the new ideas about painting, and the version of realism practised by the Impressionists lost its charm as I contemplated the miracle of imagination introduced into the colour and composition." His friend Friesz was swayed by his enthusiasm. Matisse, in a mood of fantastic creativity, painted a series of brilliantly coloured pictures which were to be the crux of the scandal at the Salon d'Automne. A kind of competition broke out between Matisse, Vlaminck and Derain. Derain had taken Matisse to Chatou to see Vlaminck's works and Matisse was deeply impressed. He returned the following day and told Vlaminck, " I couldn't sleep last night. I want to see it all again." After these meetings he invited Vlaminck and Derain to join his group and exhibit with them at the Salon des Indépendants. This was the only time that Fauvism looked like becoming an organized movement.

The summer of 1905 was a time of supreme importance. At one stroke the Fauves, either by processes of reasoning or abandonment to their instincts, reached a high point of colour intensity. At Collioure, Matisse and Derain painted their boldest and most brilliantly coloured pictures in the pointillist technique of the Neo-Impressionists, but soon the rediscovery of Gauguin, or rather a deeper understanding of his works, led them in a new direction. Maillol, who had settled in his native region, had, through his contacts with the Nabis, retained a deep admiration for Gauguin which was increased by a knowledge of the late works owned by Daniel de Monfreid in his house at Corneilla de Conflent, a few miles from Prades. Maillol took Matisse and Derain to see the pictures, and their overwhelming strength made a profound

Matisse : article published in *La Grande Revue,* **December 25, 1908**

" What I seek above all is expression. On occasion I have been conceded a certain amount of knowledge, but critics have added that my scope is limited and does not exceed the purely physical satisfaction that the sight of a picture can bring. But a painter's feeling should not be considered apart from his style, for his feeling is only valid inasmuch as it is served by a style that becomes more complete (and by complete I do not mean complicated) as the inner content becomes deeper. I cannot distinguish between the idea and feeling I have of life and the manner in which I express it.

For me expression does not reside in passion, which breaks out on a face or is indicated by a violent gesture. It is in the whole arrangement of my picture: the place occupied by the body, the empty spaces around it, the proportions, all have their part. Composition is the art of arranging in a decorative manner the various elements which express the painter's feelings and ideas. In a picture every element is visible and plays its proper part, whether principal or secondary. Anything that is of no use in the picture from this point of view is of its nature harmful. A work implies a general harmony: for the spectator, any superfluous detail takes the place of an essential one.

Composition should aim at expression, which is of course modified according to the surface to be covered. If I take a sheet of paper of a certain size, the design I draw on it will bear a certain relation to that size and shape. I should not repeat it on another sheet of a different size or of different proportions—rectangular, let us say, rather than square. But if I had to transfer it to another sheet of the same size but ten times as big, I should not merely be satisfied with making the sketch ten

impression on Matisse, the effects of which were to be felt for a very long time. He discovered the impact of pure colour applied in broad flat areas, and the importance of the dark line surrounding and emphasizing it. It was while under the influence of this visit that he painted *Fenêtre ouverte à Collioure,* which marks the transition from the pointillism of Signac to the broader treatment of Gauguin.

His change of course became even more marked after his return to Paris. Gauguin is the operative influence behind his portrait of his wife wearing a flowered hat, the famous *Femme au Chapeau,* the key picture of the scandal provoked by the Fauves at the Salon d'Automne. The face is yellow and green, the hair red. All the shadows are green. The colours, however, are carefully orchestrated, vivid, but fresh and clear, not brutal and rudimentary like those of Vlaminck. The whole of Matisse's future development is adumbrated in this picture. Also from this period dates another portrait of Mme Matisse : here her face is bisected by a green stripe. The pointillism of Saint-Tropez is completely absent from these two works.

Gertrude Stein and her brother, always in search of something new and sensational, visited the Exhibition and immediately chose *La Femme au Chapeau* for which they made an offer of four hundred francs. The price in the catalogue was five hundred and Matisse, encouraged by his wife, refused to lower it. Mme Matisse reasoned that if the Steins could afford four hundred they could go up to five hundred. The extra hundred francs would allow her to buy winter clothes for their daughter. She was right, and the Steins gave in. At the same Salon, Matisse sold pictures to Maurice Level, Vollard and Thénard.

A short-lived but close friendship grew out of this meeting with the Steins : they frequently entertained Matisse in their apartment in the rue de Fleurus, and visited his house on the Quai Saint-Michel. " Mme Matisse occasionally gave them a lunch," Gertrude Stein relates in *The Autobiography of Alice B. Toklas,* " this happened most often when some relation sent the Matisses a hare. Jugged hare prepared by Mme Matisse in the fashion of Perpignan was something quite apart. They also had extremely good wine, a little heavy, but excellent. They also had a sort of Madeira called Rancio which was very good indeed."

Friendly relations became cooler when Matisse realized that the Steins were interested in Picasso. " Miss Gertrude likes local colour and theatrical effects. A person of her worth could not possibly have a serious friendship with a man like Picasso," he said harshly. Nevertheless, he exchanged pictures with Picasso, whom he met at the Steins. Unkind friends hinted that each artist had chosen the worst he could find amongst the other's work in order to show it around. This is not altogether true, because the portrait of *Marguerite* given by Matisse to Picasso is first-class, and it is difficult to believe André Salmon

times larger. The drawing should have an expansive force that will give life to the things around it. If an artist has to transfer a composition from one canvas to a larger one, he should not merely square it up but conceive it all over again ... The main function of the colour should be to serve the general expression as best it can. When I apply my colours, I have no favourites. If at the beginning, perhaps without my being aware of it, a tone has charmed and attracted me, I usually find that when the picture is finished I have respected this tone, though I have progressively modified and transformed all the others. I respond to the expressive qualities of my colours in a purely instinctive way ... My choice of them is made without the benefit of any scientific theory; it is based on observation, on feeling, on experience, and on my own sensitivity. An artist like Signac, remembering certain passages of Delacroix, takes great care with complementary colours, and his theoretical knowledge leads him to use certain colours in certain places. But I simply try to put on colours that will give a certain feeling. There is a necessary proportion of colour that can lead me to modify the shape of a figure or to transform my whole composition ...

If I put red, green and blue on a canvas, each new application causes the last to lose its importance. I have to paint an interior, and before me is a cupboard that gives me a very vivid sensation of red. A relation is established between this red and the white of the canvas. If I put a green beside it, and paint the floor yellow, further relations between the yellow, the green and the white of the canvas will be established and they will satisfy me. But these different colours diminish each other. It is essential that the colours I use must be balanced in such a way that they do not destroy each other. Therefore I must get my ideas in order, and then the relations between the tones will be established in such a way that they will support rather than spoil each other. A new combination of colours will succeed the first, and thus give the whole of what I wish to represent ...

when he tells us that Picasso's guests at the Bateau-Lavoir used it as a dartboard (" One in the eye for Marguerite! ").

The hostility between Picasso and Matisse has been greatly exaggerated. In spite of certain ironic remarks, the two men admired each other; Matisse felt concern for Picasso's work right up to his death, while Picasso bought pictures from Matisse. Matisse explained their differences by saying, " Picasso is Spanish and I'm French. It's as if you asked me to explain the difference between an apple and a pear. It's in the nature of things."

In spite of—or because of—the attacks and jeers aroused by the fourteen pictures exhibited in the Salon d'Automne, Matisse was regarded as the leader of the new movement. Many young painters came to him for advice, and he opened his first studio in a former convent in the rue de Sèvres. Then, as the number of his pupils rapidly increased, he took a studio in the Hôtel Biron, where Rodin and Rainer-Maria Rilke were already living. This was the beginning of what came to be known many years later as the School of Paris. The painter Léopold Survage, who was one of Matisse's first pupils, recalls that there were many foreigners, amongst them the American, Bruce, Hans Purrmann, a German, Isaac Grunwald and Nils de Dardel. Slavs were particularly numerous. These artists, especially the Germans, made Matisse's name known abroad, and spread the Fauve theories of pure colour.

Matisse remembered Gustave Moreau's principles and advised his pupils to concentrate on the construction of the picture and the balance of the figures. " Paint straight onto the white canvas," he used to say, " if you put a colour onto a primed surface you begin with a false harmony that will get in your way as you go on ... A single tone is only a colour, two tones make a harmony, something alive ... A colour is only of value in relation to its neighbour ... Fix your impression from the beginning and stick to it ... Feeling counts most of all." And he would add, " Don't kill yourselves trying to make an exact copy of nature."

Although admired by a few young painters, Matisse was nevertheless attacked on two fronts, by the upholders of the academic tradition, and by certain young painters of Montmartre. The following inscription appeared on a wall in Montparnasse: " Matisse drives you mad ... Matisse is worse than absinthe " (referring to an official campaign against alcohol). For some time, Utrillo was suspected of being its author. In 1906 Matisse sent his *Bonheur de Vivre* to the Salon des Indépendants. Roars of laughter greeted both this and the Douanier Rousseau's *Liberté invitant les artistes à la 22e exposition des Indépendants*. Once again the Steins' judgment was correct and Leo bought *Le Bonheur de Vivre*, which was painted entirely under the influence of Gauguin, and which may be considered, together with *Les Demoiselles d'Avignon*, as one of the key pictures of the twentieth century.

Victory was in sight. Apollinaire, who called Matisse the *fauve des fauves*, published a long article on him in *Phalange*. It was his second article devoted to a contemporary painter, the first being on Picasso. Matisse himself wrote an important article, a confession of faith, and the first real commentary on his work, in the *Grande Revue*. This was the first of a long series of similar writings. Few artists were so intent on explaining their work; this was probably the outcome of the long period of incomprehension and rebuffs.

From this point, he was considered a painter of importance, and having accomplished what he set out to do, he kept his distance from the other Fauves, not wishing to be lumped together with the other members of that hot-headed group. His influence abroad increased, especially on the painters of Dresden and Munich. When he visited Germany in 1908 and 1910, he was greeted and honoured as a master.

The times of material hardship were at an end. Thanks to several collectors, notably the Steins, Shchukin and Marcel Sembat, he was able to look after his family properly, and they all moved to a house at Issy which had the almost unknown luxuries of a bathroom and a conservatory. A contract with Bernheim, signed in 1909, delivered him from money troubles—or almost : during the first World War, his wife had to go back to making hats.

His success coincided with the dispersal of the Fauves and the decline of the movement. Cubism had already arrived. He had watched it grow out of the pipe-smoke of the Bateau-Lavoir and the Montmartre bistro Azon, where various young painters gathered round Picasso. Although Matisse kept apart, he played an indirect part in the formation of the new doctrine which was to replace Fauvism. It was in his house that Picasso discovered Negro art which, although not the principal source of Cubism, was nevertheless its prelude.

Max Jacob, who is in many ways a more accurate witness than Apollinaire, described the birth of Cubism in an article in *Les Nouvelles Littéraires* in 1928 : " M. Matisse lived with his family at 19, Quai Saint-Michel. He did not go out much. I was present at some of his excellent discussions with Picasso. He would often expound his theories on colour, and the relation between the painted surface and the brilliance of the colouring, etc. ... His gold-rimmed spectacles made him look like a scholar and his remarks proved that he was one. I mention him intentionally. One evening, Salmon, Apollinaire, Picasso and I were dining with him at the Quai Saint-Michel. I think we even intended to have a weekly dinner there, but I wouldn't swear to it. Matisse took a black wood statuette from a sideboard and showed it to Picasso. It was the first Negro wood carving we had seen. Picasso held it in his hand for the rest of the evening. The following morning, when I arrived at the studio, the floor was covered with drawing paper. On each sheet was a big drawing, each one almost the same as the next : a woman's face with one eye, an elongated nose merging into a mouth, and a lock of hair on her shoulder. Cubism was born. The same head reappeared in paint; instead of one woman, there were two or three. Then came *Les Demoiselles d'Avignon*, which is as big as a wall."

As will be seen, it was Vlaminck who discovered the plastic possibilities of Negro sculpture. He pointed them out to Derain, who brought them to the attention of Matisse with whom he was very close at this time. From then on Matisse began to collect Negro sculpture.

Although not deeply influenced by early Cubism, Matisse was not entirely unaffected by it, as can be seen in several of his pictures. The great Cézanne retrospective in the Salon d'Automne of 1907 gave him a clearer insight into this master's work and he developed a more tightly knit construction and a broader handling of colour. He discovered the importance of neutral tones in conjunction with brighter ones. His *Nu bleu*, painted after a journey to Biskra, is the first example of this new trend. A second journey to Morocco in the spring of 1913, in the company of Charles Camoin and the Canadian painter James W. Morrice, brought another change of direction. Pictures painted at this time show a tendency towards the geometrical synthesis of the Cubists which is particularly noticeable in *Les Marocains, Jeune fille au bain, Le Rifain,* and the *Leçon de Piano*. To this must be added the fact that he had been equally impressed by the icons he had seen in Moscow in 1911 and by the examples of Muslim art he was able to study in the important exhibitions in Paris and Munich in 1903 and 1910 respectively. These had revealed to him the evocative power of linear arabesque, and his delighted surprise is reflected throughout all his subsequent work.

His interest in Cubism was short-lived. In the course of his stay in Tangier, he and Camoin had explored the red light districts and had made a number of sketches in brothels; later, in Nice, these were to be developed into pictures of languorous odalisques. His purely Fauve period was over; his art ceased to be a matter of sensations and became more and more reflective. He never, however, completely abandoned the principles of Fauvism. His arabesques and more subtle colouring were essentially a further exploration of the cruder sensations he had expressed at the time of the Salon d'Automne of 1905.

It is impossible to speak of Matisse without being constantly reminded of the presence of Marquet. Friends for life, they were inseparable as young men. They first met in 1891 at the Ecole des Arts Décoratifs; both went on to attend the Ecole des Beaux-Arts and the studio of Carrière. For many years they lived in the same house on the Quai Saint-Michel, their studios one above the other. When they had something to say to each other, they would bang on the floor or the ceiling. Such closeness implies deep affinities; in fact, it would be difficult to find two men physically and emotionally less alike. Matisse was imposing, scholarly and pedantic, a great trackerdown of essentials, given to interminable explanations of his slightest plastic intention. Marquet was self-effacing, a caustic wit whose remarks were repeated around the studios, as were those of Degas. " He was not a great talker," writes Marcelle Marquet in her moving little book on her husband, " but whatever he said was always exactly right... There was nothing more to add; the matter was finished. He was remarkably clear-sighted; his explanations were like his drawings, neither too much nor too little, going straight to the heart of the matter." He had no interest in intellectual speculation, although he was extremely intelligent, and like any other artist, capable of explaining his work, but he was only interested in painting and willingly left the commentaries to others. For him, painting came first. Matisse and he understood each other without too many words, and found painting the best medium of communication.

Marquet was not essentially a colourist and the few pictures by him that could be properly described as Fauve were painted under Matisse's influence, more or less experimentally, " to see what was in it," rather than from a deep conviction. He never had a completely Fauve period; he could paint in a subtle grey and bistre colour scale one day and use pure bright tones the next. "Sometimes," he remarked, "I would start a picture in brilliant colours and go on to finish it in greys." He was a Fauve by association, but he never claimed the title.

His most characteristically Fauve qualities are to be found not in his occasional highly coloured pictures, but in his simplified conception of the picture surface, his use of unmodelled areas of local colour, and above all, his allusive drawing. He was fascinated by movement and life—unlike Matisse, who, with the exception of *La Danse*, preferred to show his subjects in repose—and liked to sketch in cafés, music-halls, or the street; with a few strokes of the pencil or a brush dipped in Indian ink he would create mordant and astonishingly life-like outlines. This gift for capturing the essence of a subject never failed him. Even his landscapes are portraits.

In spite of their differences, or perhaps because of them, he and Matisse got on well together. They shared similar backgrounds and very fixed ideas of creative freedom. They were united, moreover, by the hostility that their work aroused. Both were quiet men, little attracted to a Bohemian way of life, preferring the simpler pleasures of music, reading and the open air. In some respects, their relationship was like that of vassal and overlord, or younger and elder brother. Matisse protected Marquet, the younger man, all his life, less by virtue of his superiority as an artist than by his greater experience of the world. In practical matters, Marquet was like a bewildered child. When dealers came with offers of exhibitions and contracts, Matisse gave him the advice consonant with his legal training. Later he told him how to invest his money (Marquet, who had a Balzacian streak in his character, developed after 1910 the habit of speculating on his own works, and even kept his pictures in the strongroom of a bank. " An artist must also be a business man," he used to say).

Marquet allowed himself to be managed, although not without a trace of irony. One day, when they were both famous, Matisse advised him to buy gold. " Why ?" said Marquet, " are Matisses going down ?" Another reason for his self-effacement was his physical appearance. It is no insult to his memory to say that his great lumpy head and pince-nez made him look like Toulouse-Lautrec, whom he also resembled in his height and gait. André Salmon describes him in *l'Art Vivant* as walking about town " in a venerable felt hat, which he never took off, his eyes gleaming behind his glasses." His unlovely appearance earned him the cruel nickname of Aesop among his fellow students at the Ecole des Beaux-Arts.

His lack of physical beauty had not embittered him, although it may have sharpened his caustic wit. Matisse was well aware of the tender heart behind the gross exterior. Marcelle Marquet relates that when he came to her to plead Marquet's cause, he said, " Have you realized how kind he is ?"

Albert Marquet was born on March 27, 1875, and was of even humbler origins than Matisse. His father, about whom little is known, worked at the railway station at Bordeaux. He was extremely absent-minded and registered his son's birth a day late. Many years later, Marquet had his horoscope compiled by the amateur astrologer Mainsieux. " It's a curious thing," said Mainsieux, " nothing in your life agrees with what I see, but it would all fall into place if you had been born a day earlier." " But I was born a day earlier," replied Marquet in astonishment, " my mother always told me so."

At the age of four he was already covering his school books with sketches, and his greatest pleasure, before he went to Paris, was to draw in the harbour. His work reflects his consistent love of water, harbours and ships. Marquet's father did not approve of his son's becoming an artist. " You'll end up on the waterfront," he said, a curiously prophetic remark. His mother, however, took his side, and it was to her that he owed his artistic education. A canny, witty woman, Mme Marquet sacrificed her security and her married life for her son's desire to be an artist. Realizing that he could not train properly in Bordeaux, she sold a small piece of land she owned in her native Le Tech, and on the proceeds left her husband, went with her son to Paris, and opened a little draper's shop in the rue Monge. The tiny income from this paid for their keep and her son's schooling. For long periods, mother and son lived on a sack of lentils which they had brought with them from Bordeaux.

In 1890, at the age of fifteen, Marquet went to the Ecole des Arts Décoratifs; Matisse, who was to help him to discover his own particular talent, enrolled there the following year. Their formation and development were intimately connected. Like Matisse, Marquet took the advice of Gustave Moreau and made copies in the Louvre. His choice of artists shows that he instinctively admired the great colourists: Veronese, Rubens, Claude Lorrain, Corot, and Chardin. Moreau also encouraged his habit of sketching out of doors. He was immensely gifted, and Léon Werth relates. " I remember one evening in Rotterdam. A crowd had gathered outside a bar where two men were fighting, possibly with knives. It would have been wiser to pass on, but Marquet approached them as calmly as possible until he was practically under their noses." He wanted to get their expressions down in a quick sketch.

" Let's go and draw cabs," he would say to Camoin, when the two had got tired of Cormon, Moreau's dreary successor. He was particularly fond of cabs and made many sketches of them. " I intend to become a cab driver," he told Vlaminck, who took him seriously. " I shall earn a good living and I can draw while I'm waiting for fares."

When he was not out sketching with Matisse, he would go off with Charles-Louis Philippe. Behind their spectacles, they looked like a couple of clerks on the loose. They would explore the Marais, the red light district around the Boulevard Sebastopol, and the Place Maubert, observing the secret life of prostitutes and petty criminals for their illustrations for *Bubu de Montparnasse* (an obtuse publisher turned these down). It is worth noting that Marquet was the only Fauve painter who was in close contact with writers like Léon-Paul Fargue, Léon Werth, Francis Jourdain and Marguerite Audoux. His first pure colour period coincided with that of Matisse; while the latter was in Corsica in 1898, Marquet was in Moreau's studio, painting a male nude in crude reds and blues. Shortly after, Mme Matisse was the model for a *Femme au Chapeau* in an interior, also painted in very bright colours.

As he himself recognized, this was his most violent phase: "I painted in pure colours only at Arcueil and in the Luxembourg gardens," that is to say in 1898, when he ground his own colours in order to get absolutely unadulterated tones. This conflagration quickly burned out into greys and subtler colour harmonies: intense colour was not his vocation. Nevertheless the ashes flared up from time to time. Thanks to his mother, Marquet was spared the poverty that nearly killed Matisse (who had a wife and family to support). It was probably to comfort and encourage Matisse that he went with him to work for Jambon at the Grand Palais. " Only six more hours and we can go home," he would murmur as they painted the laurels. " Shut up, or I'll murder you," was Matisse's reply.

Less extreme, less agressive than those of his friends, Marquet's paintings were more popular with collectors. Berthe Weil noticed his work at the Salon des Indépendants and exhibited it in her gallery in the rue Victor Massé. Overcome with joy at her son's success, Mme Marquet began to keep accounts of his sales: one pastel, twenty francs; four pictures, three hundred francs ... In 1905 and 1906 he underwent a second conversion to colour. On a visit to

Matisse and his family at Saint-Tropez during the summer, he painted admirable landscapes of the harbour and hills in a broad technique which owed nothing to Signac and the divisionists. He was never again to find such breadth and natural ease of execution. He was then in full possession of his powers, perhaps superior to Matisse who reached his maturity in slow groping stages. This flow of inspiration continued throughout a holiday spent in 1906 on the Normandy coast with Dufy, a close friend in spite of Matisse's antipathy for him. Under the influence of Dufy's vigorous personality, he painted in pure colours—or almost pure; he didn't altogether abandon his black and earth tones—and the two men's pictures of this period are so similar in subject matter and handling that it is possible to confuse them. The pictures of the fourteenth of July celebrations at Le Havre, and of sailing boats at Fécamp and Trouville, which give Fauvism its particular atmosphere of happiness, date from this period. But the manner did not last. In 1907 Marquet returned for good to a subdued palette and subtle tones applied in flat broad areas, simple harmonies which are an accurate reflection of his temperament.

His mother died in her native village where she had retired to spend her last days. She died at peace. Her goal had been attained; her son was over his difficulties and on the way to becoming a famous painter. In the year of her death, Charles-Louis Philippe wrote in the *Grande Revue*: " Marquet has a sense of balance and of the density of things which preserves him from all extravagance and aberration."

Alone, Marquet began a long period of wandering that lasted until his death. He lived on the Quai Saint-Michel in order to be near Matisse, but he was hardly ever in his studio, forever setting off for Naples, Hamburg, Tangier, Rotterdam, Sète, Venice, Norway, Morocco, Algeria, Egypt, Rumania, Sweden, Russia, always painting harbours and seas and ships from a window or balcony. From early days his limp had made it difficult for him to go out in search of subjects, and he had adopted the habit of setting up his easel before a window. Hence the characteristic plunging perspective which is almost a hallmark of his works.

Fauvism was only a short episode in Marquet's career but he never forgot its lessons of simplicity and simplification. He reverted to a traditional conception of reality that owes much to Corot, and he expressed himself with wonderful felicity in terms of grey, bistre, and other muted shades. His joy in painting ended only with his last breath.

Colour plates 1—16

1. MATISSE. ÉTUDE DE NU. ATELIER CARRIÈRE. Collection particulière, Paris.

2. MATISSE. NOTRE-DAME. Collection Mme Ginette Signac, Paris.

3. MATISSE. LUXE, CALME ET VOLUPTÉ. Collection Mme Ginette Signac, Paris.

4. MATISSE. LA DESSERTE ROUGE. Musée de l'Ermitage, Leningrad.

5. MATISSE. CYRANO. PORTRAIT DE LUCIEN GUITRY. Mr. and Mrs. William S. Paley Collection, New York.

6. MATISSE. ARBRES A COLLIOURE. Mr. Robert Lehman Collection, New York.

7. MATISSE. NATURE MORTE AVEC LA DANSE. Musée de l'Ermitage, Leningrad.

8. MATISSE. JEUNE HOMME A LA CASQUETTE (portrait de Pierre Matisse). Mr. and Mrs. Leigh B. Block Collection, Chicago.

10. MARQUET. AUTOPORTRAIT. Musée des Beaux-Arts, Bordeaux.

11. MARQUET. NU DANS L'ATELIER. Collection Mme Albert Marquet, Paris.

12. MARQUET. LE PORT DE SAINT-TROPEZ. Collection Mme L. Jäggli-Hahnloser, Winterthour.

13. MARQUET. LE PONT-NEUF. National Gallery of Art, Washington D. C. Chester Dale Collection.

15. MARQUET. FÊTE FORAINE AU HAVRE. Musée des Beaux-Arts, Bordeaux.

16. MARQUET. LE SERGENT DE LA COLONIALE. Musée des Beaux-Arts, Bordeaux.

IV   The School of Chatou

The School of Chatou had no more existence as a real movement than had Fauvism itself. It is in fact little more than a convenient term to describe the activities of those two friends from the suburbs, Vlaminck and Derain. One might just as well describe the activities of Matisse and Derain in 1905 as the School of Collioure. Nevertheless, it is a practical term.

The School of Chatou was invented and maintained by Vlaminck, who was also convinced that he had invented Fauvism. He had no contact with the artistic circles of the capital, and knew nothing about the colour theories of Valtat, Matisse, and various other members of Moreau's studio, whose researches date from long before his own. He did not meet Matisse until 1900 at the Van Gogh exhibition and had little to do with him before 1905, when the two men compared their work. He was a solitary; he discovered the new style independently, and for that reason we have no right to correct him when he claims to have invented the Fauve movement.

Painting was for Vlaminck both a means of expression and a safety-valve. At the age of twenty he painted as others throw bombs: to show his opposition to society in its every aspect. " I painted in order to clarify my thoughts," he said later, "to assuage my desires, and above all to acquire a little purity. The idea of becoming a professional artist never occurred to me. If anyone had suggested that I should take up painting as a career, I should have laughed in his face. Painting is no more a career than anarchy, love-making, running, dreaming, or boxing. It's an accident of nature ..." At the end of his life he added, " God knows what would have happened to me if I hadn't been able to paint."

Vlaminck's life reads like a novel. At the age of eighteen, he was generally recognized as a superman: over six feet tall, weighing fifteen stone (about a hundred and eighty seven pounds), red-haired and overflowing with energy which he devoted to championship cycling, sculling at Argenteuil, wrestling with professionals in suburban circuses, and games of chance in the bistros of Bougival, Chatou and Argenteuil. He was born in 1876 near the Halles in Paris, where his grandmother had sold vegetables, and he grew up as free as a bird. He was the eldest of the five children of a strange musical couple. His father taught the violin, was head of the choral society of Chatou, and choirmaster at the church of Saint-Merri. Of Flemish origin (Vlaminck means " the Fleming"), the father was not greatly concerned with his children's future; he gave them a roof and a bed and set them free when they were old enough to earn their own living. His mother, a former Conservatoire prizewinner, gave piano-lessons. A native of Lorraine, she was a Protestant, and with her husband's consent she brought up her children in her own religion. This perhaps explains certain puritanical aspects of Vlaminck's character : he drank nothing but water, disapproved of pub-crawling, and was a great moralist. His Flemish blood explains his orgiastic colouring, his taste for juicy impasto, his energy, and the Baroque movement of his work.

Speaking of his childhood, he says that he was " born to music." " From my earliest years I ate, slept, and woke to the sounds of the violin and the piano," he writes in his book, *Tournant Dangereux*. " I grew up to the sounds of my father's pupils doing their exercises, the *Carnival of Venice, The Maiden's Prayer,* and the sonatinas, scales, and duets which were a permanent background to our lives." His father taught him music, and until the age of thirty he earned his living as a violin teacher. " I didn't think there was much money in painting," he confesses.

Vlaminck, who represents instinct as opposed to reflection and research, is the complete antithesis of Matisse. He wanted to burn down the Ecole des Beaux-Arts, whereas Matisse proclaimed that he had never rejected its teaching and would enumerate the influences he had undergone. Vlaminck insisted that other people's painting had no interest for him and claimed that he had never been inside a museum. This was completely untrue, and he later admitted it. " I often stated that too much museum visiting corrupted the personality, just as a close acquaintance with the clergy leads to a loss of faith. But don't misunderstand me. I am not against the lessons that a museum can teach. I don't say it's a waste of time to look at a picture by Poussin or Courbet. I remember too clearly what a revelation Van Gogh and the Douanier Rousseau were for me. But I do say that it is dangerous to look at other people's pictures, and even more dangerous to copy them."

At the age of twelve, he began to copy the coloured pictures—usually of landscapes of the Seine, a subject to which he long remained faithful—which were given away free with packets of chicory. Robichon, an academic painter who lived in Chatou, gave him a certain amount of advice. Vlaminck claims that he also learned a great deal from a harness-maker at Croissy who painted crude portraits in red and blue varnish, and in fact bright reds and blues were to be the characteristic colours of his Fauve period. He had a knowledge of Impressionist painting (discovered for himself in the galleries of the rues Laffitte and Le Pelletier), and all his life he had a fervent admiration for Monet, an admiration which dates from his childhood.

His mother was in favour of his painting because it would " keep him out of bad company," but his father was strongly opposed. " That won't butter your bread," he would say, and encouraged him to become a racing cyclist, a much more lucrative profession. Four hundred francs a week, in 1894, was a considerable sum for a boy of eighteen.

It was only after his meeting with Derain that he made a definite decision to become an artist and ceased to consider painting as a pastime. In his Memoirs Vlaminck has frequently described the circumstances in which he met Derain (to whom he always referred, for some reason, as Dérain). He dates this meeting in July, 1900, but this may be open to doubt. Alice Derain says it took place in 1897, and the truth lies somewhere between the two. If one remembers that in 1896 Vlaminck, aged twenty, went off to do his military service, he must have met Derain a few weeks after his release, i.e. in July, 1899.

Both men, however, give the same account of their meeting, in a railway accident. They already knew each other by sight : Vlaminck had often wondered about the man who walked round Chatou with a paint-box in his hand. On this particular morning, they met face to face in the train going to Paris. Vlaminck was in uniform, and he remarked that it would soon be Derain's turn. That evening they met again in the same train. At Garenne-Bezons the engine was derailed, and rather than wait for the relief they decided to walk to Chatou. In the course of their walk along the track they discovered their mutual passion for painting. They arranged to meet the following morning under the bridge at Chatou, this time with their painting equipment. Vlaminck, who was waiting for his demobilization papers, was spending his last leave with his family. He was already a mature man, with a wife and children : at eighteen he had married Suzanne Berly, and they had two daughters. " The sum total of our ages was less than forty," he relates.

Military service is a great trial to many people, to Derain, for example, whose reaction was a severe nervous depression. But Vlaminck's three years contributed greatly to his development and maturity. He was drafted into the military band, and spent his free time reading. " The barrack-room, with its twenty beds and its stink of tar, boot leather, stew and sweat, rocked to the rhythms of the regimental march," he remembers. The library contained books by Karl Marx, Kropotkin, Le Dantec, Pascal, Diderot, Victor Hugo and Zola, and it was in the course of barrack-room discussions that he became an anarchist. It was the right doctrine for him. He was against everything : family, education, the church, the army. Camille Mauclair, right for once in his life, describes him as " a professional rebel." Vlaminck lost no time in putting his new convictions into practice; he sent fiery articles to *Le Libertaire*, denouncing the reactionary mentality of the officers in his regiment, and together with a sympathizer, Corporal Fernand Sernada, outlined the plots of several novels. His collaboration with *Le Libertaire* was short-lived; its exclusiveness, its sectarian blindness, and its narrow-mindedness soon got him down. But every year, until 1939, he gave them a painting, the sale of which was intended to defray their printing costs. His literary career was more serious; he saw in the writing of hack novels another means of feeding his wife and children. " Painting," he said, " takes too long and costs too much. To write a novel all you need is a pen, some paper, and a few ideas." He had plenty of ideas. With Sernada, he threw together—literally—two novels, *From one Bed to Another* and *All for that* ...!, whose titles are a good indication of their literary worth. Later, still with Sernada, he wrote another novel, *Mannequins' Souls*, which, he said, almost won the Prix Goncourt. Apparently it was published too late to be read by the Ten and this cooled his ardour for a time. Literature's loss was painting's gain. But he retained his literary aspirations for the rest of his life, and in fact published more than twenty novels, books of reminiscences, and collections of poems.

Vlaminck always claimed that it was he who inspired Derain to paint. This is an exaggeration; Derain had been painting since he was an adolescent. While still a pupil at the Lycée Chaptal he consulted the painter Jacomin, a friend of Cézanne. His curiosity was insatiable; he went to museums and galleries, and attended drawing classes at the Académie Carrière, where he met Matisse in 1898 or thereabouts. Vlaminck has left an amusing description of Derain, who was four years his junior (he was born on June 17, 1880) : " I can still see Derain, aged twenty, aimlessly roaming the streets of Chatou, tall, lanky and gangling, like a law student. He would pass without transition from bitterness to high spirits, from lassitude and boredom to enthusiasm, from confidence to doubt and despair. He was young! "
The local children called him " cream cheese " (his parents had a dairy) and yelled after him as he went on his delivery round. He was the only son of well-established shopkeepers who had their own small house on the main square of Chatou. They wanted him to be an engineer; he was only interested in painting, and regularly cut the classes in which he was supposed to be studying. There was a scene when his mother discovered that the " Polytechnic " he was presumably attending had gone bankrupt and closed down several months earlier. Derain had said nothing, lulling them with regular reports of his progress.
Derain and Vlaminck had little in common, and their ultimate quarrel is less surprising than the fact that they had managed to agree on anything in the

first place. In his *Portraits avant Décès*, Vlaminck wrote, " Odd as this may seem, Derain and I were completely antithetical. But although our methods were different, our aspirations were of the same quality. We had the same ideal." Both adored painting, but while one believed only in instinct and abandoned himself spontaneously to colour, the other was open to every influence, perpetually harried by doubt, and ready to start all over again from the beginning. " At eighteen," said Derain, " I had as many reproductions of famous pictures as I could. What is the point of being ignorant ? "

He pursued his desire to understand so far that he eventually got lost in the process. " He suffered from too much intelligence and too little under-standing," writes Robert Rey, very accurately. " He wanted to understand everything in the world, including himself. He watched himself act, listened to himself talk, and judged himself without mercy. His lucidity did not in-cline him to be indulgent either to others or to himself. The more weaknesses he discerned in himself, the greater his pride." He himself recognized his faults when he said, elliptically, " The greatest danger in art is too much knowledge."

For the fifteen months during which they worked together, Vlaminck forced Derain to follow in his own footsteps. In this sense his influence was consid-erable : the hesitant Derain was obliged to do something positive. When Vlaminck was finally demobilized, they rented a room for ten francs a month in the former Restaurant Levanneur, a dilapidated relic of those canoeing parties immortalized by Renoir and Maupassant.

In 1900, Chatou was no longer the idyllic spot celebrated by the Impressionists. Bicycles had replaced sailing-boats, and the famous restaurants and guinguettes, "La Grenouillère", "Au Rendez-vous des Pêcheurs", "Le Bal des Canotiers", had fewer and fewer customers. Sunday was the only day when the Restaurant Fournaise, where Renoir had painted *Le Déjeuner des Canotiers* in 1889, came to life again. But the village still had its Bateau-Lavoir moored near the bridge, its red roofs, and wooded banks. The two painters had an excellent view from their room in the old restaurant, although they often had to contend with the ironic and occasionally ill-disposed comments of the locals. They were considered dangerous, and not without reason : if they worked hard, they played hard as well. Derain, in the quietest possible way, had a marked and masterly taste for mystification, which was generously acknowledged by Vlaminck. The entire village was aroused one morning when the two arrived in a cab from Paris, having just wound up a wild night in Montmartre, and disembarked in the main square with a couple of half-dressed prostitutes. "I told you that Vlaminck was a pimp," cried Mme Derain to her son. Vla-minck remarks, " We were not real bohemians, just non-conformists. We didn't belong."

When not painting at Chatou, Derain would brave Vlaminck's ironic comments and copy in the Louvre. It was at this time that he made the grisaille copy of Ghirlandaio's *Carrying of the Cross* which was to move Vollard so deeply. Indignant visitors complained to the attendants and he was moved on before he could finish it. He was not now so much under Vlaminck's influence as Vlaminck later tried to make out. In an interview published in *Comedia* in 1942, Derain said, " The Louvre was my obsession. I hardly missed a day there. I was wild about the primitives, who seemed to me the true, the pure, the absolute and only painters ..." Only on one occasion did he manage to get Vlaminck into a gallery, to the retrospective exhibition devoted to Van Gogh eleven years after his death. This event was of more decisive importance for Vlaminck than for Derain who was on the eve of his military service and unable to communicate his emotion through his painting.

Derain became a real Fauve only during his stay with Matisse at Collioure in 1905. His widow, Alice Derain, still has a picture painted when he was on leave in 1903. It is a bluish-green *Bord de Seine*, very far in feeling from the fiery certainties of Fauvism. Vlaminck was overwhelmed by Van Gogh, a fact on which Matisse, to whom Derain introduced him, commented : " I was at Bernheim's one day in the rue Laffitte," he relates, " when I saw Derain, accompanied by an enormous and vociferous young man. ' You see,' he was saying, ' you must paint with pure cobalts, pure vermilions, veronese greens !' I still think Derain was a little afraid of him, but he admired him for his warmth and enthusiasm. He came up to me and introduced Vlaminck."

In Van Gogh, Vlaminck recognized an instinctive painter, a painter without theories, a man who felt as he felt. He was quite wrong, but he drew from this discovery a conviction that he was on the right track, and saw in it encouragement for his own spontaneous and uncalculated painting. Technically, he owed a great deal to Van Gogh. Up till then, in spite of its violence, his style had been awkward and indecisive. His portrait of Bouju, called *L'Homme à la Pipe*, one of the few paintings that survive from this period, shows that he was still painting in muddy browns. The general effect is dull and heavy, despite the brutal brush-strokes that lash the canvas. After his discovery of Van Gogh his palette changed. He abandoned earths, browns and blacks in favour of pure colours, and he learned to draw with his brush, applying his paint in long parallel strokes. He never had recourse to divisionism, as Derain later did, or to the broad flat colour areas of Matisse. No transitional works are known. There is no connection between *La Fillette à la poupée*, painted under the impact of Van Gogh, and the earlier portrait of Bouju.

Derain went off to do his military service in the autumn of 1901. It was a difficult time for him; he had always had the comfort of a bourgeois home in which to recuperate from the effects of his bohemian activities. He felt crushed by the army's impersonal and mechanical system; he suffered from the promiscuity, the crudeness and the dirt, and his letters reflect a profound moral crisis. He wrote frequently to Vlaminck—who, from lack of money for stamps, did not reply as often as Derain would have liked—telling him of his feelings of despair and the problems that troubled him. Like Vlaminck, he went through a literary phase and wrote little poems about military life in a style which owes something to Mirbeau and Zola. Nevertheless, he emerged from these three wretched years more mature and with a stronger will.

Vlaminck for his part was passing through the most difficult period of his life. He was desperately poor and so continually hungry that when he did manage to get hold of some money he was capable of eating an entire leg of mutton and a couple of pounds of potatoes all by himself. He kept his gargantuan appetite until his death at the age of eighty-two and remembers tremendous eating contests with Derain and Apollinaire. The three would sit down in some restaurant and order everything on the menu. The one who gave up first had to pay the bill. " I never had to pay," he remarked. " Sometimes, after the pudding, we would begin all over again."

He used to tell fantastic stories about his years of struggle and poverty. One Sunday morning he set out on foot (and on an empty stomach) from Nanterre to walk to Paris, where he had a pupil living in the Avenue Victor Hugo. He gave the lesson and set off, again on foot, for Chatou, where he hoped to find his parents still at table. Alas, when he arrived, his mother was just removing the tablecloth. " Living entirely on hope," he relates, " and not at all put out by this bad luck, I made for the Pont de Chatou and went to see Alphonse Fournaise. Fournaise used to hire out canoes. Like all once-successful men, he liked young people who reminded him of his own great days. He liked me. That day, there was a regatta organized by the local people under the patronage of Maurice Bertaux, the Minister for War. I had only one idea—to win the prize. There were a dozen competitors, and I took my place in a canoe lent by Fournaise. In spite of the twenty-four kilometres I had done since the morning, I would rather have died than lose the prize. I won, and a few minutes later, to the cheers of the crowd, I mounted the rostrum. The *Marseillaise* played; my trembling hands received a superb metal reproduction of the *Victory of Samothrace*. Stowing it in the bottom of the boat, I set off again, gave the canoe back to Fournaise and thanked him, then made straight for the pawn-broker on the corner of the bridge. He gave me thirty francs, and the *Victory of Samothrace* underwent a rapid transformation into a four-pound steak."

In order to support his family, then living cheerlessly in a bug-infested house at Nanterre, he played the violin in various dance-halls, wearing gipsy costume. This sleazy life was a great trial to his puritanical nature, and he never came to terms with it. He got a job as second violin at the Château-d'Eau theatre and with it material security for several months. In a frenzy, he painted a picture every day : if his work did not satisfy him, he would rub it out on the grass and start all over again.

When Derain returned from the army, Vlaminck was at the height of his enthusiasm for colour; Derain followed him to a certain extent in *Les Péniches au Pecq* and *Bal à Suresnes*. The two friends had never been closer, and their pictures painted at this period are so alike as to be indistinguishable. Derain's brief moment of assurance soon passed, however, and he decided that a style based on instinct was not sufficient for his needs. He went back to the Académie Julian and to Carrière to get a thorough technical training. There is no doubt that Matisse played some part in this decision.

This marks the end of the School of Chatou. Derain and Vlaminck remained close friends until 1914, but they saw less of each other. They had many discussions, and their frequent arguments revealed the fundamental antithesis between their natures. The first break in their friendship occurred almost imperceptibly when Derain went to Paris. He settled in a studio in Montmartre, in the rue Tourlaque, and joined a group of young painters with whom he could smoke his pipe and discuss painting. He was less of a talker than Vlaminck, but was extremely fond of the kind of discussion—usually very long drawn out—that gave him a chance to clarify his ideas. He became a more positive character, with a wide range of interests: history, metaphysics, magic, astrology. By 1904 he had begun to collect primitive objects and old musical instruments, and he taught himself to play the organ and the harpsichord.

Vlaminck, although fond of talking, loathed discussions on art. To him, painting was like cooking : " One doesn't lecture about it, one enjoys it." Throughout his life he said extraordinarily little about his own work, and when visitors came to his studio he would stow away his most recent pictures. To underline his contempt for the intellectual and abstract conceptions of the Bateau-Lavoir, he exaggerated his noble savage tendencies. Vollard, who caught sight of him in the rue Laffitte before he knew who he was, was struck by his labourer's get-up, the red scarf tied round his neck accentuating the blue of his eyes. Symbolically, he held in his hand a blazing picture of a sunset painted in slabs of pure colour.

The meeting between Matisse and Vlaminck, arranged by Derain in the summer of 1905, led to the crystallization of the Fauve movement. Matisse, who was going through a slightly regressive phase as far as colour was concerned, was surprised by the violence of Vlaminck's pictures. He saw that he had taken a wrong turning, and his constrained manner did not altogether disguise his concern. The next day he was back again. " I couldn't sleep last night," he said, " I want to see everything again."

Derain: "I see the future only in terms of composition"

L'Estaque, 1905.

"Now I am working... but how badly! I find nothing of myself in it, and I don't know what I'm going to bring back. If this continues, very little!
However, I feel I am working towards something better, in which the picturesque will count less than it did last year...
Actually we are at a very difficult stage of the problem. I am so much at a loss that I wonder what words I can use to explain it to you ... If you are not aiming at decorative effects, the only thing you can do is to purify your transformation of nature more and more. We have not done this intentionally so far except in regard to colour. We have ignored drawing. There are many things lacking in our conception of our art.
In brief, I see the future only in terms of composition, because when I paint from nature I am the slave of so many trivial things that my emotions are driven the other way. I doubt if the future will follow up our experiments; on the one hand we are trying to do away with objectivity, and on the other it is our point of departure and our justification. To be perfectly honest, I don't know the logical line to take over this. If we make obvious compositions, that is to say, paint like Maurice Denis, we are only painting versions of stage scenery. I think the problem is rather to group forms in light and to harmonize them concurrently with the material at our disposal."

Collioure, July 28, 1905.

"... So I have two important points, concerning which this trip has taught me a great deal:
1) A new conception of light, which is as follows: a complete negation of shadow. Here the light is very strong, shadows are very thin. Shadow is a whole area of clarity and luminosity, which is very different from the light of the sun. In other words, it is a world of reflections.
Up till now we have both ignored this, but in the future, as far as compo-

The sequel is well known. Vlaminck and Derain were invited to join Matisse and his group and to exhibit with them at the Salon des Indépendants. Matisse's visit and his interest in their work convinced Vlaminck and Derain of the worth of their own experiments. Their elders took them seriously; they were not alone. They were also encouraged by a measure of material success. Vlaminck sold one of his pictures, *La Seine à Nanterre, Quai Sganzin*, for 100 francs, which covered the costs of his wife's confinement (she had a third daughter). Derain was even luckier, for he sold four pictures and was offered an exhibition at Berthe Weil's.

The great moment of self-realization came for Derain during his stay with Matisse at Collioure. Under the influence of the older man, and also of the later works of Gauguin which he saw at Daniel de Monfreid's, he abandoned the highly coloured and brutal approach of Vlaminck. He adopted a divisionist technique and worked in lighter fresher colours, rose-madder, violet, lemon-yellow—colours which were to reappear in his London period—closer to those of Matisse. He cared less about making a sensational effect than about producing colour harmonies. He began to think about rhythm and arabesque, matters to which Vlaminck was utterly indifferent.

That summer at Collioure was of capital importance for the future of Fauvism. Derain's artistic personality took shape; Matisse returned to pure colour and painted his most Fauve works: *La Fenêtre ouverte, La Femme au Chapeau, Portrait de M*^{me} *Matisse*. In the Salon d'Automne of the same year, Derain and Matisse were the real centre of the Fauve scandal, receiving more abuse from the critics than Vlaminck himself. Not that Vlaminck was spared. " André Derain," wrote Maurice Duval in *Le Nouvelliste*, " seems to have a greater concern for composition than has M. de Vlaminck. The latter throws a bowl of lemons, a vase of flowers, and a lot of red dots into a cloud of blue dashes ... We advise him to let his subjects settle down before trying to paint them." The Havas News Agency message, which went to all the newspapers, read as follows: "Fénelon denied that by mixing up a lot of letters haphazardly it was possible to obtain a line of the *Iliad*. M. de Vlaminck disagrees. He has thrown little blobs of colour at a canvas and called the result *La Maison de mon Père*. What are the red blobs? Where is the house? That remains a mystery. But M. de Vlaminck was pleased with his effort, and got some more little blobs of paint and threw them onto some other canvases. The result: *La Vallée de la Seine, Marly, Crépuscule, Jardin*. And that's that."

These criticisms acted like a goad on Vlaminck, affecting him more deeply than had the approbation of the Indépendants. He painted with fury, applying his tubes straight onto the canvas. Trees stretch vermilion branches against cobalt skies; red, orange and brilliant blue replace browns and earth colours. Vollard, with his infallible flair, chose this moment to descend on Vlaminck and carry off the three hundred canvases that he found in his studio, paying

sition goes, it is an additional vehicle of expression.

2) To learn from Matisse how to get rid of the consequences of divisionism. He goes on using it, but I have completely given it up. It is logical in a luminous and harmonious canvas, but it harms those things which derive their expression from intentional clashes.

In short, it is a world which destroys itself when pushed to its extreme point."

Derain, *Letters to Vlaminck* (Flammarion).

a price that seemed enormous to the painter—six thousand francs! Vlaminck wondered whether he were not cheating the poor dealer ... When Vollard undertook to buy everything he painted, Vlaminck decided to give the whole of his time to art. He was thirty. He gave up the violin lessons, took his family away from the wretched tenement in Nanterre, and moved to a little house in the middle of the woods at Jonchère, on the slopes of La Celle Saint-Cloud. He stayed there for ever after, except during the war when he was directed to work in a munitions factory at Puteaux. He identified himself more and more closely with the soil and the world of the farmer, and developed a fiery scorn for the promiscuity of Parisian life. This, however, did not prevent him from knowing exactly what went on there.

Now he was really a master. His style was essentially and boldly based on instinct, and his audacity led him quite naturally to a state of maturity which others reach only by painful and conscious intellectual exercise. He did not have to ratiocinate. Painting was his whole way of life. In later years he said, " I have never thought about classic, Greek or Italian art. I wanted to use my cobalts and vermilions to set the Beaux-Arts on fire, and interpret my impressions without a thought of what other painters had done before. When I have colour in my hands, I don't give a damn for other people's paintings : it's me and Life, Life and me. In art each generation should begin again ..." He added, " Painting reflects the painter. It is easier to read a man's life in his painting than in the lines of his hand. His origins, his background, his influences, his state of health, his mental balance, his blemishes, his mediocrity, his nobility, his education, his folly, his poverty or greatness of spirit are all there. If I had to judge men, I should judge them from their paintings—and I should make no mistakes."

Before calling on Vlaminck, Vollard had made a previous visit to Derain, and had bought eighty pictures for two thousand francs, a proportionately higher price than he was to pay Vlaminck. On hearing this, Derain's father exclamed in astonishment, " Your nonsense has brought you in this ? At your age I didn't have anything like as much. Perhaps if I finance you, you will work better and earn even more." Consequently he gave his son a comfortable monthly allowance.

Vollard had the interesting but unexpected idea of asking Derain to go to London to paint the Thames (Claude Monet's pictures of London had been immensely successful in Paris four years previously). The idea, like most of Vollard's, was a good one. Derain's stay in London was of tremendous value to him, although he claimed that the weather was wrong : the sun was shining and he had come to paint fogs. He was to visit London twice at an interval of a few months, and his London and Collioure periods are his best and most characteristically Fauve ones. Although most pictures were painted " sur le motif" and at a single stretch, Derain was completely indifferent to realism.

The appearance of the subject was dictated by the colour harmonies he wanted to capture : trees are blue, paths violet, etc. The divisionist touch gives way to a broader, flatter handling. His concentration on cool colours, violets, blues and greens, at the expense of warm orange and red, mark a further departure from the influence and example of Vlaminck.

Derain also brought back with him from London a collection of breathtaking English suits. Much later, when he had settled for sober navy-blue serge, he remembered them with some charm : " I had a reputation for elegance because I had brought back English clothes from London. Unfortunately, I applied the principles of Fauvism to my appearance. I had a green suit, worn with a red waistcoat and bright yellow shoes. My summer coat was off-white with light and dark brown checks; it got grubby very quickly. Picasso said, ' You look as if you're just back from Monte Carlo.' "

Vlaminck's outfits were no less stunning. William Clochard, one of his violin pupils, describes his waistcoats in pale yellow suede, tartan wool, purple velvet, or striped mattress ticking, and his bowler hat ornamented with a jay's feather. His wooden cravat caused a sensation, and Apollinaire devoted several lines to this curious feature of his dress : " Protected by an india-rubber suit and armed with a cravat, he (Vlaminck) follows one around, waiting for an opportunity to deal a mortal blow with his secret weapon. Though less famous than those of M. le Bargy, M. de Vlaminck's cravats are most interesting. They are made out of wood, are varnished in bright colours, and can be put to various uses. If M. de Vlaminck is in a restaurant and wishes to summon the waiter, he unhooks his cravat, which is held by a nail to the collar of his shirt, and bangs it loudly on the table. If he is in company and wants to organize a dance, he uses his cravat, on the back of which are stretched several lengths of catgut, as a kind of little violin, like those used by dancing masters in the old days. But he has no bow, and plays his cravat like a mandoline or guitar."

After Derain's visit to London, his relations with Vlaminck became cooler, although the two men remained on good terms. Derain was no longer the submissive novice and he took less kindly to Vlaminck's categorical statements. Vlaminck, sensing this, became more and more peremptory. Derain was irritated, and the result was a feud that lasted for thirty years. The pretext was so futile—some remarks about the Douanier Rousseau repeated by a malicious or ill-informed critic—that it is difficult to believe that this was enough to break up a friendship that had already lasted for twenty years. But Derain was delighted to make the break and refused to be reconciled.

After his return from London in 1906, Derain joined the group of Montmartre painters who met in the studios of the Bateau-Lavoir or at the Restaurant Azon. He became friendly with Apollinaire, Max Jacob, and the first Cubists : Picasso, Braque, Gleizes and Metzinger. Until his death, his best friends were Picasso and Braque.

"One afternoon in 1905 I was at Argenteuil. I had just been painting the barges and banks of the Seine. The sun was blazing down. I packed up my colours and brushes and went into a bistro. There were a few bargees and coalheavers at the bar. While I was drinking my white wine and soda, I noticed three Negro statuettes on the shelf between the bottles of Pernod and aniseed. Two were from Dahomey and were painted red, yellow, and white; the other, unpainted, was from the Ivory Coast.

I thought it was the effect of working in the sun for two or three hours, or perhaps the particular state of mind I happened to be in that day. Or had something just clicked with the ideas that were constantly in my mind? These three pieces of sculpture disturbed me. I perceived their tremendous potentialities. They revealed Negro art to me.

Derain and I had explored the Trocadéro Museum thoroughly on several occasions. We had looked at everything. But we had always accepted the exhibits as barbaric fetishes. The power of this instinctive art had entirely escaped us.

The three statuettes in the bistro at Argenteuil were quite a different matter. I was moved to my very depths. I asked the owner to sell them to me. At first he refused, but I insisted, and after all kinds of hesitations, refusals and excuses, he gave them to me on condition that I stood everyone a round of drinks. Then I carried them off.

Shortly after this incident, a friend of my father's, to whom I had shown my new acquisition, offered to give me some others that he had, because his wife wanted to throw " the horrible things " on the rubbish heap. I went home with him and took away a great white mask and two superb statues from the Ivory Coast. I hung the mask over my bed. I was both pleased and disturbed: for the first time, Negro art became clear to me in all its primitive beauty and strength. When Derain saw the white mask, he was stunned, and offered me twenty francs for it. I

The principles of Cubism were worked out in Picasso's studio and at Azon's restaurant. Although Derain denies that he ever contributed to these discussions, he played an important part in the formation of the new movement by virtue of his early recognition of the plastic qualities of Negro art, to which he had been introduced by Vlaminck. In 1904, the two had been in the habit of visiting the Trocadéro Museum—ancestor of the Musée de l'Homme—to look at the African and Polynesian collections. They regarded them simply as curiosities, and it was not until he had a flash of inspiration in an Argenteuil bistro that Vlaminck understood the true importance of primitive art. They converted Matisse and finally Picasso, who began a series of studies which culminated in *Les Demoiselles d'Avignon*, the first Cubist manifesto.

Shortly after his return from London, Derain gave way to his usual doubts and expressed his dissatisfaction with the limitations of expression through colour. " One might as well be a dye-stainer," he said to Vlaminck, " you can never get a redder red or a bluer blue than what the colour-merchant gives you." He felt an increasing need to organize his pictures and studied Cézanne and Seurat with enthusiasm. Ultimately, he felt a kind of repulsion for colour. Vlaminck, who expressed his scorn for the discussions at Azon's and thought them completely futile, was nevertheless a little disturbed. He felt that his ferocious faith in his painterly instinct was becoming standardized and could lead nowhere. Simultaneously, he had reached the maximum intensity of expressiveness and decorative effect; now he must look for something new. " Working directly from the tube like that," he confessed, " gives you tremendous facility. You bring it off every time and success leads nowhere. Pure colour and the violent handling to which I had committed myself no longer suited me. I suffered because I couldn't hit harder, because I had attained the greatest possible intensity, and because I was limited by the colour-merchant's reds and blues. It was like blowing a trombone or a saxophone until your lungs burst. I realized sadly that my compositions were only coloured rhythms ... and that the more I simplified, the more I relied on pure colour. By suppressing half-tones and all their pictorial possibilities, I had fallen into mere decoration. I was no longer going to the heart of things. The decorative spirit was making me forget how to paint. I needed an instrument of wider range. I began to need it badly ..."

Like the Cubists, he found this instrument in Cézanne. All the young painters were deeply impressed by the Cézanne retrospective in the Salon d'Automne of 1907. Few of them had seen Vollard's exhibition in 1895, so the impact was all the greater. But whereas the future Cubists fastened on the remark that " nature must be expressed by means of the cylinder, the cone and the sphere " (which may not have been intended seriously), Vlaminck concentrated on his lesson of how to construct a picture, and how to suggest volume by means of colour. He made many mistakes, hesitated and turned back many

refused. A week later, he raised the price to fifty. I was hard up at the time and accepted. He took the mask and hung it in his studio in the rue Tourlaque.

Picasso was the first to understand what could be derived from the plastic conceptions of the Polynesians and the African Negroes, and he introduced them more and more into his work. He took over the forms, lengthened them, and reshaped them. He flattened them and studded his canvas with them; the results were painted red, yellow and white, the colours the Negroes use for their idols and fetishes.

Picasso thus determined a movement of which the novelty struck people as revolutionary: the movement was Cubism."

Vlaminck, *Portraits avant Décès* (Flammarion).

times, before he attained the sovereign balance of his Cézanne period, in which he painted some of his most beautiful pictures. " The harder I work," he said, " the more difficult it becomes." Although condemning Cubism out of hand, he painted several canvases in which the obvious structural preoccupations and fragmented lines present certain similarities with Braque. The colour of such works—usually still lifes—is sombre and turgid. There is little red, but much of the original Fauve violence survives in the broadness of the handling. Derain, who was also unwilling to follow the Cubists (" he blamed Cubism," says his biographer Georges Hilaire, " for the same reason as he criticized Fauvism—for impoverishing the means of plastic expression,") nevertheless registered Cubist preoccupations, and his taste for analysis, which is already evident in his first Fauve works, gained in strength. He abandoned bright colours and reverted to half-tones. He was primarily in search of a means of emphasizing the structure of his compositions : colour and pigment were no longer of any interest to him. It was not until 1911 that he renounced his angular and schematic compositions and returned to a figurative style with a pronounced use of arabesque inspired by the Sienese primitives. The Douanier Rousseau, with his emphasis on pure feeling, was another important influence. Until the 1920's, Derain's intelligence and his authority caused him to be considered a greater painter than Picasso. Young artists went to him for advice and direction. He came to look on Fauvism as an aberration of his youth, a phase in his development. " He never spoke of it," says Alice Derain, whom he had met in 1907, just when Fauvism was on the wane. " It held no further interest for him. Fauvism was an explosion which could have no aftermath."

Vlaminck, however, after the interval of sobriety brought on by the influence of Cézanne, returned to a freer manner in the 1920's in which instinct was once again supreme. Using blacks and whites as he had once used reds and yellows, he prolonged throughout his life the fireworks of his youth and remained the only Fauve painter who survived the Fauve movement.

17. VLAMINCK.   LES BORDS DE LA SEINE A NANTERRE.   Collection particulière, Genève.

18. VLAMINCK. LES RÉGATES A BOUGIVAL. Mr. and Mrs. Werner E. Josten Collection, New York.

19. VLAMINCK. LA DANSEUSE DU « RAT MORT ». Collection M. et Mme André Fried, Paris.

20. VLAMINCK. PAYSAGE AUX ARBRES ROUGES. Musée National d'Art Moderne, Paris.

21. VLAMINCK. VOILIER SUR LA SEINE. Mr. Robert Lehman Collection, New York.

22. VLAMINCK. VASE DE FLEURS. National Gallery of Art, Washington D. C. Chester Dale Collection.

23. VLAMINCK. LE JARDINIER. Collection particulière, Paris.

24. VLAMINCK. BORD DE SEINE A CARRIÈRES-SUR-SEINE. Collection M. Guy Roncey, Paris.

25. DERAIN. PORTRAIT DE VLAMINCK. Collection Mme Berthe Vlaminck, Rueil-la-Gadelière.

26. DERAIN. LES PÉNICHES. Collection M. B.-J. Fize, Paris.

27. DERAIN. BORD DE RIVIÈRE. Mr. and Mrs. William S. Paley Collection, New York.

28. DERAIN. PORTRAIT DE MATISSE. The Tate Gallery, London.

29. DERAIN. BIG BEN. Collection M. Pierre Lévy, Troyes.

31. DERAIN. LA FEMME AU CHALE. Collection M. B.-J. Fize, Paris.

32. DERAIN. LE PARLEMENT DE LONDRES. Mr. Robert Lehman Collection, New York.

33. DERAIN. CHARING CROSS BRIDGE. Private Collection, New York.

34. DERAIN. SUR LA TAMISE. Collection particulière, Paris.

V   The painters from Le Havre

Although it is difficult enough to speak of the School of Chatou, the School of Le Havre barely existed at all. Its three painters, Raoul Dufy, Othon Friesz and Georges Braque, can hardly be considered a group. They were the last recruits to Fauvism, and were converted to the uses of pure colour by the paintings of Matisse, Vlaminck and Derain seen at the Salon des Indépendants and the Salon d'Automne of 1905. They were too young to contribute to the formative phase of the movement, which they regarded as a mere aberration of their youth, without further consequences. Matisse and Vlaminck would be considerably diminished in stature without their Fauve pictures. The opposite is true of Dufy, Friesz and Braque, who all evolved their mature style after the demise of the Fauve movement.

Despite the similarity of their background and tastes, the three men had very different temperaments. The sensuous and high-spirited Dufy took from Fauvism only enough to reinforce his own airy and highly personal style. Friesz, who had a sensual nature and a pronounced classical bias, evolved a stolid and somewhat prosaic manner which ultimately received official recognition, whereas the analytical spirit of Braque found such complete expression in Cubism that it is difficult to believe that he was ever a Fauve at all.

All three studied at the Ecole des Beaux-Arts in Le Havre, where the director, Charles Lhullier, was a kind of provincial Gustave Moreau. Like the latter he was a fashionable and much decorated painter, in constant conflict with the Ministry inspectors who frowned on his unorthodox methods of teaching. Sharing Moreau's contempt for academic taboos, he played a part in the formation of an iconoclastic style which completed the destruction of official painting. His own pictures are dry and tedious, his portraits, for which he required up to a hundred sittings, cold and stilted. Only a few of his sketches have any sort of animation. He had had a difficult career and known long periods of obscurity. Born into a seafaring family from Granville, he was a pupil of Cabanel and Picot, one of the decorators of the Galerie des Batailles at Versailles. To earn his living, he worked for fifteen years as assistant to Pils, the illustrious author of *Rouget de l'Isle singing the Marseillaise for the first time*, of text-book and calendar fame. Pils, snowed under with commissions, got Lhullier to execute most of his historical paintings, and this concentration on anecdote at the expense of pictorial considerations ruined poor Lhullier's talents. He was under no illusions about this and at the end of his life remarked sadly to Othon Friesz, his favourite pupil, " Don't work for others, work for yourself. I have wasted my life. What remains of my efforts ? Only the memory of a few pencil drawings on a café table, which the waiter wiped away with the rest of the rubbish ..."

But the man was worth more than his paintings. Clear-sighted, impartial, and with excellent taste, he could appreciate Delacroix, Corot and Jongkind, with whom he used to go out sketching. If he disliked Boudin, the most famous local painter, it was for a special reason : Boudin had carried off a municipal scholarship for which he was also competing. After six years as curator of the Museum of Le Havre, Lhullier was appointed director of the regional Ecole des Beaux-Arts in 1871. He devoted himself entirely to his work, and would get up early in order to open the studio doors at six in the morning so that young painters could come and draw before going off to their work. Like Moreau, he was adept at discerning his pupils' personalities, but, more exacting than Moreau, frequently put obstacles in their path as a trial of strength, forcing them to spend many tedious hours copying plaster casts before allowing them to draw from the life. In the museum he lectured them on the masters and set them problems to make them clarify their ideas. He asked Othon Friesz what was his favourite picture. Rather tentatively, Friesz mentioned one by Jongkind. " Good," said Lhullier, " you're a fine judge of painting."

Dufy, who was born in 1877, was the first of the three to attend Lhullier's classes. At the age of fifteen he would spend his early mornings and his lunch-hours drawing from casts at the Ecole des Beaux-Arts. His father, an agent for a metal company, had eight other children to support, and the following year was forced to find his son a job with the coffee importers, Luthy and Hauser. Dufy's particular task was to go to the wharves to meet cargo boats bringing coffee from Brazil. He adored standing on the quayside, sniffing the strange foreign fragrances, and his sense of smell became so acute that finally he could tell where a ship came from simply by its smell.

Despite its poverty, the Dufy family was a happy one. Their house, like the Vlamincks', was always full of music. M. Dufy was a choirmaster and played the organ, and two other sons, Léon and Gaston, were also musicians : one played the organ in the cathedral, the other, a flutist, became editor of the

Courrier Musical. Dufy used to say that his early years were cradled by the sea and by music; he himself sang in the parish choir and throughout his life was an ardent concert-goer.

His passion for drawing emerged early in life, at the age of seven, to be precise, when he was recovering from croup. The habit grew into a mania, an obsession. He did not do well at school, and spent his time drawing in the margins of his exercise-books. By the age of ten he knew the local museum inside out, and stated that when he grew up he would make a lot of money in order to buy pictures (but when he did make money he would allow only his own pictures to decorate the walls of his studio in the Impasse de Guelma in Paris).

His other passion was the sea. Like Marquet, like Friesz and Braque, he would spend hours on the quayside, storing up impressions and drawing all over his employers' bills of lading. He collected everything to do with the sea: ships in bottles, marine maps, timetables of tides, almanachs. The most important elements in his vocabulary as a painter were masts, sails and flags, which, together with musical scores and instruments, survived his discovery in 1923 of racecourses, horses and jockeys.

He was very soon aware of the clarity, luminosity and lyrical potentialities of colour, and it was probably this interest that drew him and Othon Friesz together when they met at the Ecole des Beaux-Arts. Cycling together along the Côte de Grâce, they would set up their easels at Honfleur and Trouville, where the Impressionists had worked twenty-five years earlier. To paint in peace, they rented a servant's room as a studio. At this time Dufy was the dominant influence on Friesz, whom he impressed by his ability to draw with both left and right hand. Dufy had taught himself this trick as a guard against too great a facility, and was able to go on drawing even when almost crippled by arthritis at the end of his life.

In 1898 the two friends went different ways, Friesz to Paris and Dufy to do his military service. Dufy had the good fortune to serve for one year only: his brother Gaston had volunteered for a post as a flautist in a regimental band, and as the law stated that two brothers could not serve at the same time, Raoul was released. Shortly afterwards he went to Paris on a scolarship obtained through the good offices of Lhullier.

He shared lodgings with Friesz in Montmartre, at 12, rue Cortot, previously occupied by Renoir and soon to house Suzanne Valadon, Maurice Utrillo and André Utter. Although quite unlike in temperament, the two men got on very well. Friesz had no interest in music—unusual in a Fauve—while Dufy economised on paint in order to go to Sunday concerts. Friesz was stolid and massive and walked with a nautical roll, while Dufy was slender, light and airy, and with his periwinkle blue eyes, fresh complexion, full lips and tip-tilted nose, looked like a choirboy. As they grew older they grew apart.

Friesz stopped looking like Delacroix and began to resemble Beethoven, while Dufy preserved a puckish quality all his life, even when confined to a wheelchair with arthritis. Both attended the Atelier Bonnat at the Ecole des Beaux-Arts. After the death of Moreau, Bonnat allowed a discreet incursion of liberalism into the academic programme and forebore to impose his manner on his pupils. A peaceful man, by no means devoid of taste and humour, Bonnat would confine his criticisms to " That's good ... Not so good as the first time ... Carry on." He was extremely generous and adept at slipping a banknote into a needy hand. Although he preferred Friesz, he was very fond of Dufy. " I think you will eventually draw very well," he told him (not a particularly glowing compliment), and he encouraged him to prepare for the Prix de Rome. Dufy, who had eyes only for the Impressionist pictures in the galleries of the rue Laffitte, said as much to Bonnat who then used his influence to renew Dufy's scholarship at the Beaux-Arts. He spent four years in Bonnat's studio, without direct benefit but also without material problems. He acquired an unusual dexterity of draughtsmanship, but this did not prevent him from declaring later that "no one at the Ecole des Beaux-Arts could teach drawing." Dufy's real masters were the Impressionists. He seldom went to the Louvre although he did look at Giorgione and Claude Lorrain, and amongst his contemporaries he preferred Monet, Renoir and Pissarro. Until about 1904 he painted seascapes and landscapes in a fairly timid Impressionist style which gave little indication of the wealth of colour that was eventually to characterize his works. But even when most under the influence of Pissarro, he paid scant attention to atmospheric realism. His main debts to Impressionism were in subject matter and colour. He was already an able and sensitive colourist, more intelligible to traditionally minded contemporaries than the other Fauves. The Nabi, Maurice Denis, was the first to recognize his talent and bought one of the pictures he exhibited in the Salon des Indépendants of 1903. At this time Dufy was a serious young man who preferred concerts to music halls, and although he lived only a stone's throw from the "Lapin Agile" he never set foot inside the place. He impressed the inhabitants of Montmartre with his clean shirts and his well-groomed, modest and clerkly demeanour, in which he resembled Marquet, to whom, indeed, he grew closer and closer after 1905. Ten years later Paul Poiret said of him that he hid his genius behind the appearance of a shop assistant.

But despite his mild temper and his ordered life, Dufy's name, like that of Vlaminck, figured on the police lists as an anarchist, mainly through his kindness to the anarchist painter Maurice Delcourt. Delcourt was a curious character who made his own clothes at a sewing machine to the accompaniment of revolutionary songs. He had pawned his watch and told the time by training his field glasses on the clock of a factory at Saint-Ouen. On foggy days the system broke down.

Delcourt lived by systematically entering a painting for every competition which offered a prize. When, as often happened, he was the only candidate, he won the prize (this was more profitable than a proper exhibition). He was against the army, capitalism and the church, and he suddenly stopped paying his rent, arguing that all the profit went to his landlord. When he was evicted, Dufy took him in and gave him a corner at the end of his apartment. Delcourt, infuriated by his recent experience, began to hold anarchist meetings in his corner. Cries of " Death to the police!... down with the clergy!... down with the army! " could be heard from the street. The police, tipped off by the concierge who was an informer, raided Dufy's flat and Dufy's name went down on the black list. Finally Delcourt left of his own accord, declaring, " In this life you need influential friends! " Many of his plumper colleagues refused to attend his meetings for fear of getting stuck in Dufy's narrow corridor. Like many other anarchists Delcourt was killed in the war while leading his men to the attack in 1918.

At the Salon des Indépendants of 1905, Dufy had a similar revelation on seeing Matisse's *Luxe, Calme et Volupté* as Vlaminck had felt when he saw the Van Gogh exhibition. At last he had discovered a way of painting that both satisfied him and enabled him to express his own vision of the world. " When I saw this picture," he said in 1925, " I understood the new conception of painting. Impressionism lost its charm for me as I contemplated the miracle of imagination that ordained the drawing and colour." His conversion was completed during the summer of 1906 when he went painting with Marquet on the coast of Normandy. It may seem strange that it was Marquet, the most temperate and uncommitted of the Fauves, who rallied Dufy to Fauvism, but it should be remembered that Marquet was going through a period of intense enthusiasm for colour, and under his aegis Dufy renounced Impressionist realism altogether. Few works in the history of modern painting are so indistinguishable as the pictures painted by Dufy and Marquet at Le Havre, Sainte-Adresse, and Trouville in 1906. After careful study it becomes apparent that Marquet depended more on blacks and certain reds, while Dufy was more concerned with decorative effect, in the belief that nature is only what we perceive it to be.

Despite this similarity, the whole of Dufy's mature style is foreshadowed in such pictures as *Les Palissades à Trouville, La Plage de Sainte-Adresse,* and *Le 14 Juillet au Havre,* which express the characteristic Fauve happiness and feeling for the plenitude of life. The colouring is light and varied and has a kind of acid freshness far removed from the heavy blatant tones favoured by certain of the Fauves. Unlike those painters who had been trained by Gustave Moreau, Dufy never had a divisionist period; he covered his canvas with areas of colour on which he superimposed his drawing. He had an exhibition at Berthe Weil's (despite opposition from Matisse who said, " We don't want this young man

Dufy : " It's a waste of time to study sunlight "

" About 1906, I was painting on the beach at Sainte-Adresse. Until then, I had painted beach scenes in the manner of the Impressionists and had reached a point of no return, because I finally understood that if I continued to track nature down in this way, she would lead me on endlessly, into her smallest, most detailed, and most insubstantial directions, and that I should always remain outside the picture itself.

One day, unable to stand it any longer, I went out with a paint box and a simple sheet of paper. I came to some likely subject on the beach, settled down, and considered my tubes and brushes. How could I use these means to express not what I saw, but what *is*, what exists for me, my reality ? This was the whole problem. I began to draw, choosing from the scene before me exactly what suited me. Then, using black mixed with white, I gave each object the relief of its outlines, leaving on each occasion the white of the paper in the centre, which I then proceeded to colour with one single and rather intense colour. I only had blue, green and yellow with me. Still, the result surprised me. I immediately understood that I had discovered what I had been looking for. From that day forward, it was impossible for me to return to the fruitless struggles with the elements before my eyes. There was no longer any question of representing the outward forms of such elements. I went back to Paris and continued to paint according to my new convictions. Blot, the dealer who had bought my Impressionist canvases, asked for more of the same kind, but he would have nothing to do with my new style. I sold no more pictures. Once —to get money in order to paint the way I wanted to—I painted a few pictures in my old manner, but my heart was not in it. I couldn't do it. Later, when I went back to Le Havre and looked again at the pictures painted in the new way, I saw the point of them all over again.

Having got through this difficult moment, I produced my Fauve pictures.

slipping in amongst us!") and he exhibited for the first time in the Salon d'Automne. This happy period came to an end in 1908 at L'Estaque, where he was staying with Braque. The Cézanne retrospective of the previous year had turned his thoughts to a style which would depend less on colour than on the organic structure of the picture. In this he was following Braque who had seen Picasso's recent experiments, notably *Les Demoiselles d'Avignon*. He gave up bright colours and during this stay worked in ochres, earths, Prussian blues and dull greens. His colour harmonies became muted, his drawing dry and schematic, but he retained his instinct for decorative effect, and the results are austere but elegant. This was his most abstract phase—he was always a resolutely figurative painter—but even this brief flirtation with Cubism was enough to discourage the few collectors who had been interested in his work, and quite suddenly he found himself poor.

In 1909 he had no money and resigned himself to a scholarship at the school for independent artists which had been established by a rich collector at Orgeville. A clause in the constitution forbade the inmates to go to Paris. This did not worry Dufy too much; he took the opportunity to break with his girl friend Claudine, a rather jealous and quarrelsome creature (she did not have a particularly easy life with him, and often went hungry. Berthe Weil relates in her memoirs that one day Dufy made a tremendous effort and sent her a twenty sou piece stuck on a postcard!)

His time at Orgeville was not wasted. He went with a fellow student, André Lhote, to Evreux to see the stained glass windows, and his colours gained in depth and intensity. More important, he executed illustrations for Apollinaire's *Bestiary*, his first full-scale undertaking and the beginnings of a real renaissance in the art of the woodcut. Unfortunately, this magnificent book was not appreciated by the public and copies were remaindered at fifty francs apiece.

He was saved by his decorative skill. His woodcuts had given him the idea of printing his illustrations for the *Bestiary* on cloth. Paul Poiret, who had just opened " Martine," his studio of decorative art, became interested in the project and advanced Dufy two thousand five hundred francs. He rented a place in the Boulevard de Clichy, and with the assistance of an industrial chemist and a handyman (a former porter at the Ritz), he launched the enterprise that was to bring Fauvism into interior decoration and "haute couture."

The earlier part of Othon Friesz's life was much like that of Dufy. He was two years younger and came from a slightly more comfortable family. Like Dufy, he discovered his vocation as a painter when he was a child of twelve. " My uncle had left a paintbox in our attic. This object, which I had been forbidden to touch, fascinated me. One day, I forced the lid and squeezed the tubes. Blues, reds, and greens squirted forth. I took a sheet of cardboard,

Then, in order to pursue my researches, I turned to dyeing and printing on cloth. But that day at Sainte-Adresse had marked a turning point. I had discovered my own system. Its theory is simple. To study sunlight is a waste of time. Light in painting is something quite apart: it is composed, it is arranged, it is coloured. What do we see in nature apart from the dazzling rays of the sun? The sunlit parts have colour, and where the sun does not fall there is no colour. Lack of colour is neutral, that is, white. There is, of course, a certain amount of colour there, reflections, etc. But what misleads people when you talk to them about light is that they immediately think of the sun and the subsequent shadow."

(Interview with Pierre Courthion, *Gazette de Lausanne*, June 10, 1951.)

on which the vestiges of a landscape were still visible, and added a roof and trees. I was astounded. Was this painting? It was so easy! A few days later I went to look for a subject in the surrounding countryside."

Before discovering the almost physical joy of painting, he had to a certain extent been conditioned by the light of the south which played such a decisive part in the orientation of most of the Fauves (Vlaminck excepted), when he spent his holidays with an uncle in Marseilles.

Anyone interested in Friesz must refer to Maximilien Gauthier's excellent monograph, which is based on information supplied by the artist himself. He came of seafaring stock and his passion for the sea was greater even than that of Dufy. Contrary to a popular contemporary rumour, his family came not from Friesland, as his name would seem to suggest, but from Alsace. His great-grandfather, a locksmith who invented the jack still used by motorists today, settled in Le Havre at the end of the eighteenth century. The grandfather was first a cabin boy, then a sea-captain, and finally a shipbuilder and owner of three sailing ships. He was a friend of Francis Arago and Daguerre and enjoyed a modest reputation as the first man to draw up an accurate map of Guadeloupe. Freisz's father and three uncles were all sailors or shipbuilders. Anthime, the father, was like a character from a novel by Conrad. Although he had commanded the first big liners, he was only really happy on long slow voyages under sail. After every trip, he appeared to his wife and children as an almost legendary figure, weighed down with souvenirs from every port of call.

Friesz's uncles were equally picturesque. They had established a prosperous maritime cooperative at Marseilles and every summer the family from Le Havre went to stay with their boisterous Uncle Othon on his property at Mazargues. In such circumstances it was natural for Othon Friesz to want to go to sea. As his parents insisted that he continue his studies, he stowed away on a Danish ship but was discovered and sent home. He was fifteen, and as a substitute for escape he turned to painting. His mother, who was half English and half Creole, was quite happy about this: she had been trying to get him to play the piano since the age of six, without success. Friesz next persuaded her to go and see Lhullier at the Ecole des Beaux-Arts in Le Havre, and one evening when his father was absent she took him along with her. "Lhullier," says Friesz in his little book on his master, "was in his dining room with his wife and two nieces. The room was small and modestly but tastefully furnished: the walls were decorated with ceramics, "objets d'art," and sketches by himself and Jongkind. In the dim light he seemed to me very tall and very old—he was then sixty-seven—and his broad square shoulders gave him an air of strength. His flowing moustache, once red, was now white, and a little skull cap hid his bald head. He was smoking a fruit-wood pipe. He looked rough and kind.

"My mother explained why she had come and told him of the talent she was sure I possessed. Calmly he turned to me and said, ' First you will work from reliefs and plaster casts of heads. When you can manage the head, you will go on and do the complete body. Then, in two years, you can draw from the life. After that, we'll talk about painting.'

"I was disappointed. I thought that the minute I entered the school I should be allowed to go to work with paint and canvas. Instead, Lhullier was calmly proposing a long and arduous journey to my impatient spirit."

Friesz submitted, however, and for several years attended the dawn classes before going on to school. He soon had only one idea : to leave school and become a full-time student at the Ecole des Beaux-Arts. His mother was against this, and Lhullier, who believed that an artist should be a cultivated man, supported her. One day, when his father was home from sea, Friesz summoned his courage and told him what he wanted to do. There was a scene. The captain smashed the dining-room lamp, then, having worked off his rage, gave in. He was very fond of his son and didn't really believe there was much future for seamen since sailing ships were on the way out. He disappeared on another voyage and Othon Friesz never went back to school. He entered the Ecole des Beaux-Arts in 1892, the same year as Dufy, and stayed until 1897, when he went to Paris on a scholarship awarded by the municipal council. In the drawing room of a distant relative, he had the good fortune to meet two of the reigning art pontiffs of the day, Bonnat and Bouguereau. Bouguereau gave him a disappointing reception. "Quickly!," he said, " into the lobby and hurry up. Every minute is costing me a hundred francs! " Friesz untied his sketches, never dreaming that one day he would occupy the same studio in the rue Notre-Dame-des-Champs. After a brief glance, Bouguereau dismissed him with the words, " Go back to school and I'll correct you."

But Friesz went to Bonnat who liked him and invited him to his country house in the fine weather. The canny Friesz combined these visits with a quick tour of the local junk shops, buying up antique furniture which he resold to dealers in Paris. Bonnat soon sensed that his pupil was a rebel, that he preferred the Impressionists to the style of his master, and he was only partly rewarded for his pains when Friesz took to going to the Louvre where his Baroque tastes led him straight to Veronese, Rubens, Gros and Delacroix.

Like Dufy he abandoned bitumen, earths, ochres and the traditional colours in favour of the Impressionist palette, which was based on cadmium yellow, cobalt blue, vermilion and crimson lake. A meeting with Pissarro, whom he met one day while painting on the Pont-Neuf, hastened his development along these lines. Pissarro had given him some advice but had assured him that the picture on which he was working would not find a buyer. In the foreground stood a urinal plastered with advertisements ...

Friesz was the only member of the Havre group to lead the classical life of Montmartre. He and his friend Alphonse Allais, who was from Honfleur, were well known for their stories in dialect. He was famous for his practical jokes although he sometimes went too far. One day he produced a purse containing forty francs and ordered a meal for himself and his friends. After they had eaten it, he confessed that he had found the purse in the street. " He has a girl friend," says Apollinaire, " who tears his canvases when she is angry and speaks perfect Javanese." Friesz kept his extrovert habits throughout his life, and his former pupils at the Atelier Scandinave, where he taught from 1924 on—Tailleux, Yves Bonnat, Buffet, Cortot and Busse—still remember excursions made in his company until the outbreak of the second World War. No studio party in Montparnasse was a success without him. At the same time he was universally respected as an art teacher.

He left Dufy in Montmartre and moved to 15, Place Dauphine. He mixed with the poets and writers who met regularly at the Closerie des Lilas, forming a particularly close friendship with Fernand Fleuret, whose portrait, painted in 1907, is Friesz's masterpiece and one of the great works of the Fauve movement. Fleuret was a minor poet with a rich fantasy life : he believed that he was descended from Louis XIV, and at the end of his life was convinced that he was being persecuted by the Jesuits. Other friends at the Closerie des Lilas were Paul Fort and of course Apollinaire.

Friesz was extremely adaptable and was one of the first Fauve painters to enjoy the favours of the public. While still at the Ecole des Beaux-Arts (he did not leave until 1903), he was selling pictures to collectors in Le Havre. In 1907 he managed to sell eight canvases for two thousand francs to Druet who became his dealer. Berthe Weil, to whom he had been introduced by Dufy, stated flatly that she didn't like his style. " The bitch," was Dufy's comment. Durand-Ruel told him that his colours were too dark. Surprised and extremely disappointed, Friesz wrapped up his canvases and went out into the street, where people were looking at the sun through dark glasses. He rushed back to Durand's shouting, " There's an eclipse! " Durand understood, lit the gas, and looked at his work again. " Very good, young man. Now keep working, and come back to see me again."

He painted in a Neo-Impressionist style until 1904. A meeting with Cézanne in the Dutch room at the Louvre, had little effect on him. When Camoin introduced them, Friesz could think of nothing to say. Cézanne murmured, " Ah, yes, our ancestors! We must admire them and question them again and again, then go out and forget all about them." This was not bad advice, but a meeting with Matisse had more positive results. Friesz was dissatisfied with Impressionism, and considered its devotion to sensation mediocre and limiting. His own temperament veered more instinctively to strength and solidity. The works of Matisse were as much of a revelation to him as they had been to

" Fauvism, which began about 1900 and flourished until about 1908, was not just an attitude, a gesture, but a logical development, a necessary means by which we could impose our will on painting while still remaining within the bounds of tradition. It was both a continuation of, and a reaction against, our Impressionist and Neo-Impressionist predecessors, whose work we admired. What we called orchestration of colour had the immediate effect of simplifying the palette, and marked a break with the realist and documentary spirit which had ruled until then. We perceived that a picture could not be constructed without first transforming our ordinary, direct, and mediocre vision of reality. We began by demanding that this transformation should be effected through colour. This is the essence of Fauvism, which has really been the inspiration of all subsequent artistic movements."

(Quoted by Maximilien Gauthier in *Othon Friesz*, Pierre Cailler, publisher, Geneva.)

Dufy. From that moment his development was rapid and by 1907 he was a complete Fauve. He co-opted Braque, who was still not connected with the movement, and took him off to Antwerp to paint. He had paid his first visit to Brussels and Antwerp in 1900, and always preferred the silvery light of the north to the brilliance of the south. The two painters installed themselves on the banks of the Scheldt in a deserted casino, a huge rotting building full of water and mosquitoes. But they had a wonderful view of the river from their balcony and could paint the boats in the harbour without leaving the studio. As is the case with Vlaminck and Derain, and Marquet and Dufy, Friesz's and Braque's pictures of this period are almost indistinguishable.

But they were not heart and soul in the Fauve movement. For them Fauvism was only a borrowed means of expression; it did not meet the deeper demands of their natures. There is no real Fauve violence in their colour harmonies, which are on the delicate side with strong tones used only for contrast. Friesz used not only blues and reds, but creams and greys, and, like Matisse, that dangerous colour, violet. Moreover, Friesz was probably the only Fauve concerned with fine craftsmanship. His colours are applied not in thick layers but modulated by light glazes, with the white of the canvas allowed to show through.

At L'Estaque, with a return to the south of his boyhood holidays, his colours became more vivid, though less vivid than Braque's. During a stay at La Ciotat in 1907, he resolutely turned his back on colour as a means of expression, and transferred his attention to drawing, composition, and the internal structure of the picture. In the Provençal landscape he reached a clearer understanding of Cézanne. He subdued his colours, choosing ochres, browns and emerald green, as did all the Fauves in their transitional periods. " We who created Fauvism were the first to destroy it," he said. " Colour ceased to dominate the canvas; composition regained its importance, and colour became simply a pleasant addition." Later he advised his pupils to " distrust bright colours and to use them as sparingly as a chemist uses dangerous drugs in his prescriptions."

The strongly articulated planes of the Provençal landscape converted him to careful drawing and composition. Cubism, which was following a similar line of development, did not interest him, and although the influence of Cézanne is apparent in the pyramidal structure of his works, actual Cubist influence can be discounted altogether.

By 1909 this interval of asceticism had come to an end. His robust and sensual nature favoured a direct means of expression, and the result is the *Travail à l'automne*, now in the museum of Oslo, a rhythmical work in which arabesque and relief have more importance than colour. He continued to paint in this vein until his death. An exceptional craftsman, Friesz's pictures are generous and direct, completely divorced from doubt or ratiocination. Unfortunately he was not always conscious of his facility and a tendency to carelessness, exasperated by his constant need for money, especially in his later years. It is interesting to note that although Friesz's work finally received official approval to the extent that he was offered the directorship of the Ecole des Beaux-Arts, the critic Camille Mauclair, a fervent opponent of Fauvism, continued to harry Friesz for the rest of his life, and thus gave him the consolation of believing that he had not altogether repudiated his early ideals.

Georges Braque, who was born in 1882, was the latest recruit to Fauvism. The youngest of the Le Havre painters, he took no part in the first Fauve exhibitions, and joined no particular group. He did not meet Matisse, Vlaminck and Derain until 1907, at the Salon des Indépendants, although he already knew their work. By this time, the pioneers of Fauvism were already thinking along other lines. Braque's name is indissolubly connected with Cubism, although in 1906 and 1907 he painted about forty Fauve pictures and was generally considered to be a member of the group.

Today, Braque hardly ever mentions this period, which was for him only a phase, a step on the way to Cubism, the style in which he expressed himself completely. However, two Fauve pictures, painted at La Ciotat and at L'Estaque, and now hanging in his house in Paris, give sufficient indication of his particular contribution to the Fauve movement: a quality of distinction. Painted in subdued tones, they have a lightness and a rhythmical quality to be met with in the work of no other Fauve. Arabesque and colour are perfectly balanced.

Of all the Le Havre painters, Braque was the most profoundly influenced by the Impressionists in his youth. As he spent his childhood at Argenteuil and his adolescence at Le Havre, he was more or less conditioned to this state of affairs. His father, Charles Braque, was a decorator and a Sunday painter, extremely proud of the fact that he had exhibited in the Salon des Artistes Français by the side of the masters. He and the boy's godmother, who owned the Moulin d'Orgemont where Monet used to paint, told him many stories of the Impressionists. Braque's father, painting on the banks of the Seine, would point out to his son the figure of Caillebotte.

Braque says of himself that he was born into a pot of paint—his grandfather was a house painter—and he has no memories of consciously studying technique. He learned how to imitate marble and wood and paint letters almost as a game, and this ability served him very well in his Cubist period. In 1890 his father moved from Argenteuil, where business was poor, and opened a paint shop in Le Havre. Braque's regret at leaving the Seine was compensated by the joy of discovering the sea, the harbour, the ships and the long beaches. He loved music, and learned to play the flute, the violin and the accordeon from Gaston Dufy (music plays a large part in his work: Bach or

Mozart scores appear in many of his pictures). He was not good at school. " My education," he says, " took place on the wall of the building across the street. When a billsticker put up a poster by Toulouse-Lautrec or Steinlen, I would go and pinch it. I also learned a lot from *Gil Blas*," whose illustrations he copied, and in whose pages he read Baudelaire, Verlaine and Rimbaud.

When he was fifteen his father saw that it was useless to keep him at school and got him a job with another decorator, Roney. He also put him down for evening classes at the Ecole des Beaux-Arts. He wanted his son to be a real artist, but his native caution insisted that the boy learn a trade. " If you get fed up with it," said his mother, " you can always come into the business." Thus Braque received his training. In 1900 his parents decided to send him to Paris to perfect his drawing and at the same time to work as assistant to the decorator Laberthe. He set off by bicycle, his equipment tied to his saddle. In Paris he settled in Montmartre, in the rue des Trois-Frères, and took the job with Laberthe as arranged. He did a great deal of work for this man in an impeccable Art Nouveau style, but it has all gone. In the evenings he attended a municipal art school in the Batignolles. For relaxation he boxed, played the accordeon and the flute. On Sundays he would go dancing at the Moulin de la Galette, wearing an elegant cycling outfit which cost him nineteen francs at the Samaritaine. His carriage, his height and his charm won him many admirers but he knew how not to get involved, and though he loved company and gaiety he probably preferred the solitude of his own little room.

His best friends were Friesz and Dufy whom he used to meet at Vernin's bistro in the rue Cavalotti, made famous by Max Jacob. His military service, from which he emerged with the rank of sergeant, was done in 1901 and 1902 and did not greatly disturb the pattern of his life. On his demobilization there was no further question of his becoming a house painter. His father, convinced of his gifts and of his vocation, gave him a small allowance so that he could work in peace.

He gave up the evening classes and enrolled at the Académie Humbert in the Boulevard Rochechouart, where he drew from 1902 to 1904. It was there that he met Marie Laurencin, who was learning to paint on porcelain, and introduced her to Guillaume Apollinaire, thus initiating one of the most famous liaisons in the history of literature. He also met Manolo and Picabia. Manolo, a friend of Picasso and a highly unusual character, lived by dubious means, " lifting " purses or selling tickets for lotteries with one of his non-existent sculptures as the prize. " I'm afraid you haven't won," he would say, if anyone asked the result. Francis Picabia was less picaresque. He had just left Cormon's studio at the Ecole des Beaux-Arts and was trying to shake off his academic training. He was one of the last painters to be affected by Fauvism, as can be seen in some violently coloured seascapes painted at Saint-Tropez in 1909.

A visit to Braque

A rainy evening in autumn. Shadows fill the great olive green room in the rue du Douanier. On each side of a Spanish table sit Braque and his wife, she in a leather armchair, he in a wheelchair with a blanket over his knees. Although the room is heated, he wears a big black and white tweed greatcoat. He seems very old and very frail. He answers questions readily, but there are long silences; he does not proffer information. He is tired. His fine face rarely relaxes into a smile. Only his tuft of white hair, on which the light falls, seems truly alive.

On the wall opposite the window are two Fauve pictures: one of L'Estaque, the other of La Ciotat. The latter was bought back by Braque two years ago. " You see," he says, " it hasn't changed in fifty years. They used to say to me, what will your pictures be like in twenty years time, with the chemical colours you use ? Well, it's as fresh as it was the day I painted it."

Contrary to popular report, he does not repudiate his Fauve period. " Fauvism was important, very important. I came to it when it was nearly over and I didn't paint many pictures."

" How many ? About twenty ? "

" A few more than that, I think. They liberated me, permitted me to try other forms of expression. I was very young..."

October 18, 1961.

For two months Braque also attended the Atelier Bonnat, probably in order to keep in touch with Dufy and Friesz. He soon lost interest, went back to the Académie Humbert, or painted from the nude in his studio in the rue d'Orsel. At this point his style was as far removed from Fauvism as it was from academic art : the Impressionists were the major influence on his work until 1904. Unfortunately we know little about this period as he destroyed most of his pictures. We simply know that they reflected his admiration for Renoir. He also admired Van Gogh, but cared nothing for Gauguin and knew little about Cézanne.

His first sign of individual taste was his fondness for Egyptian and archaic Greek art. In the Louvre he looked not only at Poussin and Corot, his favourite painters, but spent long hours in the sculpture galleries, committing to memory forms and rhythms which he was later to use in his post-Cubist compositions. A first indication of Fauvism appears in his *Bateau dans le port du Havre*. After his visit to the Salon d'Automne of 1905, he quickly decided in favour of the style, realising that a subjective use of colour would free him from his own dependence on Impressionism. He was also temperamentally in favour of the violence and idealism of the Fauve movement. The dozen or so pictures which he painted in Antwerp with Othon Friesz are completely Fauve works but, like those of Friesz, are insidious rather than peremptory. Like Friesz he uses notes of sharp green, violet, cream and pink. He sold his Antwerp pictures to collectors in Le Havre, and on the proceeds went to L'Estaque to stay at the Hôtel Maurin, which was to become a favourite rendezvous for Fauve painters.

As he himself has said, this stay was one of the happiest periods of his life. " I am still transported by the memory," he says. He discovered the sky, the sea, the gulf that Cézanne had painted; in a state of euphoria he completed the greater part of his Fauve production, working in a kind of rudimentary divisionism, almost like mosaic, and in his restricted use of colour—some reds, blue, yellow—manifesting an early taste for an almost monochrome canvas. His care for rigorous construction and internal rhythm is also already discernable.

The pictures painted at L'Estaque were hung in the Salon des Indépendants of 1907 where they were extremely well received. Some were bought by the German art critic Wilhelm Uhde. Matisse, Vlaminck and Derain came to make his aquaintance and to congratulate him. He was now numbered among the Fauves, but the movement was already on the decline.

In May he went back to the south, this time to La Ciotat, with Friesz, and painted a further series of Fauve pictures. By the autumn of the same year his participation in the Fauve movement was at an end. He returned to L'Estaque and worked with the emphasis on drawing and neutral tones. His interest in construction replaced his earlier interest in colour. These studies done in L'Estaque and worked up during the winter in Paris inspired Louis Vauxcelles, who had already christened the Fauve movement, to make his famous remark about Cubes and Cubism.

Though the suddenness of this change is surprising, it can be easily explained. Braque came to Fauvism at a time when the men who had created the style were in doubts as to its future. In Montmartre, at Vernin's, at Azon's, he had listened to theories which owed something to Negro art, something to Cézanne. Finally, in between his two trips to the south, he had been taken by Apollinaire to see Picasso in his studio at the Bateau-Lavoir. Picasso showed him *Les Demoiselles d'Avignon* which he had just finished. Braque disliked, even hated, it. "With all your explanations," he said to Picasso as he left, "it's as if you were forcing us to eat oakum and drink paraffin." But he was unconsciously influenced by what he had seen and heard. The Cézanne retrospective had taught him to see the Provençal landscape with new eyes, and his latent need to construct his picture and fragment his subject grew in force. When he returned to L'Estaque with Dufy in 1908 he was a Cubist. He had found his true style. This change had repercussions on his way of life. Braque, who had formerly lived a sober and vegetarian existence, now took to wearing blue overalls like Picasso. His conversation became cruder, he went dancing or played the accordeon at the "Lapin Agile" or "Chez Frédé," and was once seen riding a sofa down the slopes of Montmartre. But this interlude was brief. The rest of Braque's life has been so completely bound up with Cubism that his name is almost synonymous with it.

Nevertheless he too seems to have obeyed the law affecting all the Fauves as they grew older : his most recent works are as brightly coloured as those of his youth. *La Chaise* of 1961, for example, painted in harsh reds, yellows and greens, might almost date from 1907. Painters who first express themselves by means of colour never entirely lose the habit.

Colour plates 35—58

35. DUFY.   LE YACHT PAVOISÉ AU HAVRE.   Collection Mme Raoul Dufy, Nice.

36. DUFY. VUE DE L'ÉGLISE SAINT-GERVAIS. Musée Calvet, Avignon.

37. DUFY. LES OMBRELLES. Collection Dr Roudinesco, Paris.

38. DUFY. LE BAL CHAMPÊTRE. Collection particulière, Paris.

39. DUFY. LE BASSIN A HONFLEUR. Collection Dr Roudinesco, Paris.

40. DUFY. LA PLAGE DE SAINTE-ADRESSE. The Honorable and Mrs. John Hay Whitney Collection, New York.

41. DUFY. LE BATEAU PAVOISÉ. Musée des Beaux-Arts, Lyon.

42. DUFY. VOILIERS AU HAVRE. The Honorable and Mrs. John Hay Whitney Collection, New York.

43. DUFY. LES AFFICHES A TROUVILLE. Musée National d'Art Moderne, Paris.

44. DUFY.   LES BAINS DU CASINO MARIE-CHRISTINE A SAINTE-ADRESSE.   Musée National d'Art Moderne, Paris.

45. FRIESZ.   PORTRAIT DE FERNAND FLEURET.   Musée National d'Art Moderne, Paris.

46. FRIESZ.   LE BEC-DE-L'AIGLE.   Mr. and Mrs. Werner E. Josten Collection, New York.

47. FRIESZ. L'ESTAQUE. Musée National d'Art Moderne, Paris.

48. FRIESZ. LA CIOTAT. Musée National d'Art Moderne, Paris.

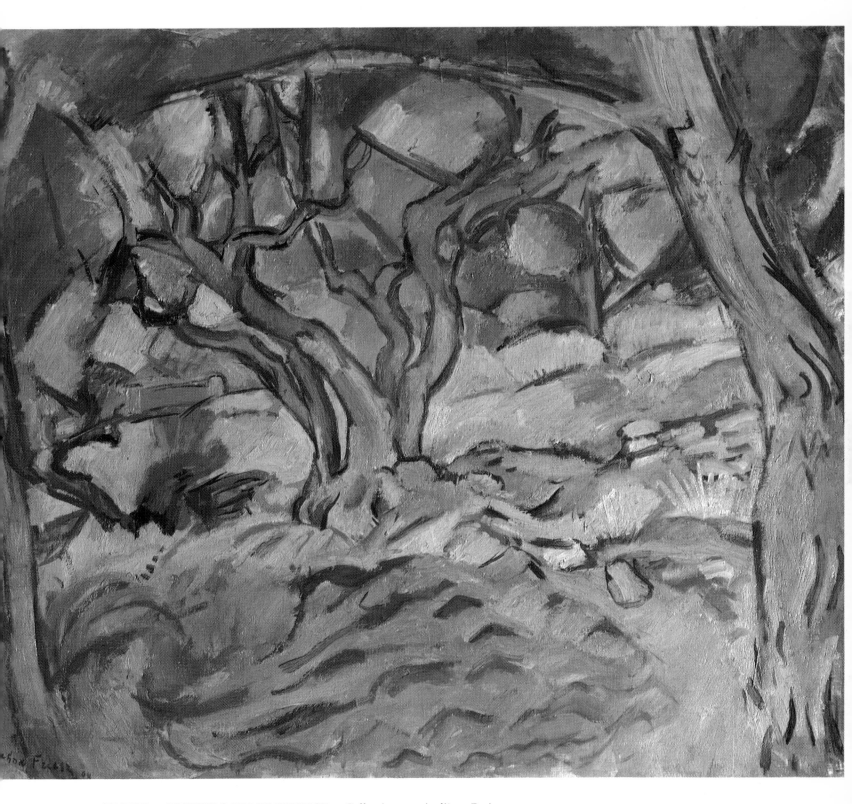

49. FRIESZ. OLIVIERS EN PROVENCE. Collection particulière, Paris.

50. BRAQUE.   L'ESTAQUE.   Collection Georges Braque, Paris.

51. BRAQUE. NU ASSIS. Collection particulière, Paris.

52. BRAQUE. LE PORT DE L'ESTAQUE. Collection particulière, Paris.

53. BRAQUE. MAISON DERRIÈRE LES ARBRES. Mr. Robert Lehman Collection, New York.

54. BRAQUE. LA CIOTAT. Collection particulière, Paris.

55. BRAQUE. PAYSAGE A LA CIOTAT. Collection Georges Braque, Paris.

56. BRAQUE. LE PORT DE LA CIOTAT. The Honorable and Mrs. John Hay Whitney Collection, New York.

58. BRAQUE.   PAYSAGE A LA CIOTAT.   Mr. and Mrs. Leigh B. Block Collection, Chicago.

Fauves and more Fauves

Rouault

Although Rouault did not belong properly speaking to the Fauve group, he must be considered in relation to it. Louis Vauxcelles defined his position when he said, " Rouault... who has always walked alone, may be considered a special kind of Fauve."

The Fauves themselves regarded him as a friend and an ally, whose spirit of revolt and indomitable independence resembled their own. Like Vlaminck, Derain and Van Dongen, he painted in a state of perpetual excitement. His character contained that seed of violence which is also to be found in most of the major Fauve painters.

In the technical sphere his position was analogous to theirs. Like the Fauves, he rejected the classic principles of linear and atmospheric perspective; he retained chiaroscuro but used it for a completely independent purpose. His methods, too, were typically Fauve, for he sought not so much to represent as to suggest, in a violent, evocative and summary manner, applying in this way one of the favourite recommendations of Gustave Moreau, whom he admired to the point of idolatry.

His rather brutal style was formed not at the Ecole des Beaux-Arts but in the workshops of the master glassworker Hirsch, to whom he was apprenticed at the age of sixteen. While helping his master to restore the stained glass windows of Saint-Séverin in Paris, he discovered the impact of pure colour

A number of fringe figures can be discerned in the wake of the major Fauve painters. Of these, the most talented and the most picturesque is the Dutchman Van Dongen, followed, in degree of importance, by Valtat, who anticipated Matisse's first Fauve experiments by two years, Manguin, Camoin, Jean Puy and Flandrin. These last four were moderates, fellow-travellers, but by no means negligible as artists. Their technique resembles that of the Fauves but in spirit their work remains close to that of the Impressionists. Their broad, generous, brightly coloured and synthetized style is free from the weaknesses and distortions of atmospheric realism.

For these painters Fauvism was only a passing phase, initiated mainly by their friendship with Derain, Matisse and Marquet. They became Fauves by a process of osmosis. As they considerably modified the excesses of the true innovators, they enjoyed a proportionately greater degree of commercial success. Their obvious good taste appealed precisely to those collectors who had been disconcerted by the truculence of the " real " Fauves.

A number of other painters are tenuously connected with Fauvism : the tender and delicate Laprade, Charles Guérin, who painted *Fêtes galantes* in the manner of Watteau, Marinot, who worked mainly in glass, d'Espagnat, a second rank Impressionist, Asselin, Ottmann, Dufrenoy, Girieud and many others. Very occasionally one can read a reference to Matisse or Vlaminck in their works. But the part they played in the evolution of the movement was very slight. This is not true of Van Dongen, a Fauve in every sense of the word, a man with a reputation as sizeable as that of Toulouse-Lautrec, Modigliani, Pascin or Utrillo, and a candidate for the position of outstanding bohemian figure of the twentieth century. The legend came into being largely after the first World War, when Van Dongen was elevated to the rank of a " typically Parisian figure," and the rich and fashionable gave him the place in their hearts formerly reserved for the pontiffs of academic art whose historical exercises

enhanced by strong light. The memory of this impression stayed with him for a long time: " As I was forced to earn a little money for myself and my family, I started by being a stained glass worker, an almost defunct trade ... I was with a master who had had copies made of all the really old stained glass windows he had restored. I spent my lunch hour poring over these ... the rest of the day I struggled through ugly modern jobs ... But that one hour was heaven ... even though the copies themselves were imperfect ..."

His style, with its emphasis on brutal compression and its preference for primary colours set off by black outlines, derives from this training.

He sent three pictures to the Salon d'Automne of 1905, including *M. et Mme Poulot*, a tribute to Léon Bloy. Although he was not hung with the Fauves he was assumed to be one of them and received the same kind of abuse from the critics.

He felt a temperamental need to underline the vices of society, to parade them on the faces of his judges, prostitutes and clowns. This attitude should have shown the critics how different he was from the Fauves, who were only interested in expression in terms of colour. Something drove Rouault to consider these technicalities only useful in relation to the moral purpose they might serve. " Between the Fauves and Rouault," writes René Huyghe, " there is all the difference of quality between a human personality, however fascinating, and a soul ...". So Rouault was no Fauve, but he felt a special sympathy for them which they reciprocated. With his friend Desvallières, he defended the Fauves and insisted that their work be received at the Salon d'Automne, of which he was one of the founders. " Rouault never let his Fauve friends down," wrote Frantz Jourdain, who knew him at that time. " Frankly, he was much more preoccupied with his own painting than with theirs, but he defended them, if necessary, with some conviction and a great deal of clumsiness ..."

The Fauves admired him. Vlaminck, whose judgments were so severe, always kept a watercolour by Rouault on his wall and never failed to point

were now relegated to the attic. He was known as Kees, Keesy, Kiki, or Van, and his appearance at Cannes or Deauville, with flowing beard and piercing eye, marked the height of the season. Millionaires, prostitutes, models, statesmen, gangsters, and showgirls from the Casino de Paris would crowd every Monday night into his studios in the rue Juliette-Lamber and dance to the accordeon of Emile Vacher. Thrifty and secretly contemptuous, Van Dongen would give them nothing to drink but mineral water served in champagne glasses by white-gloved waiters ... and they loved it! He made his name with a portrait of Anatole France, painted two years before the writer's death, which showed him as a decrepit and slobbering old man. He was then adopted as the Goya of the twenties, the darling of an international and slightly parvenu society avid for self-castigation. He was a Fauve not only in his technique but in his attitude to the international moneyed set. His portraits of Boni de Castellane, the Comtesse de Noailles, the Dolly sisters, the Aga Khan, Edmonde Guy and Sacha Guitry seem to incarnate the age of the charleston, inflation and the jazz band. In this connection he was not merely a fashionable painter but an implacable witness of his own era, and his ability to express a truth about humanity in the portrait of an individual gives him a curious resemblance to Rouault. But whereas Rouault's prostitutes, clowns and judges are painted with a ferocity all the stronger for the painter's Christian compassion, Van Dongen takes pleasure in his own pitiless satire.

There is a marked difference between the fashionable Van Dongen and the Van Dongen of the Fauve period. Like Vlaminck, with whom it is reasonable to compare him, he was self-taught and rejected all systems. Vlaminck wanted to set fire to the Ecole des Beaux-Arts and boasted of having never been inside the Louvre. Van Dongen spent one afternoon at the Ecole des Beaux-Arts, then left because the model's pose got on his nerves. As to museums, " they ruin the eye," he said to Michel Georges-Michel. " Museums are cemetaries for dead paintings. I prefer life ... House painters are the real artists; they take on an old building and turn it into something beautiful."

He neither sought nor rejected the Fauve label. " They say I was a Fauve. It's possible, but I don't remember. In 1905 I was too much in love to bother about painting." Nevertheless one is completely justified in considering him a Fauve not only on the basis of his painting but of his whole intellectual bias : his schematic drawing, his use of extreme stylization, his preference for bright colours with a marked liking for blacks and reds, his lack of interest in half-tones and shadows. His sensuality is even more directly expressed in his painting than is that of Vlaminck; he is a hedonist interested only in the rapid satisfaction of his desires. And in conclusion, he once uttered the memorable remark, " Painting is not natural, it is essentially artificial," a profession of faith of which Matisse or Vlaminck might have been proud.

it out to his guests. In his *Portraits avant décès*, which is full of singeing attacks, he has a few lines of affectionate comprehension for Rouault: " A portrait or a nude by Rouault contains the whole of the inner sexual drama, the drama of the devil and the flesh. True painting is not at all literary; that is the whole point of it. A portrait by Georges Rouault, a simple portrait, can be a terrible thing ... There is something of the saint in him, something of the martyr and the eternal vagrant. He also has the grandeur and the resignation of Christ on the cross. For those who know him, Rouault's personality is unique. With his black tweed suit, stiff white collar and black tie, he looks like a priest in lay clothing or Verlaine disguised as a waiter. But Rouault is a very great and good man! "

It was only after the death of Gustave Moreau, his master and guide, whose studio he entered in 1891 at the age of twenty, that Rouault began to discover his own personality. He was a tall, pale, gangling and sickly youth (although he lived to be eighty-seven), with a bulging forehead, pale blue eyes and drooping mouth. He was extremely poor and lived a silent and solitary existence. He abandoned the religious themes he had painted hitherto, in the style, if not the spirit, of Gustave Moreau, and began to concentrate on subjects taken from the life and inspired by Forain, Toulouse-Lautrec, and Daumier. This was the start of his admirable series of clowns, judges, and prostitutes. Prostitutes affected him deeply. " When I lived at Versailles," he said, " I saw a girl at the door of a brothel. She was beautiful, glossy with colours and light. I remained discreetly where I was and painted her." A combination of Christian piety and plebeian vitality inspired a series of images on the theme of the ugliness and misery of the world. But the cynicism and satire never conceal the profound tenderness of the Christian suffering for a fellow sinner. " When he paints a prostitute," wrote Louis Vauxcelles, " he does not take a cruel pleasure in her viciousness, as does Lautrec; he suffers and weeps for it."

Legend has it that Van Dongen arrived in Paris in 1897 on an excursion train for the 14th of July celebrations, that he had only twenty francs in his pocket, a cardboard suitcase containing a shirt, two drawing books, and two pencils, and that he was so taken by the joys of Paris that he sold his return ticket and stayed on. Naturally the truth is quite different. Cornelius Theodorus Maria Van Dongen was born on January 26, 1877 at Delfshaven, a suburb of Rotterdam, in an old seventeeth century brick house by the side of a canal. His father was a maltster (not a brewer, as Van Dongen has often claimed). He was a clever child, more interested in drawing than in his studies, and at the age of twelve he was expelled from school. This left him quite unmoved: he had just finished his first painting. "A butcher friend of my father's," he relates, " had a plaster cow in his window. He asked me if I wanted to colour it. I did so, not forgetting the green of the grass under the cow's hooves." He perfected his drawing, using as models the prostitutes who sat in windows to attract passing sailors in the red light district.

His sensible parents wanted to train him for a lucrative career by sending him to a school of decorative art to study industrial design. This was his only artistic training, and it ended abruptly when he was eighteen and ran away, like Othon Friesz, to sea. He got on a steamer going to America, of which he saw nothing because he was kept washing dishes all the time the ship was in New York.

This journey marked the end of his obedience to his family and also of his enjoyment of family security. He moved into a little room above a brothel which provided him with unlimited models, and he spent his days at the window drawing them. He became a draughtsman for the *Rotterdamsche Niewsblad* and accompanied reporters on stories to draw corpses and accidents. In this way he acquired great dexterity.

The discovery of Toulouse-Lautrec and Steinlen in the French comic journal *Gil Blas* was an important event for his art, both immediately and much later. *Gil Blas* also revealed to him the free, rebellious and iconoclastic spirit of Paris, so very different from the pompous puritanism of his native Holland. All his thoughts were concentrated on getting to Paris. His drawings of this period contain the seeds of his future development, but his painting promised nothing in particular. He had begun to paint under the influence of Rembrandt and had then gone on to work in the dark and heavy manner of Van Gogh's Nuenen period. His journey to Paris, where he arrived on July 12, 1897, was financed by his father with whom he had become reconciled. He was still uncertain which direction to take. He looked at the Impressionists in the galleries of the rue Laffitte and for some months painted in a style influenced by Claude Monet. Impressionism was at variance with his Nordic temperament, which hankered after solidity, but it freed him from

His spiritual development crystallized around his meeting with Léon Bloy in 1905. He was attracted by the latter's fierce independence, his realism, and the violence of his faith. Bloy did not convert Rouault, as has often been said, since Rouault was brought up in a devout working class family. But Bloy led him to a more ardent conception of the faith which gave a dimension of pathos to his art.

Paradoxically, Bloy did not understand Rouault's pictures, which he condemned as hideous caricatures. In 1907 he wrote to Rouault: " I have two words to say to you, after which you will be nothing more to me than a fellow carcase. Firstly... you are drunk with ugliness. Secondly, if you were a man of prayer... you couldn't paint those horrible pictures."

In spite of these savage words, Rouault loved Bloy. " It could be said," wrote Raïssa Maritain, " that he went to Bloy in order to provoke castigations of what he held most dear so that he could test the strength of those instinctive forces that were drawing him towards an unknown future and which would triumph over all obstacles."

1914 marks a definitive break between Rouault and the former Fauves. His ideal was situated far beyond their problems, and in a state of grace he turned away from his period of pessimism and prostitutes to the jubilation of his biblical landscapes. His constant search for the transcendental gave him the mystical serenity for which he is known. No better definition of his work exists than that of André Suarès, in a letter written in December, 1923: " You are less interested in form than in expression and your only interest in technical perfection is as the servant of your feelings: *ancilla domini*. I appreciate both your skill and your desire for redemption, which you pursue even when it leads you down to hell. What redeems your rogues and prostitutes and human refuse is *la belle matière* in which you clothe them. It is as if you were demonstrating that their misery is also worthy of salvation."

his dark Dutch palette. Finally, the atmosphere of Paris and his contact with cartoonists on the comic newspapers helped him to find his way.

The moment he had got out of the train he had felt at home. He was at ease in the streets of Paris, and on his first night went home with a girl whom he met in a dance hall. The following nights were less pleasant: he slept on benches at the Porte Saint-Ouen until his compatriot Ten Cate took him in. He lived precariously for several months, staying where he could, eating when he could. Some gipsies gave him shelter in their caravan until he moved into a hut on a bit of waste ground between the rue Ordener and the rue Caulaincourt. He sold newspapers, looked after the furnaces in office buildings, and was in turn porter at the Halles and at the stations, doorkeeper and house painter. In the evenings he went to fairgrounds and earned a few pence by acting as stooge for the professional wrestlers. He looked so like a tramp that he dared not speak to Renoir, Degas, and Toulouse-Lautrec when he saw them in the streets of Montmartre. At the end of a year, he had had enough of this life; he went back to Rotterdam and his old job on the newspaper and saved his salary in order to make another start in Paris.

This second attempt took place in about 1900, but things went no better than before, and, with a wife and child to support, his needs were all the greater (on July 11, 1901 he had married Augusta Preitinger, a student he had met in an art school in Rotterdam, at the Church of Saint-Pierre de Montmartre). " I did all sorts of things," he relates, " I set up my easel in a square and painted portraits of anyone I could catch. Most of my clients were nursemaids ... I also went back to selling newspapers, then I began to draw for the illustrated weeklies, *Rabelais, l'Indiscret,* moving up by degrees to *Le Rire* and *Le Sourire*. My greatest difficulty was to find captions for my drawings." He got round that one by looking up old jokes and drawing them all over again.

This recital of Van Dongen's material difficulties should be set against the fact that they occupied only a short period in a long and happy life, that his situation at this time was no worse than that of any other young Montmartre painter, and that he knew much joy and good fortune.

His work soon attracted the attention of the public and he sold a few pictures. The galleries of the rue Laffitte, where he had tried to show his work, sent him about his business. One day he stopped Vollard in the street to show him some pictures. The dealer was interested and asked Van Dongen his name. Van Dongen, knowing that his name was difficult for the French to pronounce, simply called himself "*le peintre*" (the painter); Vollard, who thought he was being facetious, walked away. His luck changed when the critic Félix Fénéon saw some of his pictures in the gallery of Le Barc de Boutteville and took him under his wing. Van Dongen's anarchist associations made him an object of special sympathy to Fénéon, who was confident of the painter's talent and arranged for some of his sketches to be published in *La Revue Blanche* and an entire number of *L'Assiette au Beurre* to be illustrated by his studies of prostitutes. Maximilien Luce, another anarchist sympathiser, got him into the Salon des Indépendants and even shouldered his first costs. " We used to say what we liked," Van Dongen remembers, " shout and abuse the bourgeoisie. We were all young and all anarchists." At the Salon des Indépendants of 1904, Fénéon recommended him to Vollard. The dealer seemed surprised to realise that this painter was the lunatic in overalls and plimsolls who had once accosted him in the street, but he bore no malice and agreed to give him an exhibition. The experience was a disappointing one for Van Dongen. He had to share with a Swiss woman painter, and the day before the opening Vollard took down all his pictures and replaced them with Cézannes.

Furious, Van Dongen refused to give in. He put his pictures back on the walls and promised to sell them himself. " I've sold things on fairgrounds," he said, " and I haven't made a bad job of it." Vollard, who was a rather phlegmatic character, was amused and let him have his own way. He had already noted him as a painter of the future.

Van Dongen's exhibition, which contained a remarkable portrait of La Goulue, painted in 1902, attracted a certain amount of attention; critics stressed the violent and discordant character of his work and this helped to make his name known. He showed two pictures in the Salon d'Automne of 1905, one of them a female torso in hectic colours. Simultaneously, he had a second exhibition, this time at Druet's, and Louis Vauxcelles wrote of it in *Gil Blas*: " This landscape painter is drunk with colour and reflections; he paints at noon in mid-August; hence these torrents of light, heat, and colour." The following day he devoted his column to the Fauve room in the Salon.

Van Dongen, having defined his own personality, now began to express it clearly in his own independent language. Some of his best canvases date from this time: *Anita la Bohémienne, Nini* of Folies-Bergère fame, *Le Clown rouge*, the self-portrait of 1905, *Boxing exhibition, Mistinguett et Max Dearly dans la valse chaloupée*. For some time he confined himself to this genre, using girls from bars and music halls as his models. He seemed to be the most gifted of the Fauves, certainly the best colourist, both strong and elegant : he set off warm against cool colours with great mastery and applied his paint in a generous and succulent manner.

The previous five years had made of him, like Picasso, one of the most picturesque figures in Montmartre. Both had studios in the Bateau-Lavoir, Place Ravignan (now Place Emile Goudeau), a former factory building roughly converted into extremely primitive studios. There was only one tap for them all, and Picasso had to light a candle to show his pictures. Van Dongen, whose studio gave onto the ground floor, was nicknamed " the concierge," since the building had no caretaker and visitors used to ask their way from him.

The inhabitants of this fortress of talent and poverty shared everything: Fernande Olivier, Picasso's mistress, often looked after Van Dongen's little girl, and made her a doll out of an old stocking stuffed with rags, on which Picasso painted a face. (The child called Picasso " Tablo ".)

At this time Van Dongen was better off than Picasso, who lacked the former's ability to throw off an amusing sketch for the newspapers. Both artists used to exhibit their pictures on the footpath outside the Cirque Médrano and steal milk and croissants from doorways in the mornings.

Their hard times together forged solid links between the two men although they never exactly handled each other with kid gloves. " Dubuffet," said Picasso recently, " paints with bitumen, but Van Dongen manufactures it." Van Dongen replied, " Picasso's painting ? I've often seen it but I can't say I've ever looked at it." He added, " I don't envy him. He used to be so cold : I can still see him shivering."

In 1907 Van Dongen began his upward progress to fame and fortune when Kahnweiler gave him his first contract. The contract was renewed in 1908 by the Bernheim brothers, when Kahnweiler decided to devote himself to Braque and Picasso. Van Dongen, who now had an assured income of nine thousand francs a year, moved to a decent studio at 35, rue Lamarck. This was a euphoric time for him. He was as indifferent to Cubism as he was to Cézanne: even today he regards them as jokes. He travelled widely—to Uruguay, for some unknown reason, to Italy, Spain, Morocco and Egypt—and purely for pleasure. He brought nothing back from these countries except from Egypt. " It's just as well," he said, " that we live in a country that is not too beautiful. They have no painters in the East because everything is so beautiful already. I had only one desire when I was there, to lie down and look at it all ... Painting is an invention of the north! "

His style entered a new phase of development after 1912, prompted not by boredom, like Vlaminck, or the influence of new ideas, as in the case of Derain and Dufy, but because he found that pure colour was an inadequate form of self-expression. He gave up painting in broad unmodified areas, using paint straight from the tube, and began to mix his colours, thereby obtaining a wider and more subtle range. Nevertheless he remained a Fauve at heart; in Elie Faure's words, he wanted to express " the sensual poetry of existence." As portrait painter to the world of fashion, he painted innumerable portraits of men, but these in a sense merely serve to set off his peculiarly feminine qualities of grace, sensuality, and lavishness. His masculine portraits are unidealized, fierce caricatures in which the sitter's character is investigated without pity. " All women are beautiful," he said. " They must be allowed to do as they please, for they pose better than men. They know how to arrange themselves so that everything they have shows up to advantage. Men don't bother; they think they're handsome enough as they are."

His life changed in 1913 when he met Countess Cassati, the famous Jasmy, known as " *la divine*," who was his companion throughout the wild years that lasted until 1934. Elegant and eccentric, she was the model for most of his portraits of elongated and sophisticated women with vast eyes and sparkling jewels. With her, his life became a round of big hotels, casinos, beauty competitions, and *concours d'élégance*. Then, when he had become the most famous painter of the post-war period, she suddenly left him. One morning she emerged from her suite superbly dressed and wearing all her jewels. " Where are you off to ?" he asked, laughing. " A wedding ?"
" Yes," she replied, " my own. I am going to marry General Azam."
This incident, in 1934, marked the end of their years together.

Though Louis Valtat's story has none of the picturesque qualities that distinguish the life of Van Dongen, there is a tenuous similarity between the two men. Like Van Dongen, Valtat discovered his own brand of Fauvism before Matisse investigated the possibilities of pure colour : his *Fiesta*, painted at Dieppe in 1896, in broad washes of red, green, and yellow, is one of the most violent pictures in the whole Fauve range. As a painter Valtat has been consistently overlooked; his shyness and his lack of contact with the art world contributed greatly to this state of affairs while he was still alive. " Patience," said Vollard. "One day people will see that you are a great painter." Bonnard, who owned one of his most sumptuous still lifes, *La Bouillabaisse*, was of the same view, as was Renoir who admired his colour harmonies, and Monet who described him as " the beginning of a new state of grace in painting." Valtat followed the same path as the others : the studio of Gustave Moreau, the Académie Julian, the Salon d'Automne of 1905, but he never became seriously involved with any particular group. He was friendly with both the Nabis and the Fauves, but he was interested in painting only as he himself felt. He took no interest in Cubism, although his admiration for Cézanne pre-dated that of Matisse and his friends by some ten years : in 1905 he executed a bust of Cézanne which is now in the Méjane library in Aix-en-Provence. Like Friesz he made contact with the world of southern light and colour while he was still a boy, and it was the inspiration behind his finest work. When he left the south to return to Normandy and the Ile-de-France, his painting became dull and weak. It recovered its strength only at the end of his life, when failing eyesight forced him to heighten his colours. Less fortunate than Monet, he was totally blind for four years before his death in 1952.
Valtat, whose father was a ship-owner, was born in Dieppe on August 8, 1869, and spent his childhood between Versailles and the Côte d'Azur. His family owned a few acres of land at Anthéor, and after his early marriage he built himself a house there. He introduced the region to the many friends

whom he invited to stay with him; in recognition of his services the railway company gave him a free pass for life.

Valtat was one of the few Fauve painters who received encouragement from his family. His father, an amateur painter, was proud and pleased when his son's work was hung beside his own in the Salon des Indépendants in 1892. When he left school Valtat enrolled at the Ecole des Beaux-Arts under Gustave Moreau and got to know Matisse and Marquet; after Moreau's death, he followed the others to the Académie Julian, where he met Vuillard and Bonnard (who became his life-long and dearest friend) and Albert André. André recounts that when Bouguereau and Benjamin Constant came round to correct in the class, Valtat, who greatly disliked both men, would go out and smoke his pipe in the street. He preferred to spend his time in the Louvre copying (notably Delacroix's *Justice of Trajan*) or studying the Impressionists. At the Académie Julian he had less contact with the future Fauves than with the Nabis, with whom he felt instinctive sympathy. This sympathy is reflected in his work, for like Jean Puy, Valtat is the only Fauve, or sub-Fauve, with a feeling for bourgeois interiors. He was particularly friendly with Maillol whom he accompanied to Banyuls, and in later life he remembered with feeling that he had helped the sculptor to execute his first terracotta figures. Although never a member of the Nabi group, he contributed to their publications, providing drawings for the pro-Nabi *Omnibus de Corinthe* and designing the scenery for a Hindu fantasy, *Le Chariot de terre cuite*, produced by Lugné-Poë.

He was completely indifferent to the problems that preoccupied Matisse and Derain, and considered that the former wasted far too much time talking. He preferred to let his instinct work for him. In 1900 he was working in a broad and richly coloured style, close to that of the Neo-Impressionists in subject matter and the divisionist application of primary colours. He exhibited five pictures in the Fauve room at the Salon d'Automne of 1905 and was therefore classed with the other members of the group. He then took the curious step of withdrawing from the movement altogether just when it was on the point of becoming famous. It is unlikely that he was prompted by any reason more sinister than a desire to work on his own. The major influences on his artistic development were Renoir, who used to motor over to see him at Magagnosc, near Grasse, and his own delicate health and voluntary absence from Paris with its artistic fashions and discussions. His style became progressively closer to Neo-Impressionism; his pictures of this period place him somewhere half-way between Renoir and Cross.

His painting is characterized by a certain happiness and freedom of spirit, and by dexterity of handling of a very high order. He had no trouble in making contact with both dealers and collectors. Vollard gave him a contract as early as 1900 : Valtat was, in this sense, his first Fauve. And as the painter had money of his own he was not obliged to sell or exhibit, and simply let his canvases pile up in his studio. The rest of his life was uneventful : he was a good son, a good husband, and a good father, a " complete bourgeois," an intelligent, cultivated and peaceable man whose painting is an exact reflection of these very qualities.

Manguin and Camoin were also fortunate and uncomplicated. On June 14, 1910, Apollinaire wrote in *L'Intransigeant*: " M. Manguin is a voluptuous painter. He is exhibiting fifty pictures of throw-away sensuality at the Galerie Druet. He is a colourist, and he specializes in contrasts which give him the opportunity to exploit curious light effects. These strange colours clash with the academic drawing of his nudes. A painter and a draughtsman exist quite independently in him. The result is an authentic but disconcerting charm arising from the dichotomy between the two. His nudes have a pagan frankness. His enchanted landscapes reflect the wonder of ruins at sunrise in midsummer. His still lifes are well constructed and more likeable than his other pictures. Here the colourist is given free rein, untroubled by the preoccupations that caused a conflict in the painting of the nudes."

Apollinaire's fairly tortuous evocation nevertheless conveys the impression of euphoria and sensual enjoyment for which Manguin's paintings are known. As a colourist he is closer to the Impressionists than to the Fauves, but what distinguishes him from Camoin and Valtat is the strength and solidity of his draughtsmanship, a lesson learnt from Cézanne, whom he came to appreciate much earlier than his friends in the studio of Moreau. While the other Fauves were lost in admiration for Gauguin, Manguin realized how much Gauguin owed to Cézanne.

Manguin had no great problem to surmount. His only need was to paint, but he felt this need to an extreme, almost maniacal degree. At his home in Saint-Tropez he would get up at five in the morning, work till lunchtime, spend the afternoon looking for new subjects, and frequently paint again in the evening. His daughter Lucile remembers a car journey from Paris to Saint-Tropez that lasted three weeks. He stopped the car and set up his easel every time he saw something worth painting.

Like Valtat, he was spared the material difficulties which made life so difficult for the other Fauves before they made their names. He was the richest member of the group. Berthe Weil was rendered speechless by his way of life, his country house, and his income of three thousand francs a year. Manguin, who may have felt a little ashamed of his good fortune, dressed the part in velvet gaiters, flowing cravat, and broad-brimmed hat. To Marquet, who showed surprise at this outfit, he replied, " You don't want me to look like an iron-monger, do you ? "

He was born in Paris in 1874. His family did not oppose his desire to be a painter, and he became a pupil of Gustave Moreau in 1895. Moreau did not influence him as strongly as he did Matisse and Rouault, but he did stimulate and inspire him. He copied in the Louvre with Matisse and Marquet. A natural taste for grisaille developed, under the influence of Matisse, into a love of pure colour. Renoir and Bonnard also encouraged him along these lines, and his evolution was accelerated after Moreau's death, when his own vast studio in the rue Boursault became the favourite meeting place of Matisse, Marquet, Camoin and Puy.

He was a handsome young man with a long beard and curly hair, and patriarchal tendencies. By the age of thirty he was known as Papa Manguin, a name which stuck to him for the rest of his life. His most violent period, comparatively speaking, can be dated at the beginning of the century, when he used violet, rose madder, cadmium and cobalt with a freshness and enthusiasm that inspired the phlegmatic Vallotton to make the remark, " These pictures are warming me through! "

1905 is an important date in his career. A visit to Signac at Saint-Tropez impressed on his mind the beauties of the little cape, and he bought a large property, " L'Oustalet," at the entrance to the harbour, where he lived until it was destroyed by the Germans in 1944. He would go back there after his frequent journeys to Italy, Morocco, Holland, Norway, and Egypt, to exchange impressions with Signac, another great traveller. The special light of Saint-Tropez, which is caused by the northern aspect of the peninsula, attracted him as it attracted so many other painters : the sun strikes the landscape like a searchlight, emphasizing the dark greens and violets of the sea, and the gorse covering the mountains. Also in 1905, he exhibited with Matisse and Marquet at the Salon d'Automne, but like Valtat he had little interest in theory and only cared for his own particular manner. He is one of the few Fauve painters whose style remained consistent throughout his life.

Camoin, one of the last surviving Fauves, still has a studio in the Avenue Junot filled with odds and ends collected in the course of a lifetime. He says of himself, " I was born to paint. My family had a decorating business in Marseilles. My mother painted quite well herself, and it was she who took me to see Gustave Moreau." He became a pupil of Moreau's in 1897, when he was eighteen. " I stayed there about four months, "he says. " He only corrected my work about two or three times. When he died, I left. I'm sorry I didn't know him better. He had such a wonderful knowledge of the Louvre, but stated firmly that he ' preferred Fra Angelico to that rubbish by Degas.' " But in those four months Moreau was able to teach him the importance of the old masters, and he learned much from copying Titian, Rubens, Chardin and Fragonard. His earliest works show that he was an instinctive colourist;

he still points with pride to a little picture of a fish-stall, painted in Marseilles in his sixteenth year, which is as brillantly coloured as the work of his later Fauve period. His *Cabaretière* of 1900 is done in a flat bright synthetist style very close to that of Gauguin, and in fact the picture, which is now in Sydney, was for many years believed to be by Gauguin. " Colour was in the air," he says, " and I had probably absorbed it without knowing." And he adds, " Nobody influenced me. I paint by instinct. I never took any notice of the theories of Matisse, who once told me that the one essential instrument in painting was the plumb line—that was long before his Fauve period, of course! Some time later, he took up this idea again. I have a letter in which he describes himself as a romantic and a scientist existing side by side ... "

Although one cannot speak of influences in his work, his meeting with Cézanne in 1901 played an important part in his general development. " I met him while I was doing my military service," he says. " I had spent a year in Avignon and Arles, where I met Dr. Rey who had looked after Van Gogh and who was using Vincent's portrait of him to block a hole in the chicken house. Then I was sent on to Aix. In Paris I always stopped to admire the Cézanne in Vollard's window on my way to the Ecole des Beaux-Arts. I was one of the few to do so; most people preferred Renoir and the Impressionists. The very evening of my arrival in Aix, I asked for Cézanne's address. No one knew it. At last I found out that he lived in the rue Boulegon. I went there and rang the bell. Mme Bérenguier answered the door. I explained why I had come. ' Cézanne is not here,' she said, but she asked me to wait in the dining room. For some reason I lost my nerve, told her that I would come back another time, and made off for the nearest café, where I blamed myself for being such a fool.

"I told myself that if I didn't go back at once, I would never go at all. I rang the bell again. A shutter was pushed back on the second floor, and Cézanne's head emerged, covered with a night-cap. The housekeeper had already told him that a soldier had called, so he was not surprised to see me. He came down with a candle and we went back into the dining-room. I blurted out how much I admired him, and I think he was touched. ' Listen, young man,' he said to me when I left, 'when you can express that stove-pipe jutting out from that wall, you'll be a painter.' He was already full of his theory about the sphere, the cylinder and the cone."

A friendship grew out of this meeting, and during the three months that Camoin spent in Aix, Cézanne used to call for him at the gate of the barracks and take him out walking in the country, delighted to have found an intelligent companion at last. They made a curious couple, the tiny figure in frock coat and Homburg hat gesticulating beside a tall youth in red trousers, white gaiters and pom-pom cap. He talked freely about everything that interested him. " They should put a thousand painters to death every year," he once said excitedly.

" Who would choose them ? "

" We would, of course! "

Once, in the heat of conversation, he exclaimed, " I need a man like you beside me! " Camoin modestly made no reply.

When Camoin was transferred to Paris, he and Cézanne corresponded regularly until the latter's death. Camoin still has Cézanne's letters, carefully preserved behind cellophane.

On his demobilization, he found himself alone in the world with fifty francs, a present from an uncle. His worries were soon over, however; his pictures were already selling and enjoying a modest success. Berthe Weil, Druet and Kahnweiler all bought from him. In 1904 he sold all six of the pictures he exhibited in that year's Salon des Indépendants, one to Signac. On the proceeds he and Marquet went off to Provence, theoretically on holiday. They painted all day long. " We were crazy with enthusiasm," he says. Signac invited him to Saint-Tropez, where he fell in love with the boats, the sea, the mountains, and the pink and yellow-washed houses. He bought himself one of the most beautiful villas on the peninsula, " Le Maquis," which he sold in 1926 to Dunoyer de Segonzac, who lives there still. Camoin still spends long periods in his studio on the Quai Jean-Jaurès in Saint-Tropez, but times his departure to coincide with the beginning of the tourist season. Like his friends Valtat and Manguin, Camoin remained unmoved by the theoretical aspects of Fauvism and Cubism. " They bored me to tears," he says. " Cubism meant nothing to me. Our period has been dominated by the need to establish certain theories, but as far as I'm concerned, they all go back to Cézanne."

The evolution of his style really dates from 1912, when he met and was influenced by Renoir. The memory of Cézanne faded; Camoin's painting became less concerned with drawing and construction, freer, more flowery, and more brightly coloured. A genuine crisis had preceded this line of development. Returning from a trip to Tangier with Matisse and Marquet, Camoin slashed eighty pictures and threw them away. Fifteen years later, he was surprised to find them put together again and hung in an exhibition organized by Francis Carco. He had to take legal action to have them removed.

His true gifts lie in his ability to convey certain sensuous properties : the sweetness of fruit, the velvety softness of flowers, the heat of a summer's day and the sound of the sea on the beaches of the coast of Provence.

Only in the broadest sense of the word can Puy and Flandrin be said to have been associated with the Fauve movement. Certainly one can find Fauve qualities in their work, but they remain very far indeed from the impetus of

movement at the Ecole des Beaux-Arts and the various academies they subsequently frequented, but their interest in pure colour was brief and temperate. They really only evolved a personal style once Fauvism was over.

Puy's qualities of moderation and sensibility seem to place him more properly in the orbit of the Nabis, with whom he was friendly, particularly with Bonnard; his preference for nudes, children and interiors was stronger even than Valtat's. His understanding of subtleties and feeling for atmospheric values show that he was really in opposition to the Fauves, who were hostile to these particular qualities. His only Fauve characteristic is his sensuality, which he possessed in abundant measure, as may be judged not only in his paintings but from his way of life, and certain "illustrated" letters. But unlike the Fauves, he usually managed to keep this under control.

A true solitary, with a passion for boats and the coast of Brittany—he spent several months a year sailing at Belle-Ile—Puy always painted in isolation, seeking neither fame nor money. Permanently dissatisfied with his work, he burned a great deal of his annual output. He ultimately felt unable to make contact with the times in which he lived, and when the Galerie Vendôme staged an exhibition of his works in 1905, the year before his death, he took fright at the idea of having to use the Métro and had to walk home.

He was born in Roanne in 1876, into an austere, upper middle-class, provincial family, and as a boy studied modern architecture at the Ecole des Beaux-Arts in Lyon. His father was disappointed when he came to prefer painting, but a compromise was reached and for several terms he studied both. His master was Tony Tollet, a well-known portraitist and pupil of Cabanel, whose teaching methods had something in common with those of Moreau. In 1897 Puy overcame family opposition and went to Paris to complete his studies. His only wish was to become a history painter, but this soon changed after he met Matisse, Derain and Laprade at the Académies Julian and Carrière, and was introduced by them to the works of Pissarro, Monet and Renoir. Matisse converted him to colour, to the great disgust of Carrière. The influence of Matisse is evident in all his early works and in some of his best ones, certain nudes which show an elegant use of arabesque and fresh but not exaggerated colours. His pictures, which reflected a muted version of Matisse's palette were soon sold through Berthe Weil and Druet, in whose galleries he exhibited as well as at the Salon des Indépendants. He shares with the Fauves a keen sense of form, a feeling for stylization, and strong powers of synthesis. He transposed his Fauvism into the domain of taste; he gave less cause for alarm than his more famous contemporaries, and was much more easily and rapidly appreciated.

In 1905, however, trouble came along. On the advice of Matisse, Vollard had offered him a contract. From then on, all Puy's pictures went straight into Vollard's basement. They are still in the basement of Vollard's heirs. The dealer liked Puy personally but was not greatly interested in his work : he paid for the pictures and stowed them away. He preferred Puy as a draughtsman, and asked him to provide illustrations for his pastiche of Jarry entitled *Père Ubu à la guerre*.

Puy instinctively detached himself from the Fauves and drew nearer to Bonnard and Vuillard. At the end of his life he was almost a post-Impressionist. He went back to Roanne in 1927, after the termination of his contract with Vollard. He lived a secluded life with his family, and spent his last years in an old barn which he converted into a studio. The pictures of his Roanne period are practically unknown; many of them are still *in situ* on the walls of rarely-opened salons. As a painter, Puy has not yet been fully discovered and appreciated.

Flandrin is even less of a Fauve than Puy. Born at Corenc, near Grenoble, in 1871, he is essentially a provincial painter. He studied with the rest of the Fauves under Moreau, in the Louvre etc., but unlike his companions he took a particular interest in Puvis de Chavannes, from whom he gained an ability to execute large decorative compositions on folk themes, with full complement of flocks, shepherds, and allegorical statuary.

He aspired to nothing more revolutionary than the right to exhibit in the stuffy Société Nationale des Beaux-Arts, but his Fauve connections came to life again in 1909 when he painted a series of studies of the Russian ballet. The influence of Fauvism in this connection is probably more important than that of Slav folk art : Léon Bakst, the designer, had followed the experiments of the Fauves since their earliest days. Flandrin thus came back to Fauvism by an indirect route, and in this way painted the best pictures of his entire career.

He was friendly with most of the group and especially with Marquet, who was his neighbour on the Quai Saint-Michel. He lived there for forty years with his eccentric mistress Jacqueline Marval, a former corset-maker who had come to painting by way of concubinage. Marval, whose real name was Marguerite Vallet, and who was originally from the same region as Flandrin, arrived in Paris with a painter who had done his military service in Grenoble. She deserted him for Flandrin. In many respects she was a more thoroughgoing Fauve than her lover, who adored her and compared her with Phidias and Raphael. She enjoyed a modest success until Flandrin abandoned her, married one of his pupils, and went back to his native Dauphiné. She died of cancer in 1932, preceding her unfaithful lover by fourteen years. They have since been reunited in oblivion.

Colour plates 59—89

59. ROUAULT. AUTOPORTRAIT. Collection particulière, Paris.

60. ROUAULT. NU. Musée d'Art Moderne de la Ville de Paris. Collection Girardin.

61. ROUAULT. LES « POULOT ». Collection Philippe Leclercq, France.

62. ROUAULT. LA NOCE A NINI PATTE-EN-L'AIR. Collection particulière, Paris.

63. ROUAULT. LA PARADE. Collection Max Bangerter, Montreux.

64. ROUAULT. NU AU MIROIR. Musée National d'Art Moderne, Paris.

65. VAN DONGEN. AUTOPORTRAIT. Collection M. et Mme Kees Van Dongen, Monaco.

66. VAN DONGEN. ANITA. Collection M. et Mme Kees Van Dongen, Monaco.

67. VAN DONGEN. LE PROMENOIR DES FOLIES-BERGÈRE. Collection M. et Mme Kees Van Dongen, Monaco.

68. VAN DONGEN. PORTRAIT DE FERNANDE. Collection particulière, Paris.

69. VAN DONGEN. LE CLOWN. Collection Mme Lucile Manguin, Paris.

70. VAN DONGEN. LA BALLERINE BORGNE. Collection particulière, Paris.

71. VAN DONGEN. LA FEMME AU CHAPEAU. Collection particulière, Paris.

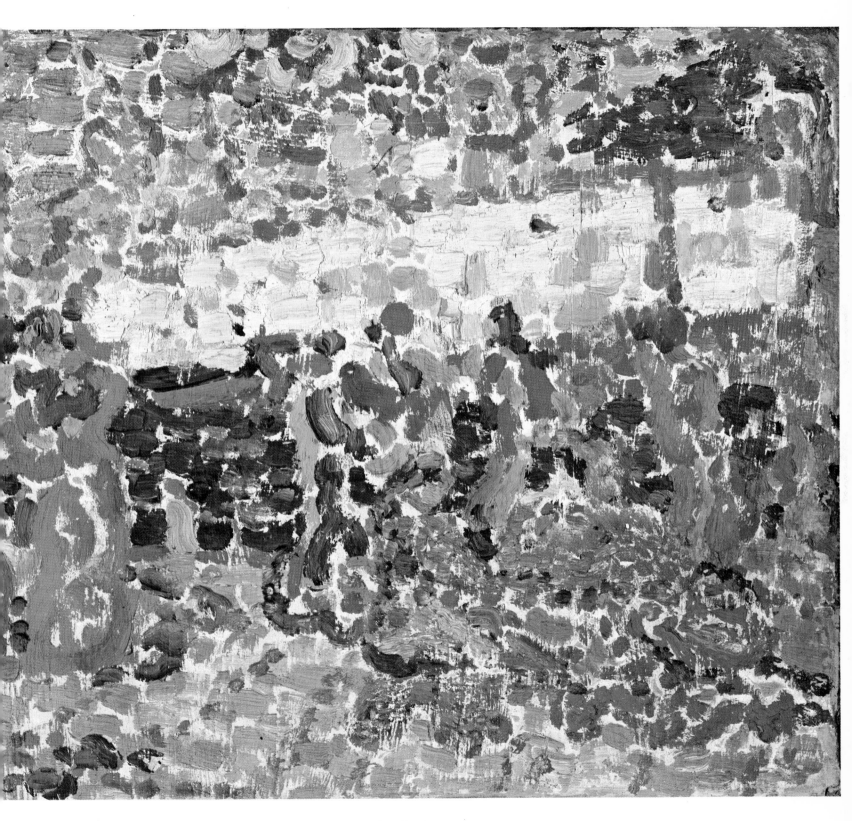

72. VALTAT. LA FIESTA. Collection Dr Jean Valtat, Paris.

73. VALTAT. LA JETÉE. Mr. and Mrs. Henry Ittleson Collection, New York.

74. VALTAT. VOILIER DANS LA BAIE D'AGAY. Collection Dr Jean Valtat, Paris.

75. VALTAT. FEMME SUR UN BANC. Collection Dr Jean Valtat, Paris.

76. VALTAT. LES ROCHERS ROUGES D'ANTHÉOR. Collection Dr Jean Valtat, Paris.

77. CAMOIN.   LA RUE BOUTERIE.   Collection Mᵐᵉ Ginette Signac, Paris.

78. CAMOIN. LE MOULIN ROUGE. Musée de Menton.

79. CAMOIN. LE PORT DE MARSEILLE. Nouveau Musée du Havre.

80. CAMOIN. PORTRAIT DE MARQUET. Musée National d'Art Moderne, Paris.

81. MANGUIN.   QUATORZE JUILLET A SAINT-TROPEZ.   Collection Mme Lucile Manguin, Paris.

82. MANGUIN. PAYSAGE AVEC PERSONNAGES. Collection Mme Lucile Manguin, Paris.

83. MANGUIN. NU. Collection Mme Lucile Manguin, Paris.

84. MANGUIN. PORTRAIT DE MME HENRI MANGUIN. Collection Mme Lucile Manguin, Paris.

85. MANGUIN. FEMME A L'OMBRELLE. Collection Mme Lucile Manguin, Paris.

86. PUY. NU. Collection particulière, Paris.

87. PUY. LA FEMME AU FAUTEUIL. Collection Dr Paul Gay, Saint-Jeoire.

88. PUY. FEMME LISANT. Collection particulière, Paris.

89. PUY. NU COUCHÉ. Collection M. Oscar Ghez, Genève.

VII   Death and resurrection of Fauvism

A mere two years after the scandal at the Salon d'Automne of 1905, the Fauve movement had already lost impetus. During the winter of 1907-8 and the spring that followed, many of the Fauves turned their attention to other matters. The founders of the movement were not slow to recognize the limitations of expression by means of pure colour, a programme which could not be expected to satisfy the younger members of the group. The style, which depended on immediate effect rather than a long process of evolution and thought, contained the seeds of its own destruction. Vlaminck suspected that he was becoming decorative and repetitive, and Derain, with his memories of classical art, declared, " The most inert or monotonous colour may possess explosive power. The great masters have an emotive force that surpasses mere technique."

A reaction therefore set in against Fauve methods and painters began to search for other forms of expression based less exclusively on the senses. Many possibilities were open; innumerable movements and counter-movements were in the air. The most important trends were a deeper knowledge of Cézanne, the discovery of Negro sculpture and of popular art, and the vogue for the Douanier Rousseau, which began as a joke.

Cubism, which began as a brutal reaction to Fauvism, offered painters vast fields for experiment, and was soon understood, by Apollinaire and others, as the full flowering of many of the trends adumbrated in the works of the Fauves. In an interview in *Le Temps* of October 14, 1912, Apollinaire stated, "...Maurice de Vlaminck's taste for primitive and Negro sculptures, and André Derain's speculations along the same lines, together with the fact that the Impressionists had already freed painting from its academic chains, were to have a great effect on the future of French art.

"About the same time, there lived in Montmartre a youth whose mobile eyes and face recalled those of Raphael and Forain. This was Pablo Picasso, who at the age of sixteen was already known for his pictures which bore more than a passing resemblance to the malicious works of Forain. Picasso had suddenly abandoned this manner in order to paint mysterious pictures in shades of blue ... I knew him in 1905. His fame did not extend beyond the boundaries of Montmartre ... That same year, André Derain met Henri Matisse and this meeting gave birth to the famous Fauve group which counted in its ranks many of the young painters who were afterwards to become Cubists. I note this meeting to emphasize the part played by André Derain in the development of the movement... The following year he joined Picasso, and the result was the birth of Cubism, an art of painting new syntheses based on conceptual rather than visual truth."

Apollinaire's account is inaccurate, particularly about the meeting between Matisse and Derain, but we may accept his estimate of the important part played by Derain in the evolution of Cubism, and also note the contribution of many other Fauve painters. There is additional proof that Braque and Dufy, as well as Derain, contributed to the movement in its early stages. Le Corbusier and Ozenfant confirm that Matisse had much to offer in the discussion that took place at the Bistro Azon. According to them, " Matisse permitted Cubism," and it is interesting to note that Matisse was the first to speak of cubes (not without irony) with regard to a picture by Braque in the Salon d'Automne of 1908. Vauxcelles took up the phrase and used it in *Gil Blas*. Although not all the Fauves went over to Cubism, they were without exception influenced by the lesson of Cézanne, and after their orgy of colour most of them used his example to improve on their early Fauve experiments. Braque, Derain, Marquet and Friesz broke completely with the movement. Van Dongen evolved a sort of fashionable expressionism in which colour was used more or less as a relish, while the lesser Fauves ended up as uncomplicated post-Impressionists. Only Matisse, Vlaminck and Dufy remained faithful to their original ideals, and at the end of their long careers made a partial return to the brilliant colours of their early works.

As is usually the case, once the leaders of the movement turned their attention elsewhere, a number of less gifted and less audacious artists took over their discoveries and converted them to pleasing but minor ends. It can truly be said that the style of the Salon d'Automne between the two World Wars was formed by the Fauve heritage, and today Desnoyer and Czobel are the last practitioners of the style.

Although Fauvism died out in France it had an important posterity in the rest of Europe. A splinter movement in Belgium was led by Rik Wouters who died blind in 1916, but its greatest influence was in Germany, where it stimulated important subsidiary developments in Dresden and Munich.

But before examining this German development, it might be fitting to take a look at the later years of the French Fauves.

Shortly before 1914, Matisse went through a phase which, if not completely Cubist, was at least marked by a taste for geometrical synthesis. This phase, although brief, produced the *Nu bleu, Les Marocains, La Leçon de piano*, and *Le Rifain*. He then settled in Nice during the war, and this move coincided with a prolonged Neo-Impressionist phase. He arrived in pouring rain on December 20, 1917, but the next day was bright, and Matisse was so charmed by the brilliance of the sea, the elegance of the palm trees, and the somewhat subdued life that went on behind the blinds of his hotel, the Beau-Rivage, that he stayed on.

His Nice period, which lasted until 1939, is famous for the series of *Odalisques*, which show the unmistakable influence of Renoir, *Fenêtres ouvertes*, and *Intérieurs*. He went to Cagnes to pay his respects to Renoir, who was astonished at Matisse's pompous tweeds and gold-rimmed spectacles but also glad to find that he was talking to a real and experienced painter. He had heard bad reports of him. " They told me," he remarked, " that Matisse paints like this " (and he passed his brush through his legs), "but it's not true. He takes a lot of trouble."

Matisse paid further visits, and Renoir told him the story of Impressionism and inspected some of this pictures. At this time Matisse shows a strong preoccupation with grace and linear elegance; his colours are precious and subtle, and although less vigorous than those of his Fauve period, are more expressive and attractive. This was a happy and fruitful time, marked by the least personal but perhaps most accessible of all his styles. It was this period that made of him a famous painter.

In his later years, incapacitated by a serious internal operation which he was forced to undergo at the beginning of the Occupation, he abandoned painting for paper cut-outs, to which he gave all the weight of a new genre. He had already experimented with these *papiers découpés* when preparing *La Danse* for Dr. Barnes in 1931 and 1932, and in his *Jazz* volume of 1937 he had returned to the attack, working directly with scissors and coloured paper. During and after the war he perfected his new technique and used paper washed with body colour. " Paper cut-outs," he said, " enabled me to draw in colour. I saw them as a means of simplification. Instead of drawing the contour and inserting colour, so that the one modifies the other, I draw directly into the colour, which is all the better proportioned for not being transposed. Thus the two processes become one ... This is not a new departure; it is an arrival." Once more he became deeply interested in colour, and Camoin was astonished to hear him praise a Rouault of great brutality of tone which hung on the wall of his studio. " That is what I've always been trying to do myself," said Matisse. Installed in his specially designed bed or in an armchair in the middle of his studio, which housed a collection of three hundred tropical birds, he would supervise the activities of his secretary-housekeeper, the mysterious and silent

Lydia Delectoroskaia, who came to him after his separation from his wife in 1934. She would arrange outlines of leaves or human figures against sheets of white cardboard tacked to the wall until he was satisfied with the rhythms and colour harmonies obtained. This technique was radically different from the *papiers découpés* of the Cubists. Braque, Picasso and Juan Gris all cut out their shapes according to a prearranged plan, whereas Matisse followed his intuition as he worked directly with the scissors. Only when a particular combination satisfied him were the sheets of cardboard mounted on canvas. The colours of his papers were so violent that his doctor ordered him to wear dark glasses when he was not working, to rest his eyes.

In the last years of his life he executed not only the great decoration of the chapel at Vence but a series of other large-scale compositions : *Bêtes de mer, Poissons chinois, Danseuses, Tristesse, Négresse, Acrobates*, in which the dynamism and joy of his Fauve period reappear. Both the volume and the quality of these works are astonishing when one reflects that they were done by a total invalid at the end of a long career.

Matisse, who had always lived for painting, whose only distractions had been two trips to America and the South Seas, spent his last years in a state of slow-burning exaltation, sleeping only a few hours each night, unwilling to waste the time which he felt slipping away from him. He worked up to the last day of his life, and was just finishing a large composition commissioned by the King of Sweden when he died suddenly from a heart attack on November 3, 1954. He had imposed his work on the times in which he lived and fulfilled Moreau's prophecy that he would " simplify painting." He knew he had succeeded, and said, " I have laboured for years in order that people should say, ' Matisse's painting ? Nothing to it! ' "

It may seem paradoxical to include Vlaminck with the Fauves who remained faithful to the principles of colour. It is true that when he abandoned his early violence, his work reflected the influence of Cézanne for a long period of time : drawing and construction were dominant, colours were limited to bistres, Prussian blues and emerald greens, and later blacks and whites which made people say, " There are always storms in Vlaminck's skies." But his bias towards instinct, temporarily subdued by the discipline of Cézanne, came back in full force after the war. A greater anarchist than ever, he returned to a violent synthetic style, using brutal hatchings of white, black, vermilion and cadmium yellow in a crescendo which reached its peak a few years before his death. He was fully conscious of this development, which he put down to living in primitive surroundings.

" At first I was disconcerted by the atmosphere of a place dominated by the earth," he said. " These immense distances were very different from the more orderly landscape around Paris. Here nature is great, naked, bare, and rich in essential colours. Clouds chase each other across an endless sky filled with rooks ... Haystacks the colour of rotten straw ... Earthen walls the colour of clay ... Trees bent by the wind. Green fields filled with apple trees and grazing cattle and flocks of chickens and ducks ... I wanted to paint all this and to express the dual quality, peaceful and tragic, timeless and impermanent, with which all things are stamped." His romantic expressionism took him back to the primitive style of his youth.

After a triumphant exhibition at Druet's in 1919, Vlaminck had no further financial worries. He left Paris for good, but despite his detestation of the city he never travelled much beyond its outer suburbs, where he could keep his physical and moral distance and at the same time remain in touch. He went first to Valmondois then, after his second marriage in 1925, to Rueil-la-Gadelière, on the borders of Normandy and Le Perche, an ordinary little village which he discovered in the course of an afternoon walk. He lived in a local house which he jealously maintained in a state of original rusticity, refusing to install running water or central heating, and for thirty years lived the simple yet comfortable life of a gentleman farmer, subsisting on the produce of his farm and receiving innumerable guests and admirers at his table. Writers like Duhamel, Vildrac, Louis Bromfield, Roger Martin du Gard, Mac Orlan, Eugène Dabit, Malaparte, Céline and Louis Pauwels frequently visited " La Tourillière," as did picture dealers, politicians, and Montmartre layabouts brought by friends for his amusement. Vlaminck's jokes, his roars of thunderous laughter, charmed and deafened his guests. He had opinions on every subject, though he rarely mentioned painting (" It's talk of that kind that makes the Mona Lisa smile," he would say). He would give, without hesitation, his views on finance, social security, penicillin, and literature, and he would read to his visitors, no matter who they were—the butcher from Vernon or a professional writer—passages from his novels or memoirs, watching their reactions very carefully, seizing on the slightest nuance of criticism, and purring openly at the most outrageous compliments paid to his ability as a writer.

Vlaminck always enjoyed life enormously and his last years were a kind of wild apotheosis, crowned by his reconciliation with André Derain, the loss of whose friendship he had always regretted, and the retrospective exhibition of his works held at the Galerie Charpentier in March 1956.

The meeting between Derain and Vlaminck, which took place in 1954 in a hotel in Pontchartrain, had no aftermath. A few days later Derain was knocked down by a car near his house at Chambourcy and died on September 8. He too in his last years had made a return to the bright colours of his youth, but the great formless heads of fauns and satyrs, which are still in his studio, are the terrifying visions of an imagination gone mad.

In spite of his sometimes hasty execution, which critics were quick to call commercial, Vlaminck did much good work in the last years of his life. " To reproach me for always doing the same thing," he would reply to his detractors, " is like blaming Wagner for always composing Wagnerian music or Beethoven for being recognizably Beethoven." The pictures of flowers and the gouaches executed a few months before his death have the same fiery verve and liberality of his early landscapes of Chatou. Though his methods of execution varied, Vlaminck remained a pure Fauve, and the vein of plebeian poetry apparent in his pictures of 1905-7 never ran dry.

His death and burial were in the same spirit as his life had been. He died suddenly during the night of October 11, 1958 and was buried at dusk on the evening of the following day, a Sunday. As he had wished, the coffin was placed on a farm cart drawn by a neighbour's horse, and the silence of the country evening, broken by the sound of the percheron's hooves, was the only requiem he desired.

Before his death he had written a testament which sums up his experience as a painter and constitutes a moving creed for younger artists: "I give freely to all the deep emotion, which I still remember keenly, and which was given to me by the works of Ruysdael, Breughel, Courbet, Cézanne and Van Gogh ... and I also give, without the slightest regret, such things as pasteurized milk, pharmaceutical products, vitamins, anything synthetic, ' decorative ' painting, and abstract art.

" ... It is not money itself that spells death to a painter or writer, but the facility it brings; the new desires it stimulates are morbid elements, virulent microbes, which modify the appearance of life, change our innermost feelings, atrophy the fresh and veracious flower of our beginnings. The destiny of a work of art is that of a seed which germinates, grows, and flowers. The painter is not an inventor, and painting should not be an invention. Truly personal and original expression is rare. More often than not, the artist has at his disposal means which have been used before but which he may be able to revive and expand ... How difficult it is to bring forth what we see in our mind's eye! How difficult to select the real feelings from all those that rush pell-mell from the brush or the pen!

" To young painters I bequeath the flowers of the fields, the banks of streams, the black and white clouds that pass over the plains, brooks, woods and great trees, hillsides and the road, little villages covered with snow in winter, meadows with their magnificent harvest, birds and butterflies ... These inestimable treasures which are reborn every season, these inestimable treasures of light and shadow, the colours of the sky and of water ... should we not remind ourselves occasionally that they are a priceless heritage and a constant inspiration of masterpieces? This treasure, not subject to tax or death duties, can be rightly bequeathed by an old painter whose wondering eyes still hold the image of those fields and meadows, and whose ear still hears the sound of the streams... Have we enjoyed these things enough? Have you admired them enough ? Can you fully appreciate all the emotion that the dawn and the day which will die and never return, can stir up in you ? Can you get this deep and eternal feeling onto your canvas ?

"I have never asked for anything. Life has given me everything. I have done what I could, and I have painted what I have seen."

Like Matisse and Vlaminck, Dufy returned to the colours of his youth in his last years. In point of fact, apart from a brief Cubist period, he had never abandoned colour; colour and drawing remained the essential components of his work, but something of his original boldness flared up again just before he died.

His long association with the dress-designer Poiret and the silk merchant Bianchini, for whom he had executed several hundreds of sketches, had given him an opportunity to experiment on a very large scale. Finally, in about 1922, he evolved a style that could be called truly personal. In his pictures of racecourses and regattas, the drawing is superimposed on the coloured areas. His lines became more and more independent of the colour patches, and his style increasingly vital and dynamic.

The colour of his pictures is fresh, almost acid, rarely violent, always tender, rich and varied. Jean Cassou, considering his canary yellows, Indian reds, cyclamen violets and cerulean blues, unhesitatingly calls him " a colourist of colourists." A sparkling and volatile character—Poiret compared him to champagne and would tell waiters to bring him " some Dufy "—he acquired stability and depth as he went on, probably under the effect of illness.

His family had suffered from rheumatism, and early in life he began to notice the symptoms of arthritis. " What do you expect ?" he said. " There were eight of us in the family. My parents were crippled with rheumatism. My brothers and sisters were spared it. I've inherited the lot." Work became torture. The second World War and the Occupation brought him troubles that nearly turned to tragedy. He had sought refuge in the Pyrenees and was captured at Saint-Gaudens during fighting between the Maquis and soldiers of Vlasov's Russian division which had gone over to the Germans. He was taken for a member of the Maquis and was nearly shot.

After the Liberation his condition got worse. In April 1950 his case came to the attention of Dr. Homburger, of Boston's Jewish Hospital, who admired his work and who chose Dufy as the first patient on whom the new cortisone treatment would be used. The drug was still rare and very costly. The doctor explained to his colleagues that since they could pursue their experiments on only a few selected patients, it would be a good thing to give the benefit of a possible cure to an artist, whose renewed health would give satisfaction to many others beside himself. Dufy accepted and went to the United States, where he was admirably treated. He returned to France greatly improved

The painters of Die Brücke

NOLDE, Emil Hansen (1867-1956). Nolde, who was originally a cabinet-maker, was a self-taught artist whose training was limited to evening classes and a course in draughtsmanship. He was appointed an instructor at Saint-Gall, where he taught at the school of applied arts. Having had some commercial success with a series of postcards printed with his own designs, he was able to devote himself entirely to painting, and after a spell in Munich, went to Paris. He is known to have attended the Académie Julian and to have made copies in the Louvre, notably of Titian's *Avalos Allegory*. After nine months he went to Copenhagen; his love for the small fishing villages of the Baltic coast dates from this period. In 1901 he married and abandoned his family name of Hansen for that of Nolde, his birthplace.

His crude primitive style, with its obvious overtones of Hodler, Bœcklin and Stuck, became more personal and moved towards a form of mystical expressionism. He had a marked taste for allegory and gave colour a range of symbolic significance, but his extreme expressionism occasionally led to nightmare images that produce a distinctly unpleasant impression.

Nolde was too independent to accept the discipline of a group and exhibited alternately with the Dresden and Munich Fauves. In 1913 he went to New Guinea, and this long journey, together with the war the following year, confirmed him as a solitary. His later years were darkened by the Nazi persecution (Hitler had a thousand of his pictures removed from German galleries and forbade him to paint), but after the war he had the pleasure of knowing that his strange talent was widely recognized and appreciated.

KIRCHNER, Ernst Ludwig (1880-1938). Leading spirit of the Dresden group and, with Nolde, the most important German painter of the early years of the twentieth century. He was deeply impressed by Dürer's wood engravings, which he discovered in the course of a journey to Nuremberg in 1898, and made himself the apostle of this

and settled at Forcalquier, where he painted his last pictures in a state of euphoric contentment. Many of these pictures, of which *Le Violon Rouge* is probably the most famous example, were painted in a single colour. He called this " tonal painting." These extremely bold canvases, in which he did not hesitate to use black for the sun, are probably the strongest elements in an *œuvre* which is often considered lightweight. He went on painting until March 23, 1953 when he died of complications following pneumonia. Until the end, his subject matter—the sea, ships, sails, musical instruments—was the same as it had been since those early days in Le Havre.

As the movement died out in France, a particular form of Fauvism began to spread in Germany. There is a distinct difference in feeling between the Dresden painters of Die Brücke and their Parisian counterparts. The German painters had a taste for unity and for regulations. Strict rules governed their work and their discussions, and deviationists could be expelled from the group. There was also a spiritual difference. The French Fauves loved life; they were dynamic, direct, cared only for plastic qualities, and sought balance and harmony above all. The German artist were uneasy, neurotic—Kirchner took drugs—and obsessed with moral, religious, and sexual problems. The spirit of German Romanticism lived again. But both French and German painters shared a refusal to paint exact representations of the subject before them, a taste for synthesis, and for pure colour laid on in broad unmodulated areas.

Certain members of the Dresden group, animated by the wrong sort of chauvinism, refused to recognize the influence of the French Fauves on their own movement. Kirchner, the leader of Die Brücke and the best of the Dresden painters, went so far as to change the dates on some of his pictures in an attempt to prove that his experiments were earlier than those of the French. It is not difficult to disprove these assertions. Generally speaking, the Dresden painters were younger than their French colleagues, certainly younger than Matisse, Vlaminck, Derain and Valtat, and had hardly finished their studies when the Fauves had already produced important works. We know, moreover, that Van Gogh and Gauguin exhibitions were held in Dresden at the Galerie Arnold in 1902, 1905, and 1906, and that the painters of Die Brücke learned much from these events. Finally, French and German painters were in contact with each other and had opportunities to compare their work and exchange ideas in the course of various journeys to Dresden, Munich, Berlin and Paris. Friesz and Dufy spent four months in Munich in 1909; Van Dongen joined Die Brücke in 1908, and Matisse, who had spent the summer of 1908 in Bavaria, had an exhibition in Berlin in the winter of the same year. He returned to Munich with Marquet in 1910 for the exhibition of Muslim art. The German Fauves, who regarded him as a leader and a guide, presented him with a wreath of bay, which Mme Matisse later used for her sauces.

particular art form among his contemporaries of Die Brücke. Another important influence on his style was the exhibition of primitive Polynesian art in 1904. He joined with Schmidt-Rottluff, Heckel and Bleyl, his colleagues at the Dresden technical school, to form Die Brücke, of which he was certainly the most dynamic member.

His anxious, volatile, hypersensitive temperament is reflected in his art, which is nervous to the point of morbidity, as can be seen in his most famous picture, *The Artist and his Model*. In 1911 he settled in Berlin and took part in the demonstrations organized by the magazine *Der Sturm*. From this time dates his series of paintings inspired by the life of the great city and the anguish of modern urban man. The war threw him into a state of profound moral crisis. He volunteered for service in 1914 but was found to be tubercular and sent to various sanatoria in Germany and Switzerland. Haunted by the fear of being sent back to the front, he started to take drugs to calm his nerves. He regained his equilibrium only when the war ended.

Under the Hitler regime, his art was condemned as degenerate and six hundred and thirty nine of his pictures were seized. He succeeded in escaping to Switzerland, but the double disaster of the seizure of his work and a return of his old illness caused him to take his life in 1938.

SCHMIDT-ROTTLUFF, Karl (1884). Less complex and anxious than his colleagues, Schmidt-Rottluff (Rottluff is the name of his native village) painted correspondingly more attractive pictures, although the harsh angular manner of Die Brücke is not entirely absent from his works. He had a good knowledge of the activities of the French Fauves and Cubists which he studied during his frequent journeys to Paris. He was also in close contact with Nolde. A dreamy and slightly mystical personality, Schmidt-Rottluff was much given to painting solitary and melancholy landscapes. His best work was done during a stay in Norway in 1911. He was persecuted under the Hitler regime, but survived to be-

Further proof is supplied by Bernard Dorival's important study of Die Brücke and Fauvism published in *Art de France* for 1960, in which he establishes the connection between several pictures by Matisse and certain German works. Pechstein's *Woman at a lakeside* is compared with *La Joie de Vivre*, Nolde's *St. Mary of Egypt* with *La Gitane*, and Schmidt-Rottluff's *Young girl at her toilet* with *La Baignade*. Conservative German critics were quick to notice French influence and to condemn it.

Any attempt to represent the German painters as the true innovators is therefore ridiculous. The Dresden and Munich Fauves, especially the former, and their various groups—Die Brücke, The Phalanx, The New Artists' Association in Munich, and finally the Blaue Reiter—were responsible for an important and vigorous style of painting that played a capital part in the development of modern art. The Dresden painters opted for expressionism and the Munich group were strongly drawn towards abstract art. Their influence would have been considerably greater had the war not intervened.

Die Brücke was the creation of four young students of the Dresden Technical College who met in 1901 or 1902, and who were all equally and passionately interested in painting and in new forms of pictorial expression. The name they adopted—Die Brücke (The Bridge)—was intended to convey their desire for a new style which should owe nothing either to academic art or the fashionable Jugendstil. The leader and the oldest member of the group was Kirchner, who had been drawing and painting since childhood and had a wide knowledge of wood-engraving, and, like the French Fauves, of primitive art. His three colleagues were Schmidt-Rottluff, Bleyl, and Heckel, and they set up a studio in a former butcher's shop on the Berlinerstrasse. They were later joined by Emil Nolde, the Swiss Cuno Amiet, the Finn Axel Pechstein, and finally Van Dongen and Otto Muller. Except for Van Dongen and Muller, they lived and worked in common. They spent their holidays painting landscapes and nudes in the open air on the shores of the Baltic or the Moritzburg lake, near Dresden.

Their first exhibition, held in a former lampshade factory in 1906, had an enormous effect in Germany and brought Nolde, whom they considered almost as highly as Matisse, into the group. A native of Schleswig, Nolde was the eldest of the Brücke painters : he was thirteen years older than Kirchner, seventeen years older than Schmidt-Rottluff and Heckel, and he already had a considerable output behind him. He had familiarized himself with the works of the Impressionists and their successors in the course of a long stay in Paris in 1899. He himself painted in an aggressive and grating Expressionist style and considered that colour had symbolic and even magical properties. His ideal was a form of expression close to that of primitive religious images, and he liked to paint vast human themes such as good and evil, happiness and

come Professor of Fine Arts in Berlin after the war.

HECKEL, Erich (1883). A dreamy and melancholy artist, Heckel was even more devoted to wood-engraving than his colleagues, and he achieved his fullest self-expression in this medium. His style is the least violent and most elegant example of German Fauvism. He played an important role as intermediary between the Dresden and Munich groups.

The painters of Der Blaue Reiter

KANDINSKY, Wassily (1886-1944). Before he invented abstract art, Kandinsky had produced a considerable body of Fauve pictures during his stay in Munich. His advanced musical education, his admiration for Slav folk art, and his discovery as a young man of Claude Monet's *Haystacks*, which taught him that " painting is the real subject of the picture," conditioned him to an early understanding of the theories and precepts of the French Fauves. He was thirty when he decided to give up his position as a lawyer in Moscow to devote himself to painting. He went to Munich and entered the studios of Anton von Azbé and Franz Stuck successively. Physically a Slav version of Matisse, down to the beard, pince-nez and professorial manner, he rapidly rose to eminence in Munich artistic circles and in 1902 opened his own school of painting.

Between 1900 and 1905 he visited Italy, Tunisia and Paris, where he exhibited at the Salon d'Automne. In 1906 he was living at Sèvres and painting his most violently Fauve pictures. He returned to Germany and settled at Murnau in the Bavarian Alps; the stark landscape and the simple life marked the last stage of his evolution towards abstraction. His pictures at this time are brilliantly coloured and close in spirit to Slav folk art, but his taste for increasingly summary condensations of form combined with complete emotional freedom led him on to the next phase of his development.

Back in Munich, he became a founder member of the New Artists' Association,

sorrow, youth and age, innocence and vice. His stay with the young Brücke artists was brief. He was a solitary and a mystic, closer to Munch and Ensor than to Gauguin and Van Gogh; he loathed any form of discipline and opted out of the group in 1907.

The painters of Die Brücke wanted above all to escape from the dryness of academic art and the fake charm of the Jugendstil, the German version of Art Nouveau, then at its height. They sought inspiration in a return to the old German tradition of wood-engraving as practised by Dürer, and to a lesser degree in primitive art and French Fauvism. Many of them were also lithographers or engravers on metal, a fact which influenced the style of their painting. Their drawing was dry, angular and deliberately exaggerated, their colour applied in broad flat patches. The influence of wood engraving is never very hard to seek.

Their work reflects feelings of revolt, anxiety, and obsession, qualities which are totally absent from the painting of the French Fauves. This expressionism became stronger after 1910, when many members of the group settled in Berlin. Their street, circus and café scenes reflect the anguish and solitude of urban man. After three exhibitions, the group dispersed in 1913, and its members moved on to personal fulfilment and a more excessive and aggressive form of expressionism.

The second German Fauve group, which had its centre in Munich, was dominated by the personality of the Russian Kandinsky, whose history is bound up with the history of abstract art as that of Braque is bound up with Cubism. Munich in 1914 was an adumbration of what Montmartre was to become in the twenties. Besides a number of German artists, there were Swiss, like Paul Klee, very many Slavs, like Kandinsky and Jawlensky, Balkans, like Pascin, the star of the humorous weekly *Simplicissimus*, and even Frenchmen like the Alsatian Arp.

Munich, the artistic centre of Germany, was still dominated by the Jugendstil. But when the two Russians, Kandinsky and Jawlensky, met in 1896 in the studio of Anton von Azbé (a leading exponent of the Jugendstil) a new movement came into being.

Kandinsky, who had been a magistrate and a professor of law and was then aged thirty-two, had discovered a vocation in the course of an official journey to the province of Vologda, where he came into contact with Russian folk art. He gave up his career and went to Munich to study painting.

Jawlensky came from a different background but had had a similar experience. He was a former officer in the Imperial Guard who was also attracted to painting. Encouraged by his wife, Marianne von Werefkin, who also painted, he resigned his commission to enter the studio of Repin, and finally went on to Munich.

and in 1911 of the Blaue Reiter group. In the first World War he went back to Russia, and after the Revolution became a teacher at the State Workshops for Arts and Crafts in Moscow. When he understood the Communist attitude to the arts, he left Russia and went back to Germany. He settled first in Berlin, then in Weimar and Dessau, where he became a teacher at the Bauhaus. When Hitler came to power, he moved to Neuilly, near Paris, where he died. His various experiments in abstract painting make him one of the key figures in the story of modern art.

JAWLENSKY, Alexei von (1864-1941). Jawlensky was primarily a mystic, whose main preoccupation was his inner life. Like Kandinsky, whom he met in the studio of von Azbé in 1896, he was steeped in the traditions of Slav folk art which he never really shook off. He was in contact with the Fauves during the most critical period of their activity, and exhibited in a nearby room in the Salon d'Automne of 1905, at which period he was living in France. He was a member of the Munich New Artists' Association, but did not follow Kandinsky in his retirement to Murnau and took no part in the Blaue Reiter movement. In 1924, however, he joined up again with Kandinsky to found the "Four Blues" group (Die blauen vier), of which the other two members were Feininger and Klee. Gradually Jawlensky's overtly sensual style, with its broad flat colour areas emphasized by thick black outlines, became more immaterial; after the first World War, he returned to the faith of his Russian childhood and attempted to renew the art of the icon. His spiritual development presents certain analogies with that of Rouault. He died after a long illness at Wiesbaden.

MARC, Franz (1880-1916). An enthusiastic follower of Kandinsky, Marc foresaw the vast possibilities of abstract art when he wrote, " The art of the future will be the genesis of the form of our knowledge. It is our religion, our centre of gravity. It will be profound and solid enough to bring about the greatest possible renewal of forms."

Although deeply sympathetic to Slav folk art, Kandinsky and Jawlensky were cultivated and well-read; they had travelled widely and were fully cognizant of the developments in Western art. Both, after having settled in Munich, made many journeys to France, Italy, Tunisia, and Holland, where they made contact with the Nabis, one of whom, Verkade, became a monk in the monastery of Beuron and played an important part in cultivating relations between French and German painters. In 1904, Kandinsky exhibited in the Salon d'Automne. The following year, both he and Jawlensky had pictures in the room devoted to Russian artists organized by Sergei Diaghilev.

Kandinsky, who liked joining groups, became a member of The Phalanx in 1901. He soon rose to the rank of president and the following year opened a school under its auspices. One of his first pupils, Gabriele Münter, became his mistress. She later bequeathed the greater part of his pre-abstract work to the state of Bavaria.

The two Russians, who were greatly influenced by the French Fauves and by Matisse in particular, began to use more and more violent colours, applied without any concern for realism. Kandinsky reached the climax of his Fauve period during a long stay in France in 1906; he came to know Gertrude Stein who explained the Fauves' ideas to him. He saw their works in the Salon des Indépendants and the Salon d'Automne, and in the galleries of Berthe Weil and Vollard. But when he returned to Germany and settled at Murnau, in the Bavarian Alps, he adopted a lyrical synthetist style which verges on the abstract. He painted his first truly abstract picture in 1910. This was inspired, as he relates in his memoirs, by the sight of one of his canvases hung upside down. Its beauty struck him with the force of a revelation. " Towards evening," he wrote, " I was coming home with my paint-box, still completely absorbed in my thoughts and the memory of the work I had just done, when I caught sight of a picture on the wall that had extraordinary beauty and shone with a sort of inner light. I was nonplussed. I went closer to this puzzle of a picture in which I saw forms and colours whose significance passed my understanding, then I saw that it was one of my own, hung upside down."

Kandinsky invented abstract art but he did not altogether abandon figurative painting; the two strains alternated in his work until after the war. The remarkable thing is that his abstract art evolved under the influence of Fauve colouring, and the pictures he painted at this period, consisting of coloured strokes, arabesques and gashes, are not only among his best but are probably the most convincing examples of abstract art in existence.

In 1909, he and Jawlensky founded the Munich New Artists' Association, which counted among its members Alfred Kubin, Gabriele Münter, Marianne von Werefkin, Alexander Kanoldt, and Adolf Erbslöh. The group had a clear bias towards Fauvism and organized several important exhibitions which made Picasso, Braque, Rouault, Derain, Vlaminck, Van Dongen,

His own development, however, progressed no further than a lyrical transcription of the animal world. Animals were for him a symbol of the pure and natural life; horses and deer soon became his main subjects. Born in Munich, he grew up in artistic circles and was in closer contact with the French than any of his contemporaries. His correspondence with Robert Delaunay is essential reading for anyone studying the history of aesthetics in Europe at the beginning of the twentieth century. Delaunay's influence was more decisive than that of Kandinsky in leading him towards abstraction.

With Kandinsky, Marc founded Der Blaue Reiter and would no doubt have become one of the most important artists of his generation had he not been killed at Verdun in 1916.

MACKE, August (1887-1914). Macke was the youngest of the Blaue Reiter painters, and like Marc was killed in the War; he died in Champagne in the first days of the fighting. Less inclined to abstraction than Kandinsky, he preferred to paint the material world rather than the world of the mind; his favourite subject was a woman staring into a shop window which reflects both the motionless world of objects and the animation of the street. In 1907 he went to Paris and met Robert Delaunay, whose theories greatly impressed him. He was also drawn towards Futurism.

He visited Italy, Belgium, the Low Countries and England, and made several trips to Paris. In 1914 he accompanied Klee and Moillet to Tunis, and brought back a series of rapid, brilliantly coloured and supremely attractive watercolours. These are perhaps his finest work; he died before reaching his full measure as an artist.

Le Fauconnier, and Girieud known in Germany. But it soon split up, and a certain number of its members, headed by Kandinsky, turned towards abstract painting.

In December 1911, a crisis arose between the two parties, sparked off by the refusal of the committee for the Association's third exhibition to accept Kandinsky's *Last Judgment*. He resigned, took Macke, Marc, Kubin, Klee and Gabriele Münter with him, and immediately founded a new group called Der Blaue Reiter, after one of his own pictures. Kandinsky explained his choice of the name, " The Blue Rider," in these words : " Marc and I adopted the name at a café table in Sindelsdorf, under the trellis. We both liked blue; Marc liked horses and I liked riders, so the name came naturally."

The Blaue Reiter had its first exhibition at Tannhauser's on December 18, 1911. The catalogue was accompanied by a manifesto in which the members of the group proclaimed " the need to devote fierce attention to our inner nature and consequently to abandon the embellishments derived from the nature around us." The first exhibition contained a French section with works by the Douanier Rousseau and Robert Delaunay, whom Kandinsky and Marc admired even more than they did Picasso.

The second exhibition contained pictures by a Russian living in Moscow, Casimir Malevitch, who had been painting in a definitely Fauve manner since 1908. He was converted to Cubism in 1912 and went on to create Suprematism and paint his famous white square on a white ground. His Fauve pictures are generally overlooked by those who remember him for his adventures in abstraction.

The Blaue Reiter was different in spirit from all the previous groups inspired by Kandinsky. Jawlensky, who remained faithful to figurative painting, refused to join, although he remained friendly with Kandinsky and was sympathetic towards his experiments. After the war, he joined Kandinsky to found yet another group, "The Four Blues," (Die blauen Vier), but still refused to make any concession to abstract painting. He developed in the opposite direction, moving towards a mystic expressionism totally different in feeling from the sensuality of his early works which have much in common with Slav folk art. His later pictures are in the tradition of icon painting.

The rest of Kandinsky's career belongs to the history of abstract art, but his " dramatic " period, with its reminiscences of Van Gogh and the Fauves, is an essential part of his work, and it gave rise to an important line of abstract painters, of whom the principal members are now Afro in Italy, Hofmann in Germany, and Appel in Holland. Thus Fauvism, which persuaded painters to free themselves from the tyranny of the subject, has reached its ultimate development in our own day.

90. KANDINSKY. LANDSCHAFT MIT FABRIKSCHLOT. The Solomon R. Guggenheim Museum, New York.

91. KANDINSKY. MURNAU. Sammlung Dr Kurt Martin, München.

92. JAWLENSKY. DER ROTE SCHAL. Privatbesitz, München.

93. JAWLENSKY. NIKITA. Städtisches Museum, Wiesbaden.

94. SCHMIDT-ROTTLUFF. ATELIERPAUSE. Hamburger Kunsthalle, Hamburg.

95. SCHMIDT-ROTTLUFF. SOMMER. Städtische Galerie im Landesmuseum, Hannover.

96. KIRCHNER. MÄDCHEN VOR DEM SPIEGEL. Privatbesitz, Düsseldorf.

97. KIRCHNER.   DER MALER UND SEIN MODELL.   Hamburger Kunsthalle, Hamburg.

98. MALEVITCH. LES DÉVOTS. Stedelijk Museum, Amsterdam.

99. MACKE. LEUTE AM BLAUEN SEE. Staatliche Kunsthalle, Karlsruhe.

100. MARC. DIE ROTEN PFERDE. Collection M. et Mme Paul E. Geier, Rome.

VIII

The world of the Fauves

The world of the Fauves was small, self-contained, and bore little resemblance to the worlds of the Impressionists, Nabis, Cubists, or Surrealists, all of whom had numerous contacts with other artistic or intellectual circles. There is one obvious explanation for this difference: most of the Fauves came from provincial or working-class families and were of modest social origins. Their tastes were plebeian; they liked dance-halls, small *guinguettes* on the banks of the Seine, boating, cycling, wrestling, boxing, and snooker games in suburban bistros. None of these activities were likely to introduce them to a more elevated social circle. They were young men rebelling against the art of their time and against bourgeois society. They had no thought of making art a career; they painted simply to give rein to their own excitement. They cut themselves off from the artistic currents of the time and, unlike the Nabis, remained uninfluenced by writers, dramatists, or musicians. Only a handful of poets, Guillaume Apollinaire, Max Jacob, and André Salmon, whose enthusiasm was decisive in establishing the Fauve movement, played any part in their lives.

The most important in this connection was undoubtedly Apollinaire, who began his artistic career with a series of articles devoted to the Fauves. He was twenty-three when he first met Vlaminck, whose parents were neighbours of Apollinaire's mother, Angélique de Kostrovitsky, at Le Vésinet. It could be said that Apollinaire's introduction to the world of art was conducted in a series of train journeys between Chatou and Paris under the guidance of Vlaminck. When he had arrived from Germany, where he had been teaching, Apollinaire knew little or nothing about painting and was completely ignorant of the main modern trends. Vlaminck felt sympathy for this large young man with the face of a Roman emperor carved in lard and liked his conversation, which was gay, varied, and full of bizarre ideas expressed with the greatest seriousness.

Apollinaire, who was already a past master in the art of mystification, gave Vlaminck to understand that he was the son of a priest in the Vatican. In fact his father was Francesco Flugi d'Aspremont, a Piedmontese officer with whom Apollinaire's mother had lived for years before he had finally abandoned her. With her two sons she had then taken refuge with her lover's brother, who was the prior of a Dominican monastery in Monaco.

At the time of his meeting Vlaminck, Apollinaire was living a rather reduced life. After a period in which he had addressed newspapers for delivery, relations of his mother had found him a job in a bank, and he edited, with total incompetence, a stock-exchange journal called " The Investor's Guide " *(Le Guide du Rentier)*. The paper, which did not last long, was the cause of a tragic incident in Apollinaire's life. One of his colleagues was a noisy but winning character called Géry Pieret who came from an important middle-class Belgian family. Many years later, Apollinaire hired this man as a secretary. Pieret had stolen a number of Phoenician statuettes from the Louvre and had presented some to his employer and some to Picasso, neither of whom troubled to enquire where he had got them. André Salmon relates how Pieret used to make Apollinaire laugh by saying to Marie Laurencin, " I'm going to the Louvre. Is there anything you want ?"

Pieret, who was as foolish as he was dishonest, took to boasting of his exploits after the theft of the *Mona Lisa* from the Louvre in 1911. His revelations were badly received; Paris became " unhealthy " for him, and he hurriedly took refuge in Belgium. Apollinaire was accused of being an accomplice, was arrested, and was photographed in handcuffs. He spent a week in the Santé prison before friends obtained his release, but these six days marked him for the rest of his life and put an end to his free and fantasy-ridden outlook.

Vlaminck, who remained his friend, has left a penetrating description of the poet as he was in the Fauve period in his *Portraits avant Décès*. " He considered painting as only another manifestation of the literary imagination, an idea which he applied not only to the simplest images but to the latest Cubist and Surrealist extravagances ... Deep down, he was very naïve and for this very reason assumed the airs of a sceptic. He forgot, or pretended to forget, that in art as in life imagination is not everything ... The same paradoxical spirit that enabled him to enjoy popular novels such as *Nick Carter, Detective*, and *The Vulture of the Sierra*, would make him ask, in front of a cheap lithograph, ' Is that better than Cézanne ?,' then to affirm, ' It *is* better than Cézanne.' He played with everything, with doubt and disorder, with common sense and the absurd ... His strength lay in the skill with which he used his fantasy. It was the skill of a tightrope walker or a teacher of the Charleston : the invention of feats which he alone could perform."

The most reliable witnesses all agree that Apollinaire had no artistic perception, and that fundamentally he was only interested in art that would shock or disconcert, making no distinction between valid experiments and mere eccentricity. Francis Jourdain wrote, " I know that Apollinaire was a knowledgeable critic, and that as far as Cubism was concerned he had no rival. But he had not the least idea of what painting was about. Final proof of his incompetence and insensitivity, for me, was his *L'Art pour Tous*, in which he compares Benjamin Rabier (who drew humorous animals for children's books) with Hokusai, no less."

Gabrielle Buffet-Picabia tries to explain this : " His need for mystification was so intimately bound up with a real gift of insight into things and into people that it was difficult for him to separate them. In my humble opinion, his real genius lay in his choice of words, of people, of aspects of life, which he endowed with extraordinary values and with reasons for existence, rather than in his poetry, which in a surprising and rather disappointing way still followed classical or symbolist traditions ..."

According to D.-H. Kahnweiler, " Apollinaire was an admirable poet ... but he knew nothing about painting, and he had a real compulsion to say things that were simply not true. One of his axioms was, ' What is true is never interesting.' " Braque confirms this severe judgement, and adds: " He understood absolutely nothing about painting. You could show him two pictures, one by Michelangelo, the other by Raphael, and he would not be able to tell the difference between them. He was a great poet, but as a critic he didn't exist. We used to tell him so, but it didn't worry him. He was so kind ... he loved our painting through us."

This is surely the point. When Apollinaire became fond of people, he worked himself into a fever heat of enthusiasm over their activities. Sometimes his praise, his compliments and his reviews failed simply because they were so excessive. But the fact remains that owing to the warmth of his friendly feelings he was the most effective propagandist of Fauvism, Cubism, Futurism and Orphism. Although he bestowed equal praise on Matisse, Braque, Picasso, and the ultra-correct Albert Besnard, he always managed to draw public attention to the artists whom he admired.

These memories dated from before 1914. The war, coming soon after his entanglement with the police, left a deep mark on Apollinaire. He had received a severe head wound at the front, and thenceforward only wanted a safe career free from the uncertainties of a bohemian existence. He became art critic for *L'Intransigeant* and hoped to take up a similar post on *Le Petit Parisien*, which was edited by Vlaminck's brother-in-law. As Vlaminck said of him, " He would have ended up like Paul Valéry, decorated, a professor at the Collège de France, and an Academician, if he had lived." But Spanish influenza finished him off in a few days and fate decreed that his funeral should take place in November 1918, to the accompaniment of a rejoicing crowd yelling, "Down with William!" *(à bas Guillaume !)* to mark the end of the war : a funeral worthy of a man whose life had been one long celebration of the incongruous.

Max Jacob, another friend of the Fauves, was no less picturesque a poet than Apollinaire but was a better informed and more lucid art critic. In Apollinaire's writing it is often difficult to distinguish the true from the false, but Jacob, who had little taste for invention, is a reliable witness. After being a student at the École Coloniale, a lawyer's clerk, a piano teacher, a schoolmaster and a children's nurse, he finally turned to art criticism on the advice of the painter Alkhan. At the turn of the century he could be seen around the galleries, gravely taking notes for the *Moniteur des Arts*, wearing an outsize frock coat, a top hat brushed the wrong way, and a monocle in his left eye. One day he saw a painting by an unknown artist in Vollard's window. He was so impressed that he left a note congratulating the painter, who turned out to be Picasso, then aged twenty. Jacob looked after him like a mother and was his sole support for a number of years. They shared a room, and Jacob took a job in a shop owned by an uncle so that Picasso could continue to paint. Picasso, who would paint all night, would go to sleep in Jacob's bed when the latter left for work in the morning.

A Jew from Quimper, Jacob was distinguished not only by his exquisite manners but by the fact that everybody in Montmartre liked him. He could tell amusing stories, give irresistably funny imitations, read fortunes in the cards, and was a mine of old wives' remedies.

Vlaminck, who loved him even more than he loved Apollinaire, has left an affectionate and witty description of him : " He dressed in black—he always gave the impression that his clothes had been given or lent him—and looked rather like a Protestant clergyman. For years he lived, penniless, in the courtyard of a building in the rue Gabrielle, in a tiny shed which the concierge had formerly used for storing brooms and dustbins. His rent was a hundred francs a year and he had the greatest difficulty in finding the money... People like Paul Poiret and various members of society would invite him to lunch or dinner. He lived by his wit, his verve, and his imagination, just as others live by their skill as pianists, violinists or singers. He wrote ... He drew. He coloured his little sketches with the sort of colours that children buy at the local newsagents, or with a little Indian ink, a bit of blue, a bit of pink, and cigarette ash mixed with the dregs of his coffee. He was a delightful companion. We spent some unforgettable evenings together.

" But who dare describe the real Max Jacob ? The unhappy Max, tired of life and disgusted with himself ? The Max who buried himself in religion, attended Mass every morning at Sacré Cœur, spoke to you of the merciful Virgin, and then went back to sniffing ether and all his other vices ?

Who returned to prayer, was converted and baptized ? The Max who could be sad when he had dined well, and gay when he had gone hungry ?

" One morning in about 1906 I met him in the Place de la Trinité and he told me with the utmost seriousness of a visitation he had had from the Virgin Mary. I listened without interrupting. When he had finished, I said, ' Max, if what you have told me is an invention on your part, you are a vulgar impostor and your story is not amusing. But if you really have seen the Virgin, you'll end up at Charenton.' "

He ended his days, however, not in an asylum, but in the concentration camp of Drancy, some thirty-eight years later. The Gestapo sought him out in his retreat near the abbey of Saint-Benoit-sur-Loire, where he had been living for twenty years. On the train to Drancy he caught a chill, which developed into congestion of the lungs when he arrived at the camp. Left untended, he died a few days later, after having pleaded desperately with his captors to let him see a priest. This was the end of the man whom Léon-Paul Fargue called the greatest fantast of the twentieth century.

The part played by the critics in the Fauves' success was less spectacular but no less important. Men like Thiébault-Sisson and Arsène Alexandre of *Le Temps* and *Le Figaro* were obliged to devote their attention to the official styles of painting, but were by no means indifferent to new trends. They realized that the art of the Salon was out of date and they stated their opinions at the right moment. Roger-Marx, an important official at the École des Beaux-Arts, who admired Odilon Redon, Bonnard, and Vuillard, and had helped to establish the reputations of Cézanne, Van Gogh, and Gauguin, supported the Fauves from the very beginning, and in 1904 wrote the preface to Matisse's first exhibition at Vollard's. Wilhelm Uhde, a German critic who had been living in Paris since 1900, also took a keen and early interest in the Fauves. He was particularly interested in popular art, and with Jarry, Signac, Rémy de Gourmont, and Courteline, was one of the first to appreciate the Douanier Rousseau, well before the latter was launched as a nine days wonder by Apollinaire and Picasso. He was later to be responsible for the discovery of Seraphine Louis.

But the most faithful and most effective supporter of the Fauves was Louis Vauxcelles. A tall, thin man, hot-tempered and uncompromising, he had made his column in *Gil Blas* (a humorous paper owned by the banker brothers Mezbach), an extremely important vehicle of opinion. He came to be more than a critic, advising dealers, and showing painters what line they ought to follow. He employed two secretaries, Francis Carco and Maximilien Gauthier. It was to Vauxcelles that Apollinaire's friend, André Salmon, who was later to write on Derain, Friesz, and other Fauve painters, owed his start in journalism. Vauxcelles was accused of taking bribes—painters are always accusing critics of taking bribes—and he certainly wrote a number of excessively laudatory prefaces. This he worked into something of a speciality. When he wrote a preface simply for the money, he forced the note; the artist was charmed, but no one was deceived. He had likes and dislikes to which he remained extraordinarily faithful. He supported the Fauves but condemned the Cubists out of hand, and although he was the man who had given them their title, he never changed his opinion.

Dealers.

The success of the Fauves confirmed the importance of the art dealer in the promotion of a new style of painting. Tanguy, who had sold pictures by Cézanne and Van Gogh, and Durand-Ruel, who supported the Impressionists, showed how great the dealer's influence could be, but with the Fauves such an influence became decisive, for these artists, to whom the official Salons were closed, now depended wholly on the efforts of the dealer to reach the public.

According to D.-H. Kahnweiler, there were only about a dozen galleries in Paris, most of them concentrated in the rue Laffitte and the rue Le Pelletier. The most important belonged to Durand-Ruel, Bernheim Jeune, Mayer, Gérard, Diot, Tempelaere, Beugnet and of course Vollard, all of whom were in the rue Laffitte. Most galleries were devoted to the work of official artists like Roybet, Henner, Ziem and Chabas, Le Bail and Brispot, who were even represented by Bernheim Jeune and Durand-Ruel.

The dealers who supported the Fauves were in the main men of slender means but picturesque personalities, such as Clovis Sagot, who exhibited Braque as early as 1904 in his shop near Notre-Dame-de-Lorette, and Soulié, a former clown, who arranged pictures by Braque, Picasso, and Modigliani on the pavement outside his shop in the rue des Martyrs.

Berthe Weil was a personage of greater weight than either of these men, and one of the most important figures in the development of modern art. This tidy little woman from Alsace had a small second-hand shop at 25, rue Victor-Massé, not far from Degas' house (he was an anti-Semite and looked furious whenever he saw her). At first her stock consisted entirely of objects donated by friends, and she had to borrow money in order to pay the rent. She had an enormous flair and a sharp eye for discerning talent in completely unknown painters.

In 1900 she bought from Picasso, who had just arrived in Paris, three bull-fighting scenes for which she paid a hundred francs and which she resold to Adolphe Brisson for a hundred and fifty, a sum which delighted her. Generally

---

The Fauve market

BRAQUE
Bord de mer dans le Midi, 1907, Paris 1960. 60,000 NF.
Paysage à L'Estaque, 1907, London 1960. £ 16,500.
La Calanque, 1907, New York 1961. $ 47,000.

CAMOIN
Nature morte, not dated (post-Fauve), Paris 1961. 7,400 NF.

DERAIN
Westminster, 1906, New York. $ 9,000.
Barques échouées dans le port, 1908, Paris 1961. 164,000 NF.
La Vallée des Prus (sketch) 1906-1907, Paris 1961. 14,500 NF.

DUFY
Les Martigues, 1903 (water-colour), Paris 1959. 8,100 NF.
La Plage, 1905-1906, New York 1959. $ 5,750.
La Tribune des régates au Havre, 1906, Paris 1959. 150,000 NF.
Le Bal populaire, 1906, Paris 1959. 44,000 NF.
Le Bord de la mer, not dated, Paris 1961. 55,000 NF.
Les Pêcheurs à la ligne, 1908, London 1961. £ 5,000.
La Rue pavoisée, 1906, New York 1961. $ 26,500.
Bord de mer, 1906, Paris 1961. 75,000 NF.
Paysage de Falaise, 1902 (pre-Fauve), New York 1961. $ 15,000.

FRIESZ
Les Canaux d'Anvers, 1906, Paris 1961. 29,600 NF.
Entrée de corvette dans le port, 1904, Paris 1961. 54,000 NF.

LAPRADE
Nature morte au port, not dated, Paris
1959. 30,800 NF.
Fenêtre ouverte sur le dôme des Invalides,
not dated, Paris 1960. 4,800 NF.

MANGUIN
Terrasse à Saint-Tropez, 1906, Paris
1959. 21,000 NF.
Les Chênes-lièges, 1905 (water-colour),
Paris 1960. 5,000 NF.
La Toilette, 1905, Versailles 1961.
28,000 NF.

MARQUET
Le Coucher de soleil sur la mer, 1907,
Paris 1961. 18,000 NF.

MATISSE
Bords de mer avec pêcheuses, 1906
(water-colour), London 1959. £ 250.
Nature morte, 1895, Paris 1960
82,200 NF.

PUY
Jardin public, 1908 (water-colour), Versailles 1961. 540 NF.

VALTAT
Prunus, not dated, Paris 1960. 7,900 NF.
Bord de mer, not dated, Paris 1961.
12,200 NF.
Clairière aux pins rouges, not dated,
Paris 1958. 1,600 NF.

VAN DONGEN
La Gaité Rochechouart, 1905, Paris 1958.
27,000 NF.
Les Cavaliers du Bois de Boulogne, 1906,
Paris 1959. 32,000 NF.
Danseuse, not dated, Paris 1959.
50,000 NF.
Au Balcon, 1910, Brussels 1960.
56,400 NF.
Les Acrobates, 1904-1905, Paris 1960.
35,000 NF.
Attelage de bœufs, 1905, Versailles 1960.
43,000 NF.
Les Dolly Sisters, Versailles 1961.
70,000 NF.

VLAMINCK
Bords de rivière, 1906, New York 1958.
$ 60,000.
Fleurs dans un vase à pied, 1906 (goua-
che), London 1961. £ 3,000.
Le Pont (Cézanne period), Paris 1960.
73,000 NF.

she was content with derisory profits : if she sold a Matisse for a hundred and thirty francs she would only take thirty francs commission. Later she sold to Olivier Saincère, Secretary General at the Elysée under Poincaré, four Picassos for two hundred and twenty five francs, and to Frantz Jourdain a Marquet snow scene for fifty francs. As late as 1908 she sold a Van Gogh for sixty francs, having paid forty for it herself. And these were important deals! Most of the time she sold lithographs by Toulouse-Lautrec, Daumier, and Redon, on which she made only a few centimes profit. From 1902 on she began to mount exhibitions. She started with Matisse and Marquet, then Camoin, Dufy and Puy, and, in 1905, Friesz, Derain, Vlaminck and Van Dongen.

In addition to her extraordinary flair, she possessed the enormous talent of being able to take advice. It was on the recommendation of Dufy that she took an interest in the Fauves and later the Cubists. She could have made a fortune but she was a bad business woman, and was touchy, vain, and tactless into the bargain. If she did not like the look of a client she would show him the door. She was completely lacking in ambition, was ruthlessly honest (she refused to buy pictures which Utrillo offered her at five francs apiece), and was therefore always short of money and forced to pawn her jewellery in order to pay the rent. Artists often had difficulty in getting payment from her, and Picasso is said to have threatened her with a clasp-knife to obtain a hundred francs she owed him.

For a quarter of a century, all the young painters of note were represented in her galleries in the rue Victor-Massé, rue Taitbout, and rue Laffitte. After the Fauves, she took up Metzinger, Modigliani, Roger de La Fresnaye, Fauconnet, Gromaire, Lhote, Favory, Dufresne, Dunoyer de Segonzac, Waroquier, Bissière, Yves Alix, and Gernez. All left her once they were launched, for she lacked the prestige of men like Vollard and Druet, who stole her painters one after the other. " My role is to take the chestnuts out of the fire," she remarked bitterly. When she died in 1951, at the age of eighty-six, she was subsisting only on gifts from her former protégés.

Druet, who was often in competition with Berthe Weil, had less of an instinct for painting but a greater business sense, and an ability to bide his time and moderate his enthusiasm. He had only been selling pictures for two years when he took up with the Fauves. He was then a plump, round little man, aged about forty, whose manner revealed that his original job was running a bistro. Before setting up as a picture dealer, he had had a bar in the Place de l'Alma, which was patronized by painters exhibiting in the Salon des Indépendants in the nearby Cours-la-Reine. His familiarity with the artists and above all with Rodin contributed to change him from a modest tradesman into an important dealer. He was an amateur photographer and liked to show his efforts to Rodin when the sculptor called in from his studio. One day, he asked permission to photograph Rodin at work; the latter, amused, acquiesced, and even gave him some advice, showing him how to make intelligent use of light. After many attemps, Druet got results that pleased Rodin, who in return made Druet his official photographer. Druet never forgot, and through relatives on the town council obtained permission for Rodin to build his own pavilion for the Exposition Universelle of 1900.

His appetite once aroused, Druet took to visiting the Salon des Indépendants and, on the advice of Rodin, would buy a few pictures, particularly from the Neo-Impressionists. Once, when he resold a picture by Luce at a profit, Rodin told him, " Only a Norman like you could set up as rival to the Bernheims." So he gave up his bar and opened a gallery on the corner of the Avenue Matignon and the rue du Faubourg Saint-Honoré, which soon became as important for the Fauves as Durand-Ruel had been for the Impressionists and Le Barc de Boutteville for the Nabis. He did not give up photography, however, and kept a studio near his shop.

His success redoubled when he moved a few years later to 20, rue Royale. Until the war, his gallery was a meeting-place for painters, collectors, critics, and writers, all of whom foregathered around five o'clock in the afternoon. His guests included Maurice Denis, Marquet, Laprade, Manguin, Flandrin, Vallotton, Marval, Romain Coolus, Tristan Bernard, and Denys Cochin. They could be seen leafing through the first numbers of *La Nouvelle Revue Française* or examining the works of Gide, Claudel, and Charles-Louis Philippe, of which Druet was the distributor. But in spite of his flair, Druet, who had taken many of his painters from Berthe Weil, made the mistake of turning down the pictures which Utrillo offered him for fifty francs, and lost Matisse to the Bernheims. This was his greatest sorrow.

But of all the dealers, the most outstanding was Vollard. A heavy Creole, always asleep, he was one of the numerous offspring of a lawyer on the island of Réunion, and had come to France to study law so that he might eventually succeed his father. He became not only the most important art dealer of his time but the priest of modern painting.

In 1905 his gallery (the second he had run) was at 6, rue Laffitte, a few yards from the Boulevard des Italiens. All descriptions concur in emphasizing the sinister appearance of this dirty shop covered in peeling paint. The window contained two empty frames, but inside the pictures were piled along the walls in indescribable confusion. There were literally hundreds by Cézanne, Renoir, Van Gogh, and Degas. The furniture was reduced to a table covered with papers and catalogues, and two cane chairs.

The sultry figure of Vollard dozing and nodding in the middle of the shop did nothing to improve the impression produced by the exterior. He looked like an ape, according to Paul Léautaud, who relates that once, on a visit to

Renoir at Cagnes, he swung for a few seconds from the bough of a tree. " My dear Vollard," said Renoir, " that is not a coconut palm."

He had been a dealer since 1890 and had entered the field of modern painting with his exhibition of a hundred and fifty works by Cézanne in 1895. A further exhibition of sixty pictures by Van Gogh in 1900 had helped to consolidate his position. After the Salon d'Automne of 1905 he realized that he was on to something big and, on the advice of Matisse, carried off everything he could lay his hands on by Vlaminck and Derain.

In spite of his service to modern painting, however, it is by no means certain that Vollard had a real feeling for art. Opinions on this score are divided. Gertrude Stein, Louis Vauxcelles, Francis Carco, and Georges Besson accuse him of having no taste at all and of being unable to distinguish between real masters and second-rate painters like Innocenti, Rops and de Groux. He certainly fell down on Modigliani and Utrillo and was unenthusiastic about Cubism. Apollinaire openly mocked him because he took no further interest in Picasso after his rose period. Vlaminck, who knew him well, used to assert that he really had a good eye. " He showed me three pictures by Cézanne," Vlaminck recounts, "and said, 'I want to keep one. Tell me which is the best.'" Vlaminck replied, " 'No, you choose, and I'll tell you what I think.' The one he chose was the one I should have chosen too."

He was on good terms with Renoir, Bonnard, Vlaminck and Derain, and liked to entertain them in his basement, which was got up as a kitchen-dining room and where he would cook them violently flavoured Creole dishes. His guests would include Degas, Renoir, Cézanne, Apollinaire, Odilon Redon, Vlaminck, Forain, and Camondo. Once, for a joke, he seated the Douanier Rousseau beside Gervex, the most reactionary of conventional painters.

In spite of his rather superficial bonhomie, neither Matisse nor Rouault liked him. Shortly before his death, Matisse discussed him with the poet André Verdet : " Vollard had bought dozens of pictures from Cézanne. They were all over the place, on the walls, piled up on the floor, stacked in the corners. He had bought them for next to nothing. Cézanne knew what he was talking about when he called him a slave-driver. His exhibitions of pictures by young painters were merely a pretext to attract clients interested in established names. On the opening day he would ignore the pictures on the walls and bring out etchings by Renoir, Cézanne and others. He had no consideration for the work of younger painters ... "

Vollard made Rouault's life a torment for him. Even when he was eighty years of age and famous the world over, Rouault was still brooding over his disagreements with Vollard, working himself into a rage as he talked. " If you didn't mention his name," says Marcel Arland, " he would say :—

' Were you speaking of Vollard ?'

' Not at all.'

'But you were going to, weren't you?'

'Certainly not.'

'Well, *I'm* going to.'"   An outburst would follow.

Although he behaved like a slave-driver with Rouault, making him work against time to fulfil his part of the contract, it would not be true to say that Vollard was greedy. He accepted whatever Vlaminck and Derain brought in without so much as glancing at the pictures. Once Vlaminck found canvases he had brought in a fortnight earlier still untied at the back of the shop.

It was the same with his clients. Vollard treated them roughly, refused to sell them what they had chosen, and showed them only what he felt inclined to bring out. He openly mistrusted them, and would ostentatiously lock the door behind him when he went to get a picture from the store.

After 1908 he held no more exhibitions; he merely sold a Cézanne or a Renoir from time to time and left his enormous stock to appreciate in value. On his death this stock was seen to include eight hundred Renoirs, seven hundred and fifty Rouaults, and hundreds of pictures by Cézanne, Vlaminck, Derain, and Puy. Apart from a pronounced taste for women and good living, he had few passions. His needs were non-existent; he wore a threadbare overcoat and run-down shoes, and slept for so long on a hard bed that his kidneys were finally affected. In his youth he had lived for months on ships' biscuits in order to save money, and when he took a house in the rue de Martignac in 1924, he only furnished two rooms. The rest were used to store pictures. Rouault was given a studio in the attics.

It is possible that his greatest pleasure in life was not painting at all but publishing. He loved fine books and commissioned illustrations from the most famous artists: *Parallèlement* and *Daphnis and Chloe* from Bonnard, *La Belle Enfant* from Dufy, *Le Chef d'œuvre inconnu* from Picasso, *La Maison Tellier* from Degas, *Le Cirque de l'étoile filante* from Rouault, and *La Tentation de Saint-Antoine* from Odilon Redon. These are some of the finest illustrated books of our time. But his own *Réincarnations du Père Ubu*, written as a sequel to Jarry, is very tedious, and the book was only saved by the illustrations of Puy and Rouault. This is not true of his autobiographical *Souvenirs d'un marchand de tableaux* which earned him the enmity of many of the people he mentioned. He was killed in a motor accident in July 1939. André Suarès, writing the news to Rouault, summed him up completely: "My dear Rouault, Vollard was killed on the road to Le Tremblay. He was left there all night, without any help. His neck was broken, he suffered atrociously. The details are ghastly. I don't know what to say. Didn't I tell you that I thought his end was near? No one can take Vollard's place as a publisher. What is going to happen? My dear Rouault, your annoyance and rancour must be put aside. Whatever Vollard was like, now that he is dead one sees that he was the only one of his kind."

Kahnweiler, of whom Vollard said unkindly that his parents had given him a gallery for his first Communion, was the last of the great dealers to take an interest in the Fauves. But his interest did not last long. A few months after opening his shop at 28, rue Vignon, he discovered Picasso who had just painted *Les Demoiselles d'Avignon*, and decided to devote himself to the Cubists since, commercially speaking, he had come too late for the Fauves.

Kahnweiler, who was the son of a Jewish banker from Mannheim, was only twenty-three when he opened his first gallery near the Madeleine in the autumn of 1907. He was expected to become a stockbroker, but decided to try his luck as an art dealer. His parents, thinking he would grow out of it, advanced him 25,000 francs and gave him a year in which to succeed. He was extremely timid, had no contacts in Paris, and although he had a good knowledge of classical painting, knew next to nothing about modern art.

He was so naïve that when he bought pictures by Derain, Vlaminck, and Braque at the Salon des Indépendants, he asked for no reduction in the price, not knowing that this was done as a course. Later he changed and became known as a tenacious bargainer who would nag a painter for hours until he accepted his price.

He had not yet reached this stage in 1907, and he formed friendly and confident relations with the three leading Fauve painters. They went to see him, curious to meet a dealer who bought at the prices they asked. They were later joined by Van Dongen. Kahnweiler required his painters to promise him the whole of their production, and the agreements made, without written contracts, were honoured to the letter. Despite his lack of connections in Paris he managed to establish a reputation, mainly through the support of important clients such as Hermann Rupf, Roger Dutilleul, and the Russian Shchukin.

He gave an account of his first meeting with Picasso in a talk : " Wilhelm Uhde was the first to mention a strange picture just being painted by Picasso. He described it as vaguely Assyrian, something altogether new. I did not know Picasso, but I had heard of him, so one day I set off. I knew his address, 13, rue Ravignan ... I knocked; a young man in shorts and an open-necked shirt came to the door, took my hand, and asked me to come in ... No one can describe the lamentable poverty of those studios in the rue Ravignan. The wallpaper hung in strips from the weatherboard walls. There was dust on the drawings, and the pictures were lying on a broken-down couch. Beside the stove was a mountain of ash that looked like lava. It was terrible. Picasso lived there with his very beautiful wife, Fernande, and an enormous dog called Frika. The big picture of which Uhde had spoken, which was afterwards to be called *Les Demoiselles d'Avignon*, the point of departure of the whole Cubist movement, was there too."

This visit affected the whole of Kahnweiler's life. He decided that he was in the presence of a very great painter, and made up his mind to fight for him.

He left the Fauves and took up Picasso, Braque, Juan Gris and Fernand Léger. He remained friendly with the Fauves, however, and was Vlaminck's and Derain's dealer until 1923. For several years he shared a yacht and a motor-boat with the latter.

The 1914-18 war ruined him. His stock was seized as enemy property and sold in 1922. Eight hundred Cubist canvases were thrown on to the market and sent the prices down to almost nothing. It took Kahnweiler several years to recover his position. He was deserted by his protégés, but gradually found others. Picasso alone has remained faithful to him.

Collectors.

In spite of the low prices they asked, the few dealers who supported the Fauves had great difficulty in placing their works. The number of buyers never grew to large proportions, although early supporters were eventually joined by Fénéon, the director of the Bernheim gallery, Baron Denys Cochin, whose bedroom contained an ivory Christ and a Van Dongen, Wilhelm Uhde, who once bought five pictures in one go from Braque, and André Level, the brain behind *La Peau de l'Ours* club.

At the beginning of the century, it took a certain amount of courage to hang a violently coloured picture by Matisse, Vlaminck or Derain in a middle-class drawing-room. This explains why the Fauves depended on emancipated and picturesque characters like the former King Milan of Serbia, the restaurant owner Bauchy, who hung the walls of his Café des Variétés with pictures by Van Gogh, Cézanne and the Fauves, and Malpel of Toulouse, to whom Vlaminck gave a portrait of his daughter Yolande in return for a barrel of wine, and who supplied Matisse with the heavy and full-bodied wine of Les Corbières.

No more than six collectors were seriously interested in the Fauves and contributed to their success : Marcel Sembat, Gertrude Stein and her brother Leo, the Russians Morosov and Shchukin, and the American Barnes, who came late into the field but bought an enormous number of paintings, including many Fauve works, after the first World War.

Marcel Sembat, the Socialist deputy for Montmartre, was married to the talented painter Georgette Agutte, who had been a pupil of Gustave Moreau. He had excellent taste and contributed a remarkable preface to the catalogue of the Salon d'Automne of 1913. Matisse was his favourite painter, and he acquired the *Nature morte au tapis*, painted at Collioure, the portrait of *Marguerite*, a *Nu rose*, etc. He also owned Rouault's *Les Saintes Femmes pleurant le Christ*, and several pictures by Marquet, Vlaminck and Puy. He tried to interest his political friends in the new painters, but without success. Jaurès' tastes were confined to the conservative and academic members of the Salon, and Marcel Cachin had been converted to Neo-Impressionism by his friends Signac and Cross.

Sembat and his wife were famous in the Fauve world. They were devoted to each other and, like the Philemon and Baucis of classical legend, never left each other's side. Georgette read the same books and newspapers as her husband in order to be as close to him as possible, and accompanied him to his political meetings and rallies. When he became Minister of Works in 1916, she still went with him to the office and waited for him in an ante-room or in the car.

Their idyllic happiness came to a tragic end, for Sembat died suddenly of a heart attack in his little chalet at Chamonix in 1922. His wife shed no tears, put her affairs in order, made her will, said goodbye to her mother, and committed suicide. This almost classical death was hotly debated by the post-war public.

She bequeathed the Sembat collection to the State, at whose hands it almost suffered the same fate as Caillebotte's bequest some thirty years earlier—it was refused by the Luxembourg Museum. It would probably have been dispersed had not André Farcy, the curator of the museum at Grenoble, succeeeded through his influence in the Socialist party in getting it for his gallery, which thus became the first museum in France to have a collection of modern art.

Gertrude and Leo Stein were another remarkable couple in the history of modern painting. In many ways they played a more important part than either Apollinaire, Vollard, or Kahnweiler. She was a large, almost masculine woman, always dressed in corduroy velvet and sandals, with no stockings. " She looked," said Vollard, " like a housewife, with no contacts beyond the fruiterer, the milkman and the grocer." Her quick eyes and mocking laugh belied this appearance. He was a large, red-headed, and not particularly impressive man with a surly disposition.

They came from a wealthy family which had suddenly lost the greater part of its fortune. They received an allowance from an older brother and settled in Europe where life was cheaper than in the States. In France and Italy they led a bohemian existence and practised the nature philosophy of Raymond Duncan.

Although their income was modest, they were considered rich by Montmartre standards and their arrival in a gallery was tantamount to a fall of manna. It is true that in 1905 one did not need a great deal of money to be a collector : Gertrude Stein paid no more than five hundred francs for Matisse's *Femme au chapeau* and considerably less for Cubist Picassos and Braques.

When they arrived in Paris in 1903, the Steins were collecting Japanese prints and ivories. An Italian friend told them of Cézanne and they went to see his work at Vollard's. The meeting between Vollard and his new clients took on the character of high comedy.

This visit was followed by many others, and the Steins discovered Matisse and Picasso, who were later to meet in the Stein salon in the rue de Fleurus. For forty years Gertrude Stein's studio, its walls covered with Cézannes, Renoirs, and Fauve and Cubist pictures, was a meeting-place for all that was new in literature and the arts.

After the first World War, Gertrude was left alone—her brother went back to America—and she turned to literature without, however, abandoning her interest in painting. All the young Americans of the "Lost Generation," Hemingway, Dos Passos, Henry Miller, Ezra Pound, Faulkner, Archibald Macleish, came to do homage and to receive from her their initiation into modern art. A megalomaniac, she came to believe that she was modern art incarnate, and that the Fauves and the Cubists had come into existence through her alone. She had no hesitation in claiming this in her autobiography, but according to André Salmon, Leo was the one with the flair, and Gertrude attributed to herself merits which she did not in fact possess.

Two other outstanding supporters of the Fauves were the Russian merchant princes, Morosov and Shchukin.

Ivan Morosov had more moderate tastes than his rival Shchukin, and was more interested in the paintings of the Impressionists and the Nabis. Yet even he in a few years collected eighteen by Cézanne, eight by Gauguin, eleven by Maurice Denis, two by Bonnard, and pictures by Marquet, Matisse and Picasso, including the latter's famous Cubist portrait of Vollard.

The Morosov family possessed a certain originality. Vollard relates that Ivan had a younger brother who, in the course of a conversation, noticed a revolver on a table, said, "Do you mind if I commit suicide?" put the gun to his temple and blew his brains out.

Shchukin was literally mad about Fauvism and Cubism, bought Matisses by the dozen, and when he met the painter at the Steins, commissioned from him *La Danse* and *La Musique* for twenty five thousand gold francs. Matisse delivered them to Moscow in person. "Shchukin would come from Russia by the first train," says Kahnweiler, "whenever I telegraphed him that I had something interesting."

He was a delightful man and was very easily satisfied. He bought a *Desserte bleue* from Matisse at the Salon d'Automne and when the artist sent it to him repainted in red, he did not complain. Fernande Olivier, Picasso's first love, has described him in less attractive terms. " One day," she says, " Matisse brought an important collector from Moscow, M. Shchukin, a very rich Jew and a lover of modern art, to see Picasso. He was a small pale man with an enormous porcine head. He had a terrible stammer and had great difficulty in making himself understood. Picasso's style was a revelation to the Russian. He paid very highly for the time, bought two pictures, and became a faithful patron." Her portrait is harsh and not completely accurate: Shchukin was not only not a Jew, but a very orthodox Old Believer.

Having discovered Picasso, Shchukin henceforth became his principal patron. He did not, however, abandon Matisse. When forced to leave Russia during the Revolution, he owned forty of the latter's paintings. He settled happily enough in Paris, continued to visit the dealers, and if anyone asked him if he regretted the loss of his pictures, he would reply philosophically, " What difference does it make? I always intended to bequeath my collection to the State. The only thing I regret is not having been able to enjoy them a little longer." His pictures, together with those of Morosov, constitute the bulk of the collections of modern painting in the museums in Leningrad and Moscow.

The last collector in the field was the American Dr. Barnes, who invented the antiseptic argyrol when he was a medical student of twenty and subsequently made an enormous fortune. He was the first of the American multi-million-aires to take an interest in modern painting, possibly less through real taste than through a desire to cause a sensation.
He began by buying Leo Stein's collection. After that, his annual journeys to Europe from 1920 onwards meant the acquisition of dozens of pictures by Matisse, the Fauves and the Impressionists. He took ruthless advantage of the Wall Street crash of 1929-30 to buy important works from other collectors at rock-bottom prices. His collection finally included a hundred and twenty pictures by Cézanne, two hundred by Renoir, ninety-five by Picasso, seventy-five by Soutine, a hundred by Matisse (including *La Joie de Vivre* and *La Danse*, specially commissioned for the library of his Renaissance château at Merion, near Philadelphia), and a number of works by Seurat, Braque, the Douanier Rousseau and others.
Barnes, who was considered a lunatic by the critics and the local press, took his revenge by leaving his entire collection to a foundation for art students. Members of the public (Negroes excepted) are not allowed to see it; loans and even reproductions are forbidden. Thanks to him, therefore, hundreds of Fauve pictures, including some of the most important, are invisible. It is only recently that a legal judgment authorized two hundred people a week

to visit the galleries at Merion. This situation illustrates one aspect of the curious destiny of the Fauves. Few people can go to Russia to see the important collections there, and hundreds of pictures are still held back by the heirs of Ambroise Vollard. Our knowledge of Fauve painting is therefore still fragmentary. No doubt the most important chapter of its history still remains to be written.

Bibliography

GENERAL WORKS

Apollinaire, Guillaume : *Chroniques d'Art* (NRF, Paris 1960).
Cassou, Jean : *Panorama des arts plastiques* (NRF, Paris 1960).
Chassé, Charles : *Les Nabis et leur temps* (Bibliothèque des Arts, Paris 1960).
Courthion, Pierre : *L'Art indépendant* (Albin Michel, Paris 1958).
Derain, André : *Lettres à Vlaminck* (Flammarion, Paris 1955).
DICTIONNAIRE DE LA PEINTURE MODERNE (Hazan, Paris 1954).
Diehl, Gaston : *Les Fauves* (Editions du Chêne, Paris 1943).
Dorival, Bernard : *Les Étapes de la Peinture française* (Gallimard, Paris 1944).
Les Peintres du XXe siècle (Tisné, Paris 1957).
Duthuit, Georges : *Le Fauvisme* (Cahiers d'Art, Paris 1929-1931).
Hautecœur, Louis : *Histoire de l'Art* (Flammarion, Paris 1959).
Humbert, Agnès : *Les Nabis* (Cailler, Geneva 1954).
(L') ILLUSTRATION : for 1905.
Jedlicka, Gotthard : *Der Fauvismus* (Büchergilde Gutenberg, Zurich 1961).
Jourdain, Francis : *Sans remords ni rancune* (Corréa, Paris 1953).
L'Art officiel sous la IIIe République (Le Point, Souillac 1949).
Kahnweiler, D.-H. : *Entretiens avec Francis Crémieux* (NRF, Paris 1961).
Larguier, Léo : *Au Café de l'Univers* (Aubanel, Avignon 1949).
Leymarie, Jean : *Le Fauvisme* (Skira, Geneva 1959).
Muller, Joseph-Emile : (Hazan, Paris 1956).
Natanson, Thadée : *Peints à leur tour* (Albin Michel, Paris 1948).
Poiret, Paul : *En habillant l'époque* (Grasset, Paris 1930).
Ponente, Nello : *Tendances contemporaines* (Skira, Geneva 1960).
Raynal, Paul : *Histoire de la peinture moderne* (Skira, Geneva 1950).
Rewald, John : *Les Fauves* (Museum of Modern Art, New York 1952).
Salmon, André : *Le Fauvisme* (Somogy, Paris 1956).

Salmon, André : *Souvenirs sans fin*, 3 vol. (Gallimard, Paris 1955-1961).
Sérusier, Paul : *L'A. B. C. de la peinture* (Floury, Paris 1950).
Vollard, Ambroise : *Souvenirs d'un marchand de tableaux* (Club des Libraires de France 1957).
Vauxcelles, Louis : *Le Fauvisme* (Cailler, Geneva 1958).
Vlaminck, Maurice de : *Tournant dangereux* (Stock, Paris 1929).
Portraits avant décès (Flammarion, Paris 1943).
Weil, Berthe : *Pan dans l'œil* (Lipschutz, Paris 1933).
Zamacois, Miguel : *Pinceaux et stylos* (Arthème Fayard, Paris 1948).

BRAQUE

Gieure, Maurice : *Braque* (Tisné, Paris 1956).
Guth, Paul : *Interview with Braque* published in *Le Figaro Littéraire,* 13.5.1950.
Lejard, André : *Braque* (Hazan, Paris 1949).
Leymarie, Jean : *Braque* (Skira, Geneva 1961).
Paulhan, Jean : *Braque le patron* (Gallimard, Paris 1952).
LE POINT : *Braque* (Souillac, 1953).
Reuillard, Gabriel : Article on Braque in *Paris-Normandie,* 2.4.51.

CAMOIN

Cartier, Jean-Albert : *Charles Camoin* (Documents - Cailler, Geneva 1958).
Vildrac, Charles : *Eloge de Charles Camoin* (Brucker, Paris 1956).

DERAIN

Basler, Adolphe : *Derain* (Crès, Paris 1931).
Derain, André : *Lettres à Vlaminck* (Flammarion, Paris 1955).
Interview published in *Le Prisme des Arts*, November 1956.
Giacometti, Alberto : *Derain* (Maeght, Paris 1957).

Hilaire, Georges : *Derain* (Cailler, Geneva 1959).
Leymarie, Jean : *André Derain* (Skira, Geneva 1950).
Maunoury, R. : Article on Derain in *Le Nouveau Fémina*, no. 8.
Salmon, André : *André Derain* (NRF, Paris 1924).

DUFY

Berr de Turique, Marcelle : *Raoul Dufy* (Floury, Paris 1930).
Cassou, Jean : *Raoul Dufy, poète et artiste* (Skira, Geneva 1946).
Courthion, Pierre : *Raoul Dufy* (Cailler, Geneva 1951).
Article in *La Gazette de Lausanne*, 10.6.1951.
Dorgelès, Roland : Article in *Les Lettres Françaises*, 20.12.1944.
Dorival, Bernard : *Raoul Dufy* (preface to catalogue of exhibition at Musée d'Art Moderne, 1953).
Fleuret, Fernand : *Eloge de Raoul Dufy* in *Mercure de France*, Paris 1933.
Fournier, Gabriel : *Cors de chasse* (Cailler, Geneva 1957).
Lassaigne, Jacques : *Dufy* (Skira, Geneva 1954).
Lhote, André : Article in *Les Lettres Françaises*, 23.3.1953.
Poiret, Paul : *En habillant l'époque* (Grasset, Paris 1930).
Roger-Marx, Claude : *Dufy* (Hazan, Paris 1950).
Villebœuf, André: Article on Dufy in *Le Figaro Littéraire*, 16.5.1959.

FRIESZ

Busse, Jacques : *Othon Friesz* (Documents-Cailler, Geneva 1958).
Desnos, Youki : *Confidences de Youki* (Arthème Fayard, Paris 1957).
Gauthier, Maximilien : *Othon Friesz* (Cailler, Geneva 1957).
Héron de Villefosse : preface to catalogue of exhibition at Musée Galliéra, Paris 1959.

MANGUIN

Julien, E. : preface to catalogue of exhibition at Albi. 1957.
Terrasse, Charles : *Eloge d'Henri Manguin* (Brucker, Paris 1954).

MARQUET

Besson, Georges : *Marquet* (Paris 1920, 1929, 1948).
Preface to catalogue of exhibition at Albi, 1957.
Preface to catalogue of exhibition at Maison de la Pensée Française, October 1953.
Marquet, Marcelle : *Marquet* (Lafont, Paris 1951).
Marquet, Marcelle, and Daulte, F. : *Marquet* (Paris 1953).
Reuillard, Gabriel : article in *Paris-Normandie*, 10.12.1951.
Roger-Marx, Claude : article in *Gazette des Beaux-Arts*, March, 1939.

MATISSE

Besson, Georges : Article in *Les Nouvelles Littéraires*, 2.5.1956.
Article in *Les Lettres Françaises*, 11.12.1951.
Article in *Les Lettres Françaises*, 27.12.1951.
Butor, Michel : Article in *Le Nouveau Fémina*, no. 10.

Courthion, Pierre : *Le Visage de Matisse* (Marguerat, Lausanne 1942).
Descargues, Pierre : *Le Musée de l'Ermitage* (Somogy, Paris 1961).
Escholier, Raymond : *Matisse ce vivant* (Arthème Fayard, Paris 1956).
Fournier, Gabriel : *Cors de chasse* (Cailler, Geneva 1957).
Georges-Michel, Michel : *De Renoir à Picasso* (Fayard, Paris 1954).
Jacob, Max : *La Naissance du Cubisme*, in *Les Nouvelles Littéraires*, 1928.
Jourdain, Francis : *Au pays du souvenir* (Crès, Paris 1922).
Lassaigne, Jacques : *Matisse* (Skira, Geneva 1959).
Preface to catalogue of exhibition at Musée des Arts Décoratifs, May 1961.
Matisse, Henri : *Notes d'un peintre*, in *La Grande Revue*, 25.12.1908.
Natanson, Thadée : *Peints à leur tour* (Albin Michel, Paris 1948).
Raynal, Maurice : *La peinture moderne* (Skira, Geneva 1953).
Rico, Francis : interview published in *Ici-Paris*, 21.11.1954.
Saint-Jean, Robert de : interview published in *France-Soir*, 31.3.1948.
Salmon, André : *Souvenirs sans fin* (Gallimard, Paris 1955-1961).
Stein, Gertrude : *Autobiography of Alice B. Toklas*, The Bodley Head, 1933 (French edition published by Gallimard, Paris 1934).

PUY

Besson, Georges : article in *Les Lettres Françaises*, 10.10.1958.
Bettex-Cailler, Nane : *Jean Puy* (Documents-Cailler, Geneva 1959).
Gay, Dr : *Jean Puy* (Braun, Mulhouse, 1945).
Puy, Michel : *Jean Puy par son frère* (NRF, Paris 1925).

ROUAULT

Arland, Marcel : *Rouault* (*Le Nouveau Fémina*, no. 29).
Dorival, Bernard : *Les Étapes de la peinture française*, vol. 2 (Gallimard, Paris 1944).
Preface to catalogue of exhibition at Marseille, June 1960.
Le Point : *Rouault* (Souillac, 1943).
Rouault, G. and Suarès, A. : *Correspondance* (Gallimard, Paris 1961).
Venturi, Lionello : *Rouault* (Skira, Geneva 1959).
Vollard, Ambroise : *Souvenirs d'un marchand de tableaux* (Club des Libraires de France, 1957).

VALTAT

André, Albert : article in *Les Lettres Françaises*, 13.3.1953.
Besson, Georges: preface to catalogue of retrospective exhibition at Dieppe, 1959.

Domergue, René : preface to catalogue of retrospective exhibition at Musée Galliéra, 1956.

Warnod, André : Article in *Le Figaro*, 24.7.1949.

VAN DONGEN

Besson, Georges : Article in *Les Lettres Françaises*, 12.11.1953.

Bouret, Jean : interview published in *Les Arts*. 12.1.1952.

Cabanne, Pierre : article in *Les Arts*, 14. 9.1960.

Chabrun, Jean-François : article in *Match*, 10.10.1959.

Chaumeil, Louis : preface to exhibition at Galerie des Ponchettes, Nice 1959.

Van Dongen et le Fauvism, in *Les Arts*, Paris 1961.

Corday, Paule : interview published in *La Presse*, 10.12.1946.

Fierens, Paul : preface to catalogue of exhibition at Albi, 1960.

Life Magazine : *The Wild Beasts* (Life, 8.2.1960).

Palaiseul, Jean : interview published in *Noir et Blanc*, 13.4.1949.

Perruchot, Henri : article in *Les Nouvelles Littéraires*, 7. 8. 1958.

Poulain, Gaston : article in *Les Lettres Françaises*, April 1960.

Reuillard, Gabriel : article in *Paris-Normandie*, 29.4.1952.

Siegfried, André : article in *Réalités*, July 1959.

VLAMINCK

Carco, Francis : *Vlaminck* (NRF, Paris 1920).

Clochard, William : *Vlaminck à qui je dois...* (privately published by the author, Chartres, 1959).

Crespelle, J.-P. : *Vlaminck, fauve de la peinture* (Gallimard, L'Air du Temps, 1958).

Duhamel, Georges : *Vlaminck* (Les Ecrivains Réunis, Paris 1927).

Genevoix, Maurice : *Vlaminck* (Flammarion, Paris 1954).

Mac Orlan, Pierre : *Vlaminck* (Editions du Chêne, Paris 1945).

Vlaminck (Sauret, 1958).

Sauvage, Marcel : *Vlaminck, sa vie et son message* (Cailler, Geneva 1956).

Vlaminck, Maurice de : *Tournant dangereux* (Stock, Paris 1929).

Portraits avant décès (Flammarion, Paris 1943).

Le Ventre ouvert (Corréa, Paris 1937).

Le Chemin qui mène à rien (Denoël et Steele, Paris 1936).

Désobéir (Corréa, Paris 1936).

Werth, Léon : *Vlaminck* (Bernheim jeune, Paris 1925).

THE GERMAN FAUVES

Brion, Marcel : *Kandinsky* (Somogy, Paris 1960).

Catalogue of the exhibition, *Les Sources du XXe siècle* (Musée d'Art Moderne, Paris 1960-1961).

Catalogue of the *Nolde* exhibition, Musée des Beaux-Arts, Brussels 1961.

Dictionnaire de la peinture moderne (Hazan, Paris 1954).

Dorival, Bernard : *L'Art de la Brücke et le Fauvisme* in *Art de France*, 1961.

Langui, E. : *Cinquante ans d'art moderne* (Dumont, Cologne 1960).

Grohmann, Will : *Le Cavalier bleu*, in *l'Oeil*, Paris, September 1955.

Kandinsky, W. : *Du spirituel dans l'art* (Editions de Beaune Paris 1954).

Raynal, Maurice : *La Peinture moderne* (Skira, Geneva 1950).

DATE DUE

JAN 0 3 1980		
JAN e '80	MY 21 '80	
	MAY 22 1986	
JUN 1 9 1980	MAY 2 3 1986	
JUN 17 '80		
	AP 28 '81	
DEC 1 0 198		
DEC 3 80		
DEC 08 1981	97	
DEC 1 1 '81		
JUL 1 9 1982		
JUL 22 '82		
JUL 2 2 1982		
AER 0 4 1985		
MAR 22 '85		
AUG 5 1985		
AUG 01 '85		
AUG 0 5 1985